"A superb book written with sin
touch! I love the rooting in Luke
It is so comprehensive and so cl
really excited about this! Peter W   ͵ .͵ ouτstanding."
Revd Canon Dr Michael Green, biblical scholar, author,
and former Rector of St Aldates, Oxford

"Some years ago, I prepared to preach on Jesus' last words
to his followers, as found in Luke 24:44–49. I became
really excited as I rediscovered the incredible depth and
concentration in this short passage. In this book Peter Walker
has done us all a great service in expounding these verses –
as well as the first steps of the early church in Acts 2.
    What a great way to teach the basics of our faith and life!
What an inspiration for individuals and groups as they set
out on a journey with Jesus! I commend it wholeheartedly to
disciples old and young. Use it and share it!"
The Rt Revd Henry Scriven, General Secretary of the
Evangelical Fellowship in the Anglican Communion (EFAC)
and Honorary Assistant Bishop of the dioceses of Oxford
and Winchester

"I am really excited by this revised edition of *The Jesus Way*.
Having taught it myself, I can commend it confidently as the
best discipleship training course available, and when used it
will prove to be a great blessing to the Church."
The Rt Revd Wallace Benn, former Bishop of Lewes, diocese
of Chichester

"*The Jesus Way* is an excellent introduction to the Bible by an
outstanding biblical scholar. From my involvement with the
teaching of this material while living in the United States,
I can see the power of *The Jesus Way* to change lives and
energize people in faithful discipleship of Jesus. It will be a
blessing and great encouragement to all who use it, and I
recommend it wholeheartedly."
Revd Dr Justyn Terry, Vice Principal and Academic Dean,
Wycliffe Hall, University of Oxford

"All too often those who want to follow Jesus lose their way because they do not grasp the next steps in their walk with him. They hear the Good News and desire to move forward yet they don't have the proper tools to continue on the journey. Peter Walker's *The Jesus Way* is an excellent resource for all such people.

What the church today needs most are resources for Christian discipleship. In my work I see many people come to faith in Christ but struggle to find materials that will help jump-start them in their journey – to my dismay these are few and far between. Peter's book is easy to understand, well presented, and thorough – without being overwhelming. It is truly an ideal handbook for those starting out on the Jesus way.

This is also a superb book to take on international mission. Many people in the "two-thirds world" do not have Bibles but, when guided through *The Jesus Way*, they can access the teaching of the New Testament in just twelve easy steps.

Peter Walker provides a clear and thoughtful model for following Jesus. He has done this with the insight of a biblical scholar and the enthusiasm of a passionate believer. He shows how following Jesus is a life filled with joy, triumph in trials, peace, love, and above all, hope. *The Jesus Way* provides us with a roadmap that leads to a deeper relationship with Jesus and an experience of his abundant life."

Carrie Boren Headington, Missioner for Evangelism, Episcopal Diocese of Dallas

"*The Jesus Way* is a wonderfully clear, reliable, and biblical guide into the Way of Jesus Christ, teaching new (and old!) Christians what it means to believe in Jesus and follow after him. Whether for personal use or group study, it is an invaluable resource for basic Christian discipleship."

Revd Dr Joel Scandrett, Assistant Professor of Theology and Director of the Robert E. Webber Center, Trinity School for Ministry

"Our college students have been studying *The Jesus Way* in order to learn about Jesus and his apostles in a focused way. Dr Walker has presented his material in a way that is both evangelistic and pastoral. Yet he has done so with great simplicity, so that the book turns out to be an effective discipleship resource not just for new converts but also for the "leaned-back" disciple who is needing to get up and start walking again with Jesus."

Revd Samuel Galuak Marial, Principal of Bishop Gwynne College, Juba, South Sudan

"I love this book that Peter Walker has given us to use here in the Teso region of Uganda. I am really praying that God will use it to bring his truth to his people – in this region and beyond – in order to bring revival and transformation in this area as we teach his Word."

Pius Emesu, lay pastor from northern Uganda

"This is a book that will challenge you to love Jesus unashamedly with both your heart and mind, and then to live an authentic Christian life centred on a foundational understanding of the cross and its power. With intellectual depth, great illustrations and practical truths this book will stir your passion for Jesus."

Rachel Hickson, Heartcry for Change

The Jesus Way

Learning to Live the Christian Life

PETER WALKER

MONARCH
BOOKS

Published by
Lion Hudson Limited
Wilkinson House, Jordan Hill Business Park
Banbury Road, Oxford OX2 8DR, England
www.lionhudson.com

ISBN 978 0 85721 960 2
e-ISBN 978 0 85721 961 9

First edition 2009
This revised edition 2020

Acknowledgments
Scripture quotations are taken from the Holy Bible, New International Version Anglicised. Copyright © 1979, 1984, 2011 Biblica, formerly International Bible Society. Used by permission of Hodder & Stoughton Ltd, an Hachette UK company. All rights reserved. "NIV" is a registered trademark of Biblica. UK trademark number 1448790.

The version of the Nicene Creed quoted on p. 159 is taken from *Common Worship*, copyright © 2000 The Archbishop's Council. Reproduced by permission. All rights reserved. copyright@churchofengland.org

A catalogue record for this book is available from the British Library

Printed and bound in the UK, October 2019, LH29

This book is dedicated
to the memory of Michael Green
(with gratitude for his boundless encouragement),
to Phil and Lois Svalya
(with thanks for their prayer and support),
and to pastors and teachers throughout Africa
(the "ball is now at your feet"!).

Contents

Acknowledgments

In the first edition I was able to express my thanks to the many people in the Oxford area (in particular, at Christ Church, Abingdon or associated with Wycliffe Hall) who had seen the book in its draft stages and given me some great advice and encouragement.

Now, ten years on, I would like to thank those from around the world who have encouraged me to teach this material in their congregations or dioceses:

- in Uganda,
Bishop Thomas (in Kumi: 2005, 2007, 2017),
Bishop Stephen (in Mityana: 2017, 2019);
- in Kenya,
Archbishop Eliud (in Nairobi: 2014),
Bishop Joseph (in Kirinyaga: 2017, 2018),
Bishop Paul (in Kapsabet: 2017),
Bishop Charles (in Embu: 2018),
Bishop Moses (in Mbeere: 2018)
and Bishop Joseph (in Machakos: 2018);
- in the United States,
Bishop Jim (in Dallas: 2009),
D. Paul Thomas (in Hollywood: 2009);
Theron Walker (in Castle Rock: 2017)
as well as several churches in the Pittsburgh area (2013–17);
- in the Far East,
Bishop Rennis (teaching "in absentia": Christmas 2017);
- and, finally in the UK,
Bishop Wallace – for asking me to co-teach *The Jesus Way* with him in the diocese of Chichester throughout the weeks of Lent in 2011. It was so powerful to hear him, as an Anglican bishop, going through the material in chapter 2 and outlining, simply but clearly, the apostles' teaching on the Cross.

My thanks too to those who helped with this revised edition: Jon Oliver, Jo Stockdale and Eva Rojas (and others at Lion Hudson); Katie Black and Chris Klukas (in Pittsburgh); Geoff Chapman (for his vision of Christian discipleship being in four dimensions, which inspired some important revisions in chapter 10); and my good friend, Scott Jessel (for the great skill, as well as patience, which he has exhibited, both as a cameraman and as a video-editor).

The Jesus Way was born in Africa. In so many ways I see it as a "love-gift" from Africa. Its writing was inspired by the love and faith of the Christians I was privileged to encounter there. So I am hoping this revised edition will make it possible for *The Jesus Way*, not just to be used as a resource in the "First World", but also, in a particular way, to be given back to Africa – that the many new Jesus-followers in that great continent will be able to grow in confidence and, like Theophilus (cf. Luke 1:4), "know the certainty" of the things they have been taught.

With that in mind, I have assigned all book royalties to the Evangelical Fellowship in the Anglican Communion (see p. 256). The book is not explicitly Anglican or "denominational", but I hope that this particular organization (founded by John Stott, one of the most gifted teachers of the New Testament in the twentieth century) will be able to pick up the baton he bequeathed and use this book to entrust the apostles' teaching "to reliable people who will also be qualified to teach others" (2 Timothy 2:2). May people, all around the world, come to see the sheer brilliance of that small book, the New Testament, which Jesus has given to his followers!

Foreword to the Second Edition

In his ground-breaking book *Discipleship* David Watson (1933–84) made this sobering observation:

> Christians in the West have largely neglected what it means to be a disciple of Christ. The vast majority of western Christians are church members, pew-fillers, hymn-singers, sermon-tasters, Bible-readers, even born-again believers or Spirit-filled charismatics, but not true disciples of Jesus.

Watson's critique is enough to make any pastor lie awake at night!

Sadly, too often the word "Christian" conjures up images of institutional religion, personal piety or even a cultural hangover from a bygone era. The word, however, was first used as a kind of nickname by critics, who were trying to make sense of the incredibly dynamic Jesus-movement that had recently caused such a stir in their city of Antioch (Acts 11:26). And the term used prior to that was indeed one that emphasized the vibrancy and dynamism of this Jesus-movement – it was simply known as "the Way" (as seen in Acts 9:2 and 24:14). Quite probably, so scholars speculate, this was because Jesus had declared himself to be "the way and the truth and the life" (John 14:6) – thus making it quite clear that to be one of his followers people would need to surrender their whole life to this Jesus and in return be transformed into his likeness. Jesus was not looking for "armchair Christians", but for radical disciples!

Peter Walker has done the church a great service in this new edition of *The Jesus Way*. It's a remarkable guide – both user-friendly and yet in-depth – as to what it means to follow Jesus today. Divided into two sections, based on the two foundational chapters of Luke 24 and Acts 2, the book covers considerable ground with twelve incisive chapters outlining the essence of authentic Christian discipleship.

Robustly biblical, the guide is wonderfully holistic – including chapters that champion the centrality of the cross, the revelation of Scripture, the power of the Holy Spirit and the importance of the sacraments. And, speaking personally, I was delighted to see that all of these were set within the overall context of the importance of mission and evangelism: people need to encounter the Risen Jesus!

I am particularly excited that this new edition is now accompanied by the all the teaching resources necessary for running two short eight-week courses: "Learning the Jesus Way" (based on chapters 1–6) and "Living the Jesus Way" (chapters 7–12). This will prove an invaluable resource for pastors and home group leaders so that they can use the material in a group format that will bring maximum benefit to the participants.

In Acts 18:26 we read how Aquila and Priscilla explained to Apollos "the way of God" more fully. We can all be grateful that Peter has done this very thing for a new generation of would-be disciples in the twenty-first century. So I do encourage you to set out on the "the Jesus Way": it's full of Jesus' truth and life!

Revd Greg Downes
Director of Ministerial Training
and Dean of the Wesley Centre for Missional Engagement
Wycliffe Hall, Oxford
Summer 2019

Foreword to the First Edition

The older I get, the more aware I become of the vital need to give new converts to Jesus Christ a top quality grounding in the realities of discipleship. Granted, Christ's love and faithfulness are such that he constantly keeps safe innumerable converts who are existing in what seems a permanent baby stage – Christians who were never properly discipled and who spiritually have never grown up. (Thank you, Lord Jesus, for this further demonstration of your unfathomable love.) But our Lord's ideal, as apostolically voiced, is of steady spiritual growth through solid grounding in divine things.

Young Christians, along with veteran Christians and all Christians in between, are called to "walk" in Christ (the image is of sustained advance) "rooted and built up in him and established in the faith ... abounding in thanksgiving" (Colossians 2:6–7). This is the unchanging agenda for the high-grade spiritual education necessary for discipling both the church's children (young people, that is, growing up in Christian homes) and first-generation believers, as the Colossians were.

We live in an age in which technology is making materialists out of the entire human race: countries with a Christian heritage become secular, multi-faith communities; and Christian homes, at least in the West, are crumbling. As a result, the discipling task has become a great deal more demanding than it once was. Yet in this same age God is bringing to birth a huge crop of converts worldwide, which makes the discipling task enormously urgent at the present time.

To be done well, every teaching task requires a focused intention and strong devotion on the part of teachers, plus high quality resources to draw on. Thus in the second century, when the church seriously tackled the task of winning the Roman empire, catechetical classes for both casual enquirers and persons convinced about Christ who wanted to join the church were regularly maintained; and thoughtful writings of an apologetic-evangelistic cast were regularly produced. Then, from the sixteenth to the nineteenth century, following a thousand years of comparative neglect, this type of ministry blossomed again, as abundance of catechisms and related books (both Protestant and Catholic) bear witness.

More recently, however, this kind of material has been thought to be over authoritative, inappropriately institutionalized, and hopelessly outmoded. So catechizing in all its forms has largely dropped out of church life. The result is that good discipling material is now thin on the ground, and a renewal of both a didactic focus and catechetical resources has become urgent.

As in our time the world community has gone irreversibly global, so has the church. In saying this, I think particularly of mainstream evangelicalism which, through its many forms of denominational expression, I take to be the central and most authentic form of the Christian tradition, and which has certainly been at the heart of the extraordinary Christian expansion that has occurred since the Second World War.

Clearly, this Christian globalization needs to be reflected in both the substance and the style of tomorrow's catechetical resources. And that is why I enthuse, as I do, about The Jesus Way. It seems to me the most significant first step I have seen in this particular right direction.

As little culture-specific and denomination-specific as it well could be, The Jesus Way brings out with ingenious thoroughness and appropriate fullness all the biblical basics of personal discipleship, and presents them in a thoroughly up-to-date, enlivening way. The fact that it was born cross-culturally, in and for Uganda, no doubt gave it a head start towards achieving the world-Christian quality that seems to me to mark it out.

May it herald the era of a catechetical renewal that I, along with others, long to see.

Revd J. I. Packer
Board of Governors' Professor of Theology,
Regent College, Vancouver
Easter 2009

Introduction

Jesus Christ is worth following – worth living your life for. To use one of his own images, he is truly the "fine pearl of great value." A man is looking for fine pearls, and when he finds one that is unusually fine, he goes and sells everything he has, and buys that pearl (see Matthew 13:45–46).

However, many people set out to follow Jesus but then, sadly, get lost. Sometimes this may be of their own choosing. Perhaps, deep down, they wanted to do their own thing (using Jesus as a convenient cover) and were not very interested in actually following Jesus. They would rather follow their own agendas.

Yet others genuinely get confused. In many instances, the reason for this confusion boils down to this: they do not think of Jesus as a living person who is able to give clear instructions about how to follow him – and who does so through the pages of the New Testament. Instead, this ancient text, written by his first followers, remains something of a mysterious "closed book" – the preserve of scholars or students of history. It is rarely seen for what it is – a living book through which Jesus speaks into our lives. Jesus said: "My sheep listen to my voice; I know them, and they follow me." (John 10:27). But too often, the sheep get sidetracked and veer off the path – because they do not recognize that it is in the New Testament that they can truly hear Jesus' voice.

Follow Jesus – his way

Following Jesus, you see, is not meant to be a journey which is spent groping in the dark. Jesus has left us some fairly clear instructions. Of course, there are aspects of the New Testament that are hard to understand, or open to a variety of interpretations, but these "grey areas" rarely, if ever, affect the central core of its teaching. So it is possible to follow Jesus his way – that is, as Jesus intends, and work within the spacious frameworks which he has provided. What we have to do is listen out carefully for those instructions and guidelines – given both by Jesus himself in his own teaching and by those whom he appointed as his special witnesses. If you like, the "Jesus Way" was always meant to be followed *Jesus' way*.

Jesus can teach us how to follow him. Put another way, Jesus himself can lead us into his truth. Some people have found this diagram helpful at this point.

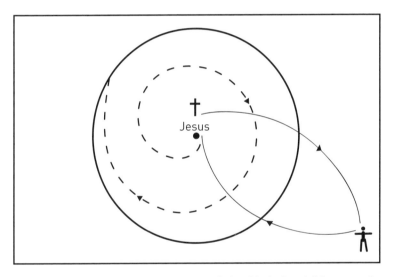

The circle represents all the truths of the Christian faith, spanning out from Jesus at the centre. Many people, when asked where they are on the diagram, place themselves outside the circle. They recognize they are not yet followers of Jesus. Some, however, would like to follow Jesus but they are a little hesitant; they are daunted by the circle (everything they don't know!) and, worse still, they don't know how to get inside the circle in the first place. The Good News is that the Risen Jesus, though he is at the centre of the circle, has the power to come outside the circle, to meet people exactly where they are, and then can take them right back to the heart of the circle. And from there it is *his* responsibility to gradually lead people outwards (in ever-increasing spirals!) into all the contents of the circle. So, if you would like to follow Jesus, or indeed have already begun to do so, you can have confidence that *he* can lead you into all his truth. Take hold of him, don't let him go, and he will then take full care of you. Let Jesus himself guide you along the Jesus Way.

How *The Jesus Way* was born

This book was born in the villages of Uganda. Invited in March 2004 to lead a team of Oxford students to meet Christian leaders in the remote area of Kumi (four hours north of Kampala), we also went out into the villages showing *The Jesus Film* (reel to reel, generated from the back of a car, under the stars!). We found that so many people wanted to follow Jesus. But we were told by their pastors that Christian faith here often proves only skin-deep. There is a mammoth task of Christian education, of training people to follow Jesus. New believers in Jesus, they said, often just do not know how to continue – not helped by the lack of teaching resources and indeed of Bibles.

It was a humbling experience. Many of the pastors – those responsible for helping others to follow Jesus – themselves did not possess a copy of the Bible. So to see their joy, as we presented each of them with their own Bible, was moving indeed. And it made me acutely aware just how privileged I was to have been taught the New Testament from a young age by those who loved Jesus. Having taught the New Testament for several years to those training for ministry in the UK and USA, I now found myself in Uganda teaching this same precious book, and together we saw its majesty and beauty coming to light before our eyes. At that moment, I saw in a new way the great treasure on which I had been sitting. The New Testament – like Jesus himself (naturally!) – is a "fine pearl of great value." It comes from him and reflects his brilliance. It's a book, therefore, that cannot be left in academic libraries, but must be enjoyed and then shared. It's a life-changing book. Indeed, it's a living book, focused on Jesus who himself is a living person, and so it must be lived out in real lives.

So, looking out on the mud huts from our jeep window as we said our farewells, I resolved to try and write a book that might introduce people to the truths of the New Testament – even if they never had a copy of it. What, I wondered, if the sum total of what people knew of the New Testament was just two chapters? Which would they be? By the time we had reached Kampala, Luke 24 and Acts 2 had come clearly into view: two key chapters (covering the climax of Luke's Gospel and the effective launch of Jesus' church), which I sensed could act together as a brilliant, clear window into the whole of the rest of the New Testament.

The Jesus Way is the result: a book in two parts, learning first from Jesus himself (in Luke 24) and then from his apostles (in Acts 2) about what it means to follow Jesus – his way. To use the imagery of the circle, my prayer is that Jesus himself would take these pages and use them to lead his people into all of his truth.

Using this book

The Jesus Way is written for anyone who wants to follow Jesus. Some may feel they have not quite started yet, but, even so, would be interested to get an overview of the New Testament's teaching. Quite rightly, before setting out on the journey, they want to know what they might be getting themselves into! Such readers may find some of the material in the Appendices particularly useful, as they consider carefully the unique claims of Jesus and the arguments for his being raised from death. This may help them get clearer in their own mind why it's so important to set out on the Jesus Way; and at the end of chapter 1 there's a prayer which could be used as a personal response to this Jesus.

Others know they have started out on the road, however falteringly. The twelve main chapters are indeed written especially for those who already aspire to be Jesus' followers today: together we tune in to what Jesus taught his first followers and then to what those same followers taught others. So *The Jesus Way* is primarily intended to help "nurture" and grow any such Christian believers who want a new grounding in their faith. Here, then, are twelve key topics that Jesus' modern-day followers need to grasp.

This book can be worked through by individuals on their own. There's quite a lot of material in each chapter, so it may be best to pace yourself – perhaps aiming for one chapter a week. You will note that there are very few illustrations or examples in each chapter, but the concentration is instead almost entirely on the text of the New Testament. This is deliberate – so that the book can be heard in widely different contexts and cultures – but you may feel it makes the material seem a bit "dense" and tightly packed. So you might find it helpful to read the book alongside someone else who has been trying to follow Jesus for a little longer and who perhaps can give you illustrations or examples from their own experience.

Alternatively, the book can be used by study groups – whether in someone's home or in a local church. In particular, church leaders might like to use it for any "follow-up" groups, perhaps for people who have been on courses like *Alpha* or *Christianity Explored*. Those who have made a new or fresh commitment to Christ – whether on such courses or through other means – often need real guidance for those next, crucial months. *The Jesus Way* might be a helpful resource here. It could also be used by those preparing people for adult baptism or confirmation, or in adult "Sunday schools" (popular in North America), or at a church's weekend away, or as part of the church's training of its lay leaders. Returning to Uganda in 2005, for example, we taught it as a course for lay ministers – those responsible for leading smaller, local churches.

For all such study groups – whether in someone's home or in a local church – there are now with this second edition some extra resources available. In particular, there is a series of short videos, in which I introduce the topic of each chapter and also interview other Christians about their experience of that topic. There is also a Participants' Workbook, with questions and activities for small groups and individuals. And – for church leaders – there are also further Teacher's Resources (with lecture outlines and presentation slides). For full details please turn to the information page at the back of the book (p.250).

All these, as J. I. Packer reminds us in his original Foreword, are forms of "catechesis" – what the first Christians called basic instruction for new believers. In modern terms we might call it a "starter kit" – either for new Christians or for those who want to go back and rediscover the essentials of their faith. Either way, it is a vital task and I hope that *The Jesus Way* might really help us at this critical point. After all, we all need to be taught by Jesus and to learn from him how to live the Christian life.

Special features of *The Jesus Way*

Several features of the book's design are worth noting. Because *The Jesus Way* is a pocket guide to the New Testament, it inevitably refers to the apostles' writings on almost every page. Many of these references are given only in verse references (for example, "Acts 19:20"); some verses, however, are quoted in full in the main text. Some key sentences from the book have also been highlighted as pull-quotes, designed to help you navigate your way more easily through the chapter. Each chapter also contains some material in boxes (often a summary of New Testament teaching on that chapter's subject).

The Jesus Way is deliberately designed for beginners, so I have tried to avoid complex jargon. Occasionally, however, it has been necessary to use a word that might require some further explanation for those unfamiliar with it. Such words are marked in the text by an asterisk after the word the first time it is mentioned in a chapter (for example, apostles*). That further explanation can then be found in the Glossary, together with a discussion of some related points of difficulty. The Glossary is thus intended to help those who may want to pursue particular matters in more detail.

By the way, one word of jargon that I have deliberately avoided using is "discipleship". Jesus' first followers have traditionally been known as the "disciples", but this is a word that is hardly used in any other context. The word used in the Gospels could equally well have been translated as "learner", "student", or "someone in training"; or we could say, they were his "followers". That's a far more everyday term and that's the word I will be chiefly using to describe anyone – whether in the time of Jesus or today – who wants to be in Jesus' school and under his instruction. Some people will thus recognize that *The Jesus Way* can also be seen as a "discipleship manual". Indeed it is, because it is designed to help you to set out on a lifetime of adventure – following Jesus.

A look at the contents page will show how the book has been deliberately structured in two equal halves, each with six chapters. Some may like to think of these as key steps along the Jesus Way. Yet, after the first three (which must be the first three such steps), the order is not that important: in other words, it is not as though you cannot proceed to the next step until you have first mastered the previous one! This is not a regimented programme that has to be completed in strict order.

Instead, then, the language of "building blocks" has been used throughout: these are twelve key ingredients – twelve key bricks, if you like – which need to be in place if we are to be effective in building a faithful Christian life. So (for reasons that become clear in the epilogue) I have developed the visual motif of an archway being constructed, with six building blocks on each side. If you find this helpful, that's great, but "no worries", if not!

Twelve key building blocks
– for following Jesus today!

PART 1

Learning from Jesus Himself

(Luke 24)

From Luke's First Book:

His "Good News" about Jesus

(Luke 24)

The resurrection (verses 1–12)

On the first day of the week, very early in the morning, the women took the spices they had prepared and went to the tomb. They found the stone rolled away from the tomb, but when they entered, they did not find the body of the Lord Jesus. While they were wondering about this, suddenly two men in clothes that gleamed like lightning stood beside them. In their fright the women bowed down with their faces to the ground, but the men said to them, "Why do you look for the living among the dead? He is not here; he has risen! Remember how he told you, while he was still with you in Galilee: 'The Son of Man must be delivered over to the hands of sinners, be crucified and on the third day be raised again.'" Then they remembered his words.

When they came back from the tomb, they told all these things to the Eleven and to all the others. It was Mary Magdalene, Joanna, Mary the mother of James, and the others with them who told this to the apostles. But they did not believe the women, because their words seemed to them like nonsense. Peter, however, got up and ran to the tomb. Bending over, he saw the strips of linen lying by themselves, and he went away, wondering to himself what had happened.

The walk to Emmaus (verses 13–35)

Now that same day two of them were going to a village called Emmaus, about seven miles from Jerusalem. They were talking with each other about everything that had happened. As they talked and discussed these things with each other, Jesus himself came up and walked along with them; but they were kept from recognizing him.

He asked them, "What are you discussing together as you walk along?"

They stood still, their faces downcast. One of them, named Cleopas, asked him, "Are you the only one visiting Jerusalem who does not know the things that have happened there in these days?"

"What things?" he asked.

"About Jesus of Nazareth," they replied. "He was a prophet, powerful in word and deed before God and all the people. The chief priests and our rulers handed him over to be sentenced to death, and they crucified him; but we had hoped that he was the one who was going to redeem Israel. And what is more, it is the third day since all this took place. In addition, some of our women amazed us. They went to the tomb early this morning but didn't find his body. They came and told us that they had seen a vision of angels, who said he was alive. Then some of our companions went to the tomb and found it just as the women had said, but they did not see Jesus."

He said to them, "How foolish you are, and how slow to believe all that the prophets have spoken! Did not the Messiah have to suffer these things and then enter his glory?" And beginning with Moses and all the Prophets, he explained to them what was said in all the Scriptures concerning himself.

As they approached the village to which they were going, Jesus continued on as if he were going farther. But they urged him strongly, "Stay with us, for it is nearly evening; the day is almost over." So he went in to stay with them.

When he was at the table with them, he took bread, gave thanks, broke it and began to give it to them. Then their eyes were opened and they recognized him, and he disappeared from their sight. They asked each other, "Were not our hearts burning within us while he talked with us on the road and opened the Scriptures to us?"

They got up and returned at once to Jerusalem. There they found the Eleven and those with them, assembled together and saying, "It is true! The Lord has risen and has appeared to Simon." Then the two told what had happened on the way, and how Jesus was recognized by them when he broke the bread.

Jesus appears to his disciples (verses 36–49)

While they were still talking about this, Jesus himself stood among them and said to them, "Peace be with you."

They were startled and frightened, thinking they saw a ghost. He said to them, "Why are you troubled, and why do doubts rise in your minds? Look at my hands and my feet. It is I myself! Touch me and see; a ghost does not have flesh and bones, as you see I have."

When he had said this, he showed them his hands and feet. And while they still did not believe it because of joy and amazement, he asked them, "Do you have anything here to eat?" They gave him a piece of broiled fish, and he took it and ate it in their presence.

He said to them, "This is what I told you while I was still with you: Everything must be fulfilled that is written about me in the Law of Moses, the Prophets and the Psalms."

Then he opened their minds so they could understand the Scriptures. He told them, "This is what is written: The Messiah will suffer and rise from the dead on the third day, and repentance for the forgiveness of sins will be preached in his name to all nations, beginning at Jerusalem. You are witnesses of these things. I am going to send you what my Father has promised; but stay in the city until you have been clothed with power from on high."

Jesus is taken up to heaven (verses 50–53)

When he had led them out to the vicinity of Bethany, he lifted up his hands and blessed them. While he was blessing them, he left them and was taken up into heaven. Then they worshiped him and returned to Jerusalem with great joy. And they stayed continually at the temple, praising God.

Enjoy Jesus' Resurrection

Why do you look for the living among the dead?
He is not here; he has risen!
Luke 24:5–6

Was Jesus really raised from the dead? Luke, the writer of this key chapter in the Bible, was in no doubt. It might seem bizarre and without any parallel, but yes, three days after his public execution in Jerusalem*, Jesus, so Luke claims, was seen by his followers.

First, he writes, Jesus' tomb was found to be empty; next, Jesus met a couple of his followers making their way to a village outside Jerusalem called Emmaus*; and finally, back in Jerusalem later that first Easter* day, he met with his followers – showing them his wounds, and eating some food to prove he was no ghost. At the start of the day, his followers had thought the first rumours were a load of nonsense, but by the day's end, sheer joy and exhilaration was evidently beginning to pulse through their lives (Luke 24:11, 41).

Resurrection at the centre

Jesus had been raised by God back from the dead! This raising or "resurrection" of Jesus has, ever since, been the central claim of authentic Christian faith – that the living God raised Jesus Christ bodily from the grave. And the news that Jesus is alive continues to this day to turn people's expectations upside down, bringing joy and new hope. This can be true for anyone – it can be true for you. Those who meet with this Risen Jesus are a given a whole new life; and those who are serious about following him are in for a life characterized by adventure and new possibilities.

Jesus wants this truth about his resurrection to become the very centre of your thinking and your life. He made that clear to his first followers on that first Easter day, and he has been doing it ever since. Jesus is truly back from the dead – he is alive!

Following a living Jesus

The resurrection has always been at the heart of the Christian message. After all, take the resurrection away and what are you left with?

> **It is love that truly stands at the heart of the universe.**

- A teacher who dies in his thirties as a failed Messiah*.
- Someone who makes great promises about God but who comes to a pitiful end.
- An example of a good, truthful person being hounded to death by human evil at its worst.

Not much good news here! No wonder there are so few people who try to follow Jesus while denying his resurrection. No wonder, if they do, that their teaching has such little impact. For why should we bother with a dead Jesus? Anything nice in his teaching (for example, about God's love) we probably want to believe already. On the other hand, anything challenging we can readily dismiss, since he's dead and gone. In that sense, we don't have to follow him at all – we're the ones who do the choosing. Above all, if Jesus remained dead in the tomb, his teaching and public ministry had evidently not been very successful. Moreover, there is no clear reason for assuming that anything he said is necessarily true.

But put the resurrection back in its proper place – at the very centre – and things start to look quite different. Now, instead, we have a Jesus in whom God was evidently at work. It becomes vital to know what he said and what he did, for it all comes with the stamp of divine approval. Moreover, because of the resurrection,

Jesus' words and actions have the power to bring God's truth and love dramatically into our lives today.

Then again, with the resurrection at the centre, hope for the future has a solid foundation: in particular, physical death need not be the end, and our present lives can be seen as infinitely valuable. We find we are living in a God-invaded world, with God himself able to become our greatest reality. Indeed, we can sense how it is love – God's love – that truly stands at the heart of the universe.

In addition, we are given a clear vision of God's purpose, not only for our own lives, but for the whole world: we are to live out Jesus' teaching, to implement his kingdom, to proclaim his rule, and to work hand in hand with the God who has the power to bring good out of evil, and light out of darkness. The true and living God is the God of resurrection power, the one who is at work to restore his broken world. We too, then, are to be an "Easter people", bringing the resurrection light of Jesus into our local worlds – into God's world.

So, no resurrection – no Good News. No resurrection – no "Christianity" worth its name. If there's no resurrection, then there's no point in following Jesus. Indeed, there's no point in walking in the Jesus Way or reading any more of this book. For we are looking together in these pages at what it means to follow a living person – not a dead one. Jesus, according to the New Testament writers, is alive – and that means alive today!

So the first "building block" as we seek to follow this Jesus – the first step along the Jesus Way – is to enjoy Jesus' resurrection and to enjoy living each day of our lives in the light of this amazing reality. If, right now, you do not feel so sure about the truth of the resurrection, or if you want to invest some time looking in more detail at the historical evidence for it, then you may find it helpful to turn now to appendix B (The Resurrection of Jesus: Can We Be Sure?) to look at the various objections to the resurrection and begin to develop your own response. It's good to build up one's confidence on this vital, life-changing topic.

In the rest of this chapter, however, we will move on to consider the implications of all this. What does the New Testament teach us about the meaning and significance of the resurrection (see Box 1)?

If the resurrection of Jesus really happened, what difference will it make? We will find it will give us a whole new vision of who God is, but also of what he wants us to do in response.

Box 1 – Resurrection in the New Testament: Some selected texts

Jesus said to Martha, "I am the resurrection and the life. The one who believes in me will live, even though they die... Do you believe this?"

John 11:25–26

Then Jesus said to Thomas, "Put your finger here; see my hands. Reach out your hand and put it into my side. Stop doubting and believe." Thomas said to him, "My Lord and my God!"

John 20:27–28

After his suffering, he presented himself to them and gave many convincing proofs that he was alive. He appeared to them over a period of forty days and spoke about the kingdom of God.

Acts 1:3

But God raised him from the dead on the third day and caused him to be seen. He was not seen by all the people, but by witnesses whom God had already chosen – by us who ate and drank with him after he rose from the dead. He commanded us to preach to the people and to testify that he is the one whom God appointed as judge of the living and the dead.

Acts 10:40–42 (Peter's words in Caesarea; see also, Paul's words: Acts 13:30–31; 17:30–31 and 26:8)

The gospel... regarding his Son... who through the Spirit of holiness was appointed the Son of God in power by his resurrection from the dead: Jesus Christ our Lord... Christ was raised from the dead through the glory of the Father... For we know that since Christ was raised from the dead, he cannot die again; death no longer has mastery over him.

Romans 1:2, 3, 4; 6:4, 9

> *Christ Jesus... has destroyed death and has brought life and immortality to light through the gospel... Remember Jesus Christ, raised from the dead.*
>
> **2 Timothy 1:10; 2:8**
>
> *For what I received I passed on to you as of first importance: that Christ died for our sins, according to the Scriptures, that he was buried, that he was raised on the third day according to the Scriptures, and that he appeared to Cephas, and then to the Twelve. After that, he appeared to more than five hundred of the brothers and sisters at the same time, most of whom are still living, though some have fallen asleep. Then he appeared to James, then to all the apostles... Christ has indeed been raised from the dead.*
>
> **1 Corinthians 15:3–7, 20**
>
> *Do not be afraid! I am the First and the Last. I am the Living One; I was dead, and now look, I am alive for ever and ever!*
>
> **Revelation 1:17–18 (Jesus' words in the vision given to John)**

The God who raised Jesus

First, the resurrection teaches us four powerful truths about God himself – the God who raised Jesus.

1. The resurrection is strong evidence for God's existence

Debates about God's existence continue unabated. Some, focusing on issues of creation or evolution, argue that science has disproved the "God theory". Others, looking at evil and suffering in the world, see no evident place for a God of power and love. Yet the resurrection of Jesus cuts into this debate with clarity, bringing something new to the table. For, if we look here – at the resurrection – we will find fresh evidence, surprisingly clear, of the activity of the God of power and love.

So, for many, the resurrection is the clearest sign that God truly exists and is able to work in his world, and that we do not live in a closed, "God-less" universe. Thus the New Testament writers (as seen in Box 1) frequently refer to the resurrection as an act of God: it was not so much that Jesus rose (by his own will), but rather that God raised Jesus from death: "God raised him from the dead" (Acts 2:24; 10:40; 13:30); "God… brought back from the dead our Lord Jesus" (Hebrews 13:20). They also see the resurrection as demonstrating God's great power:

> *That power is the same as the mighty strength he exerted when he raised Christ from the dead.*

Ephesians 1:19–20

2. The resurrection introduces us to God's holiness

For the apostle* Paul, the resurrection reveals the "holiness" of Jesus (see his words in Romans 1:4 in Box 1). It also reveals the holiness of God. This involves two aspects – both his love and his judgment. Speaking to the Athenians about the resurrection, Paul brought out this solemn theme of judgment:

> *He will judge the world with justice by the man he has appointed. He has given proof of this to everyone by raising him from the dead.*

Acts 17:31

In the resurrection, God was declaring his vindication of Jesus and of all who would then come to him. He was also thereby appointing him to be the final judge of everyone throughout the world. The resurrection is a signal that God will judge the world by his holiness at the end of time – and he will do this through Jesus.

3. The resurrection reveals God's love

In the resurrection, we see God coming back to all people with a message of forgiveness. Human beings may do their worst against God – hating him, even crucifying him – but they have an opportunity to be forgiven and restored. Peter, though he had denied Jesus three times, was given, through the resurrection, a second chance

(Mark 14:66–72; John 21:15–19). So the God who has set a future day for judgment has also made this present time an opportunity to return to him – what the Bible calls the "day of salvation", when God will save his people (Acts 4:12; Romans 13:11; 2 Corinthians 6:2). He is indeed a holy God but, deep within that, he is truly a God of compassion and grace, of forgiveness and love.

4. The resurrection reveals God's purposes

The New Testament writers saw the resurrection as the crowning fulfilment of God's purposes as already revealed in the Old Testament, by which God was now bringing the world into a new age, the age of fulfilment (1 Corinthians 10:11). Yet the resurrection also signals his purposes for the future. For just as God transformed the physical body of Jesus into a new resurrection body, so he will do the same for those who believe in him (see, for example, 1 Corinthians 15:12–57; Philippians 3:20–21). Moreover, on the basis of his raising Jesus from the grave, we can see how God is intending to bring in a "new creation", not abandoning our physical world but transforming it through his resurrection power (see chapter 12).

The Jesus who was raised

The resurrection also teaches us a vast amount about Jesus himself. Note what the New Testament writers say about Jesus in the light of his resurrection:

- He is the person appointed to be the "judge of the living and the dead" (Acts 10:42; see also Acts 17:31, quoted just above).
- He is the "great Shepherd of the sheep," who calls us to belong in his fold (Hebrews 13:20).
- He is the "Son of God," whom we must "obey" (Romans 1:5) and "listen to" (Mark 9:7).
- He is the long-awaited "Messiah" (or "Christ") of Israel* and is now the world's true ruler and king: "God has made

this Jesus... both Lord and Messiah"; "there is another king, one called Jesus" (Acts 2:36; 17:7).

- He is the "Lord". The first Christians expressed the heart of their faith in just three words: "Jesus is Lord." (1 Corinthians 12:3). First-century Jews used this title "Lord" to describe the one true God of Israel; but now Jesus' followers were applying it to this human being, recently executed in Jerusalem, called Jesus.

The whole New Testament is littered with such references to Jesus as Messiah, as the Son of God*, and as the Lord*:

> *He was appointed the Son of God in power by his resurrection from the dead.*
>
> **Romans 1:4**

Indeed, there are one or two places where it clearly hints that Jesus can be equated fully with God himself (see, for example, John 1:1–14 and fuller discussion in chapters 9 and 12). So, even if Thomas' outburst on seeing the Risen Jesus was spontaneous and not fully thought through, it was profoundly true: "My Lord and my God!" (John 20:28).

The resurrection therefore reveals and establishes the unique identity of Jesus. Yes, other aspects of Jesus' life support this claim (the circumstances of his birth, his authoritative teaching, his powerful miracles, his sinless life), but the resurrection is like the capstone in the arch. Without the resurrection, the New Testament writers would never have dared to speak in such terms. With it, they could scarcely hold themselves back!

This Jesus is unique. Though clearly human, he must also be identified with God in some way. He is the king and the judge. He is also an eternal being. As one New Testament writer said: "Jesus Christ is the same yesterday and today and forever" (Hebrews 13:8).

Meeting the Risen Jesus

If this is true, the consequences for all of us are important. The resurrection tells us that:

- we live in a world visited by God;
- God is interested in his created world and in all aspects of human life (including our physical bodies);
- there is a future for all of us after death (see chapter 12);
- the most important person – in this life and in the next – is Jesus himself.

Jesus is the centre of God's world and he must be the centre of our world too.

The resurrection thus presents everyone with a startling truth: Jesus is the true Lord of the world and we must meet him. He is God's appointed king and we must humble ourselves before him and, only so, enter into his kingdom. In the resurrection, God "gave him the name that is above every name, that at the name of Jesus... every tongue [will] acknowledge that Jesus Christ is Lord" (Philippians 2:9–11). God wants everyone to acknowledge the lordship of Jesus, his Risen Son. So Paul can write with great clarity:

> *If you declare with your mouth, "Jesus is Lord," and believe in your heart that God raised him from the dead, you will be saved.*
>
> **Romans 10:9**

So, before going any further along the Jesus Way, we have to pause and perform a vital double-check. For, if recognizing Jesus as the Risen Lord is the essential starting point of the journey, are we sure that we have truly got started? We have to ask ourselves some life-changing questions:

- Have we truly responded to this challenge of Jesus as Lord?
- Are we quite clear that Jesus is risen from the dead and therefore alive today?

There is no point in reading further through this book if we know we have not responded in this way – or indeed, if we are slightly uncertain at this point. As they say in baseball, it is vital to "get past first base".

The Bible gives us a powerful picture to help us here. It is of the Lord Jesus Christ standing outside the door of everyone's house, wanting to come in: "Here I am! I stand at the door and knock. If anyone hears my voice and opens the door, I will come in" (Revelation 3:20).

Many have found this picture helpful. They sense that Jesus has been outside their life, but unwelcomed – knocking on the door, but refused entry.

So the resurrection presents us, forcefully, with a Risen Jesus, to whom we must respond. We must "open the door". And the great news, as we see from this verse in Revelation, is that Jesus responds to any such opening of the door with those powerful words: "I will come in." This is a solemn promise, which is crystal clear and totally reliable.

Elsewhere, Jesus says: "whoever comes to me I will never drive away" (John 6:37). The Risen Jesus never rejects anyone who sincerely turns to him. Some of us may feel very unimportant or quite unworthy; others may fear that, having perhaps experienced rejection by others, Jesus might do the same. Yet this promise of Jesus stands. It is for anyone who comes to him. Similarly, in Matthew's Gospel, Jesus offers an identical invitation, matched by a firm promise: "Come to me, all you who are weary and burdened, and I will give you rest" (Matthew 11:28).

> The Risen Jesus never rejects anyone who sincerely turns to him.

The New Testament writers want us, then, to come to Jesus, to open the door of our lives to him, or – to use another of their pictures – to kneel before him as our rightful king, recognizing that we ourselves are not truly in control of our lives (but Jesus is!).

People will respond to this challenge in many different ways. Our characters and circumstances are all unique, so there is no one formula. For some, the response is a gradual one, for others a quite sudden one. Yet at some point, we will need to verbalize some kind of response to the Risen Jesus – something which establishes communication between ourselves and him, something which recognizes who he is and what he has done. In Paul's phrase, we will need to "declare with our mouth, "Jesus is Lord.'" The following words make up a simple prayer which is an example of what we might need to say to Jesus:

Lord Jesus, I now know you are the Lord
and recognize you as my true king.
You came from God; you died for me; you are alive today.
Please forgive me for my sins;
please forgive me for living my life without you.
I come to you; please receive me.
I open the door and welcome you.
Please now come into my life and stay with me,
helping me to follow you day by day. Amen**

Some of us may wish to pause at this moment and re-echo that prayer in our own hearts; others know they have already prayed it at some point in the past. Either way, the Good News is that the Risen Jesus always hears us when we pray such a prayer. We become his, and he becomes ours – forever. As an old hymn says: "Now I belong to Jesus, Jesus belongs to me: not for the years of time alone, but for eternity."

Living for him

If we have responded to the call of Jesus in some such way, then, from now on, our life is going to be bound up inevitably with this Risen Jesus. We will discover that being a Christian is not, primarily, about obeying a set of commandments, but rather means enjoying a relationship with a living person. Following in the Jesus Way is to follow a Jesus we already know!

In fact, we can now dare to think of Jesus as our "friend". Jesus said to his followers: "I have called you friends" (John 15:15). This is an amazing privilege – to be friends with Jesus. Of course, this friendship will also involve the responsibility of obedience; note that Jesus also said:

You are my friends if you do what I command.

John 15:14

He is indeed our Lord whom we must obey, our king whom we must serve. Even so, he is also our friend and, as such, we should want to spend time in his company, getting to know him better. To be a Christian, writes Peter, is to be in love with Jesus:

Though you have not seen him, you love him.

1 Peter 1:8

It is also, as Paul says, to know him:

I want to know Christ – yes, to know the power of his resurrection.

Philippians 3:10

Anyone who has responded to the Risen Jesus has embarked on exactly the same journey as Peter and Paul – an exciting journey of knowing and loving Jesus Christ better each day.

The rest of this book is designed to help you to grow in your relationship with Jesus. There will also be further explanation about how we too can share in Jesus' risen life – living our lives in the light of his resurrection power and promises (see chapters 10 and 12). For now, however, the first building block needs to be firmly set in place: it is to enjoy Jesus' resurrection.

If we are followers of Jesus, it is because he is alive and because he has called us to know him personally. We can enjoy his presence with us throughout our lives – and beyond.

Building block 1

Enjoy Jesus' resurrection – he is alive!

2

Accept His Forgiveness

The Messiah will suffer... and repentance for the forgiveness of sins will be preached in his name.
Luke 24:46–47

Luke 24, as a story, is all about the first Easter* and the resurrection of Jesus. Yet the Risen Jesus, in his own teaching here, focuses on something else – the meaning of his death. Jesus evidently wants us, as a matter of urgency, to understand why he died.

There is no doubting that Jesus truly died. The Gospel writers describe the story of his last days in Jerusalem* and his crucifixion in great detail (see Luke 19–23). It is a gripping story, worth reading in detail. We see in it things repeated so much in our human history: betrayal, plotting, secret agreements, dashed hopes, unfair trials, human brutality, and heavy-handed tactics from those abusing their power. It is also a story that poses a much deeper question: "*Why?*"

> At the cross, complete forgiveness is guaranteed.

For there is equally no doubting that Jesus could easily have escaped – after all, there was an empty desert under three miles away! Jesus deliberately went up to Jerusalem, performed some acts in the Temple which sorely provoked its leaders, and then hung around waiting to be arrested. What made him do it? What could he possibly achieve by giving himself up to such a cruel death?

Jerusalem
at the time
of Jesus

Area of the city at the time of Jesus
Route of Jesus' last days

0   250   500 metres
0   250   500 yards

N

Kidron Valley

Fish Gate

Tower Gate

Sheep Pool
(Pool of
Bethesda)

1. Triumphal entry
of Jesus

Antonia
Fortress

Israel Pool

Sheep
Gate

3. Return to
Bethany

Golden
Gate

Tyropoeon Valley

Golgotha

8. Crucifixion

Warren's
Gate

Temple

Beautiful
Gate

Mount of
Olives

2. Cleansing
of the Temple

Court
of the
Gentiles

Ophel

Barclay's
Gate

*Garden of
Gethsemane*

5. Arrest of Jesus

Gennath
Gate

Pinnacle of
the Temple

Herod's
Palace

? Palace of
Herod Antipas

7. Trial by Pontius

Aqueduct

Hulda
Gates

Kidron

6. Night hearing
before the high
priest

UPPER CITY

Valley
Gate

Gihon
Spring

Tyropoeon Va

*Hezekiah's
Tunnel*

? House of
Caiaphas

Upper
Room

From Bethany

4. Last Supper

Aqueduct

ESSENE QUARTER LOWER

Gate of the
Essenes

Pool of
Solomon

Pool of
Siloam

Water
Gate

Aqueduct

Valley   of   Hinnom

Jesus teaches about his death – *after* the event

After the resurrection, this question would press upon his followers with great urgency: why had this person with evident authority over death placed himself under it?

The Risen Jesus begins to answer this question in Luke 24. In line with Old Testament teaching and prophecy, he asserts, Israel's* Messiah* had to suffer and "rise from the dead on the third day", and also for the message about "repentance for the forgiveness of sins" to be preached to all nations (verses 46–47).

Jesus wants us to see two things. First, that his death was not a mistake: it was necessary, there was no other way. Jesus' death had been in accordance with God's plan, as already revealed in the Old Testament. So, although Jesus' crucifixion seems like a disaster, instead it is truly a cause for celebration and thanks.

Second, that his death achieved something – the forgiveness of sins. Because of his death, people from "all nations" can hear about this offer of forgiveness (Luke 24:47). We only receive this forgiveness if we "repent" – that is, we must be sorry for our sins and turn from them to God. So, because of the cross, people throughout the world are presented with a message about repentance; yet, as they respond, God gives the amazing gift of forgiveness.

Jesus' true followers, then, are those who take seriously Jesus' own teaching about his cross. We accept this vital link between his death and our sins. We do real business with God, repenting of our sins and asking truly for his forgiveness. And the Good News is that those who ask truly receive. It is a message about forgiveness – in other words, God really does forgive us. God has done everything that is necessary. At the cross, complete forgiveness is guaranteed. Jesus himself wants us to enjoy what he died to achieve.

So the second essential building block in following Jesus is to focus on the cross:

- to know that Jesus' death was no accident, but was God's intended way of bringing forgiveness for sins into his world;

- to recognize that Jesus died for my sins – and therefore for me;
- to repent before the cross and then to receive what Jesus died to bring us – the assurance of total forgiveness in God's sight.

In other words, it is to accept Jesus' forgiveness. So in this chapter we will focus on the cross, learning from the teaching of both Jesus and his apostles* concerning what it can mean for us today.

Jesus' teaches about his death – *before* the event

If you think about it, it is a remarkable thing for anyone to assure another human being that God has forgiven them. Who do they think they are? That's precisely what some "teachers of the Law" asked of Jesus, back at the beginning of his ministry. For, when healing a paralyzed man, Jesus outrageously pronounced him to be forgiven. "Why does this fellow talk like that? He's blaspheming! Who can forgive sins but God alone?" (Mark 2:7). They were right. Only God himself can forgive sins against God. Jesus, because he is God's Son, does have this authority. Through his cross, we begin to see how this can be so. He can declare us forgiven, not only because he is God's Son, but also because he himself has died in our place.

In fact, Jesus had hinted at his forthcoming death for our sins on several occasions long before the event. Consider these verses from Mark's Gospel:

- Three times he explicitly predicted his death: "The Son of Man must suffer many things and be rejected... They will kill him, and after three days he will rise" (8:31; 9:12, 31; 10:33–34).
- He spoke about carrying his "cross" and predicted (in his parable of the vineyard) that the tenants would kill the owner's "son" (8:34; 12:6).
- He praised a woman for anointing him in advance for his "burial," and went on to state that his death was predicted

in the Old Testament: "the Son of Man will go just as it is written about him" (14:8, 21, 27, 49).

- At the Last Supper, he spoke of his body being broken and his blood "poured out for many" (14:22–24).

- He summarized the whole purpose of his coming in these powerful words: "the Son of Man... came to serve, and to give his life as a ransom for many" (10:45).

So, even if his followers needed this to be explained all over again after the event, Jesus himself had been quite clear beforehand. Yes, Jesus had other reasons for going up to Jerusalem – speaking out as a prophet before the nation's leaders, challenging the Temple with his own authority, and staking his claim in the capital to be the true "king of the Jews". Yet he also went up to Jerusalem knowing it would end in agony. He would give his life, and his death would be an act of rescue, to bring God's forgiveness and freedom to many people. Jesus' followers take him at his word.

The apostles' subsequent teaching

The apostles expand on Jesus' teaching. In fact, they are always talking about the cross. They therefore talk about it in many different ways, but the heart of their message is always the same:

- Jesus' death was "for our sins" (1 Corinthians 15:3).

- His death was unlike any other death; it was not an accident but all part of God's purpose and plan (Acts 4:28).

- Jesus had not died because of his own sins – indeed they make the remarkable claim that he had no sin of his own (1 John 3:5; 1 Peter 2:22; Hebrews 4:15). No, it was because of our sins (Romans 8:3; Hebrews 10:18; 13:12).

The New Testament writers use different images to explain this great event (see Box 2). It is worth pausing and giving this material our full attention. As we do so, these pictures may appear slightly complex. Yet, remember, the New Testament writers were dealing here with the most extraordinary event in the world – the death of God's innocent Son for the sins of others – so it should not be surprising if their teaching pushes us to the limits of human language. What pictures can really be adequate to convey such a unique event?

Box 2 – Four apostolic images to explain the cross

1. Broken family relationships

The first is drawn from the world of personal relationships. Because of our sins, there was a barrier between us and God (for example, Isaiah 59:2); but now, through Jesus' death, that barrier has been removed. At the time of Jesus' death, the Temple curtain, which separated worshippers from the Most Holy Place, was dramatically "torn in two from top to bottom" (Mark 15:38); this can be taken as a sign that the barrier of sin has been removed and that we can now enter into God's holy presence (as argued in Hebrews 10:19–22). As a result, we can come running back into the arms of our heavenly Father: thus the "lost son" in Jesus' parable found a generous welcome (Luke 15:11–32). For this new welcome, the apostles use the language of reconciliation and peace, of friendship instead of enmity:

God... through Christ... gave us the ministry of reconciliation... God was reconciling the world to himself in Christ, not counting people's sins against them.
2 Corinthians 5:18–19

Once you were alienated from God and were enemies in your minds because of your evil behaviour. But now he has reconciled you by Christ's physical body through death.
Colossians 1:21–22

2. The slave market

In the second image, human beings are presented as being like slaves, but by his death Jesus paid a great price for us, which purchased our freedom – we can be free! For this, the apostles use the language of "redemption" (literally, a "buying back"), which is similar in its meanings to the word "ransom":

In him we have redemption through his blood, the forgiveness of sins.

Ephesians 1:7 (see also Mark 10:45; 1 Peter 1:18;
1 Timothy 2:6; Romans 3:24; Titus 2:14)

3. The law courts

The third image is a legal one. We were guilty and had received a death sentence from God, but Jesus died in our place and we can now walk away from the court as free people – not guilty! For this, the apostles use the language of "justification" and righteousness; we are "justified" in God's sight (that is, "put right" with him) through the death of Jesus, who himself was truly faithful and righteous:

God did this to demonstrate his righteousness... he did it to demonstrate his righteousness at the present time, so as to be just and the one who justifies those who have faith in Jesus.

Romans 3:25–26 (see also Galatians 2:16–17; 3:24)

Christ redeemed us from the curse of the law by becoming a curse for us.

Galatians 3:13

Not having a righteousness of my own... but the righteousness that comes from God on the basis of faith.

Philippians 3:9

4. The Jerusalem Temple

Finally, the apostles draw upon the image of the Temple – the place appointed by God as a place of "atonement" where the offering of special sacrifices could remove the sins of his people. Jesus' death, the apostles teach, has now become the one, true sacrifice, which has truly turned aside God's wrath – we can be counted holy in God's sight and enter his presence.

For this, they use language which sees Jesus' death in sacrificial terms (such as "propitiation" or "atonement") and they often refer to Jesus' crucifixion by talking of his "blood" – thereby emphasizing its sacrificial purpose (see Acts 20:28; Colossians 1:14; Hebrews 9:14; Revelation 1:5). These words may seem alien to us today but would have been very familiar to people who knew the Old Testament Temple.

God's wrath was now "propitiated" or "turned aside," not by the sacrifice of an animal in the Temple, but by "the precious blood of Christ, a lamb without blemish or defect" (1 Peter 1:19; see also John 1:29; Romans 3:24; 1 Corinthians 5:7; 1 John 2:2; Revelation 5:6, 9). This sacrifice atoned for our sins, covering them over in such a way that God no longer needs to consider them any more.

Christ offered himself unblemished to God... to do away with sin by the sacrifice of himself.
Hebrews 9:14, 26 (see also Hebrews 10:10)

The heart of the cross

In the light of this New Testament teaching, we can deduce several important points, which will take us to the heart of what was going on at the cross.

1. The apostles always link the cross with our "sins"

For them, Jesus' death is not just an example of heroic suffering or powerful love. Of course, it is a great act of love, but only because it achieved something for us – it did something to our sins. In one key verse, Peter refers to Jesus' "sin-bearing," which (in the light of its Old Testament usage) means receiving the penalty that our sins deserved:

He himself bore our sins in his body on the cross...
1 Peter 2:24

It is an act of salvation (or rescue) which brings us into a place of safety. The very name "Jesus" means "God saves" (Matthew 1:21) and there are frequent references to him as the "Saviour". He "came into the world to save sinners" (1 Timothy 1:15).

Sometimes we dislike this emphasis on sin:

- "Do we really have to see Jesus' death against this background?"
- "What if our sinfulness is not so serious?"
- "And, anyway, couldn't God forgive us without anyone needing to die for us?"

Such questions, however, begin to imply that Jesus' death was pointless: it's a brave person who says that to Jesus! They also overlook the seriousness of sin in God's sight. Note some key points that Paul makes in Romans concerning the seriousness of sin:

- God judges everyone by the same standard (2:11).
- Everyone has sinned and is far away from God's saving presence (3:23).
- Death has spread to the whole human race because everyone has sinned (5:12).
- Sin is something which can easily control us, gain mastery over us, and to which we can become enslaved if we do not stand against it (6:12, 16–17).
- Sin pays its wages – death (6:23).

Sin is thus a more deadly disease than we know. Jesus knew this. He too warned people that they would "die in their sins" and that "everyone who sins is a slave to sin" (John 8:21, 24, 34). Sin turns out to be the guiding principle of our lives – if lived without repentance and turning back to God in obedience.

Moreover, sin is not just about the wrong things we do with our bodies but also about the wrong things we think in our minds and feel in our hearts. We are called, says Jesus in Matthew 22:37, to love God with all our heart, soul, and mind;

but in each of these three areas of our lives we simply fail to do this. God thus sees sin:

- not just in our conscious actions, but even in our unconscious re-actions;
- not just in the ways we selfishly do things to advance our own cause, but also in the ways we defend ourselves from others;
- not just in in the things we do in public, but also in the things we do in the privacy of our own rooms and in the secret imagination of our inner hearts.

Sin is thus deeply ingrained within us, and we are helpless to save ourselves from its consequences and from its power. We need forgiveness from a holy God who is deeply opposed to our sin; we also need his strength to be set free from its ongoing power.

That's why Jesus gave his life – to rescue us from the death that will come to us because of our sins. That's also why God raised Jesus from the dead – to make us alive with him as new people, filled with his Spirit such that we can begin to live lives set free from the power of sin (see chapters 3 and 10).

So that's why the apostles always link Jesus' death on the cross with our sins:

He was delivered over to death for our sins and was raised to life for our justification.

Romans 4:25

2. The apostles understand that Jesus did something for us which we could never do for ourselves

It is not as though, with a little more effort, we could have made our own way back to God or worked out our own salvation. No, there is the frank realization that we are inept, helpless, and unable to save ourselves.

When we were still powerless, Christ died for the ungodly... While we were still sinners, Christ died for us.

Romans 5:6, 8

As a result, "it is by grace you have been saved, through faith – and this is not from yourselves, it is the gift of God – not by works" (Ephesians 2:8–9). So we should not think of Jesus just as our representative (doing something for us, as it were, as our leader) but rather as our substitute (doing something in our place and on our behalf, which we ourselves could never do). Jesus gave his life for us; but, when pressed, that little word "for" strictly means "in our place" or "instead of us".

3. The apostles express their wonder that on the cross this was God himself at work

The New Testament writers are adamant that the cross is the work of God. Jesus is not some poor human being – an innocent third party – whom God asks to die for others. No, in Jesus' death on the cross, God himself was showing his own love for us.

So Paul writes: "God demonstrates his own love for us in this... Christ died for us" (Romans 5:8). Look at this verse very carefully: it only makes sense if Christ and God are identified in some way. If they were quite separate, then the cross would only show us the love of Christ, not the love of God. Yet in fact, the cross does show us God's love, because Christ was there acting for and as God. As Paul says, God was acting directly in and through Christ – "for in Christ all the fullness of the Deity lives in bodily form" (Colossians 2:9; see also 2 Corinthians 5:19).

> In Jesus' death on the cross, God himself was showing his own love for us.

This is truly amazing. In what other religion does God love us so much as to... die for us? Look how much he gave up for us so that we might be forgiven! Effectively, if Jesus was our substitute, then we must now say that God himself substituted himself for us. In other words, when faced with the cross, we are looking at an act of divine self-sacrifice:

- "God made him who had no sin to be sin for us, so that in him we might become the righteousness of God" (2 Corinthians 5:21).

- "For God so loved the world that he gave his one and only Son" (John 3:16).

Truly, salvation is won for us, not by human beings, but only by the Lord* himself. This is well expressed in the Old Testament: "Salvation comes from the Lord" (Jonah 2:9). No one else can save us but God alone, and, through Jesus' cross, that is precisely what God has done.

Jesus' followers, then, should never move away from the cross. They should never dismiss it as elementary or primitive – something which they can now leave behind because they are too mature or because they have no need for it. On the contrary, we should return to it on a daily basis – this is the only place where we can safely stand before God. As an old hymn says, "All other ground is shifting sand."

So the cross is the bedrock of our faith. It may seem foolish and weak to others, Paul notes, but to us it is "the power of God and the wisdom of God" (1 Corinthians 1:24). Paul himself focused his teaching on "Jesus Christ and him crucified" and wanted others to fill their imaginations with the cross (1 Corinthians 2:2; Galatians 3:1). In his experience it was the only thing that a believer should ever boast about:

May I never boast except in the cross of our Lord Jesus Christ.
Galatians 6:14 (see also 1 Corinthians 1:18–31)

Coming to the cross

The cross, then, is God's greatest action in human history. Not surprisingly, therefore, we see hints of it way back in the Old Testament – as God prepared his people for the coming of his great salvation.

That's why, on the Emmaus* road, we saw Jesus pointing out "in all the Scriptures" that "the Messiah had to suffer" (Luke 24:26–27). He wanted them to put the jigsaw together, to see how the cross was the goal of God's long-term purposes. Almost certainly, at some point, he will have drawn attention to the so-called "Servant Songs" in the prophecy of Isaiah. The last of these (amazingly, written over 500 years earlier) predicts in an uncanny way the events of Jesus' crucifixion. It is worth reading all of Isaiah 52:13 – 53:12. The Lord's Servant, it says, would be "despised", "rejected", and brought down to death, but this would come about, not because of his own sins, but because of the sins of others:

> But **he** was pierced for **our** transgressions,
>   **he** was crushed for **our** iniquities;
> the punishment that brought **us** peace was on **him**,
>   and by **his** wounds **we** are healed.
> We all, like sheep, have gone astray,
>   each of **us** has turned to **our** own way;
> and the Lord has laid on **him**
>   the iniquity of **us** all.
>
> Isaiah 53:5–6 (emphasis mine)

Here again, we see the way the Bible links sin and death. Here too is someone suffering for the sins of others, receiving the punishment they deserved. This prophecy then explains Peter's clear vision (see above) of the cross as the place of "sin-bearing", as well as Jesus' own reference to his life being given "as a ransom for many" (Mark 10:45; 1 Peter 2:24). Reading this prophecy prayerfully and faithfully, Jesus would have realized that he himself was called to be the Suffering Servant of the Lord (though paradoxically, as we have seen, he was also to be identified with the Lord himself!).

Yet Isaiah's prophecy also speaks clearly about us. "We all," it says, "like sheep, have gone astray." In relation to God, we do indeed wander like sheep: we dislike his rule, cherish our independence, and go off and do our own thing. This wandering and disobedience is part of what the Bible refers to as "sin" – a short word for what is a huge problem. In God's sight "all have sinned and fall short of the glory of God" (Romans 3:23; see also 3:9–12). Is there any way back?

The cross of Jesus is God's answer. It is the place where "we are healed" (Isaiah 53:5), the place where sin is dealt with once and for all, the place where the barrier between us and God is decisively removed. For (as Isaiah foresaw) the Lord, the holy God of Israel, placed "the punishment that brought us peace... on him" – that is, on Jesus, his Son. This removes our sins, as it were, from off our shoulders and onto the shoulders of Jesus; it therefore removes the barrier of sin between us and God. The possibility of intimate relationship with God is restored.

As a result (to use a different picture), Jesus' death then becomes like a bridge from earth to heaven, from human beings to God – it is the one way through to God (for a diagram describing this bridge, see Box 6b in chapter 6). As Peter says: "For Christ also suffered once for sins, the righteous for the unrighteous, to bring you to God" (1 Peter 3:18). Through the cross, the barrier is brought down and the road opened for travel – all we now need to do is to walk along it!

So, if we want to approach God with a clear conscience with all barriers broken down, and if we want to be declared "not guilty" and included in God's family, then we must come to Jesus at his cross. We must place our sins on him, asking Jesus to carry them for us; we must repent, asking God for his forgiveness.

In God's sight, people's sins are located in one of two places: either on the shoulders of the person who has committed them, or on the shoulders of Jesus who offers to carry them. We have to ask ourselves: where now are our sins? Through the cross, Jesus wants to take this major burden off our shoulders; it is surely a part of what he meant when he said, "Come to me, all you who are weary and burdened, and I will give you rest" (Matthew 11:28). Indeed, people cannot follow Jesus if they insist on carrying their own burdens along the road. Instead we each need to confess* our sins and then give them over to Jesus.

What happens when we do this? Here is what the New Testament promises:

- We are forgiven: "I will forgive their wickedness" (Hebrews 8:12, quoting Jeremiah 31:34).
- We are reckoned as righteous (or justified) in God's sight, "made acceptable to God", and vindicated in God's court of judgment (Romans 3:24; 5:1).
- We have "peace with God" (Romans 5:1).

- We are "adopted" as God's own children into his family; those who receive Jesus in this way are given by him the "right to become children of God" (John 1:12; see also Romans 8:15–17; Ephesians 1:5; Galatians 3:26).

- We can now dare to call Almighty God "our Father" (as Jesus encourages us in the Lord's Prayer) and enjoy a personal relationship with him – so personal, in fact, that the Bible even uses the word "*Abba*"* (which means "my dad"; see Matthew 6:9; Galatians 4:6; Romans 8:15; and chapter 3).

- We become full members of the people of God (Galatians 4:7; Ephesians 2:19; Romans 3:29–30).

These are the great New Testament promises that apply to us – but only because of Jesus' cross. We may sometimes feel they are not true, but our feelings are unreliable guides. What is utterly reliable is Jesus' cross. This event is an unchangeable event in human history. God cannot, as it were, undo what he has done! So we should build our lives on this solid rock. We should take God at his word and humbly receive what he promises: total forgiveness.

So the second building block in the Christian life is to understand the cross and to enjoy God's forgiveness. In some ways, this could have been our first building block. For, when individuals first come to Jesus, they must always know their need for his forgiveness – hence the reference to Jesus' death in the sample prayer in chapter 1. Even so, it was helpful in chapter 1 to focus on the resurrection, because without the resurrection, Jesus' cross lacks any power. The cross on its own – without the resurrection – is only half the story. After all, a Jesus who stays dead is ultimately no Good News at all.

Yet as soon as we affirm Jesus' resurrection, we see the cross in a whole new light: as God's appointed sacrifice, gladly accepted by God, and as the moment of Jesus' greatest glory – where he won a resounding victory over evil and the powers of darkness (John 12:23; 2 Corinthians 13:4; Colossians 2:15).

So the cross and the resurrection belong together. Some people may find that they first come to Christ through pondering the truth of the resurrection, others through hearing about the cross. Yet everyone needs to move on to discover the other half of the story: the Risen Jesus also died for us; and the one who died for us is alive today.

> *I am the Living One; I was dead, and now look, I am alive for ever and ever!*
>
> Revelation 1:18

Everyone needs to move on to discover the other half of the story: the Risen Jesus also died for us; and the one who died for us is alive today.

Living under the cross

So this is where our Christian life begins – at the cross of the Risen Jesus. If it does not begin here, it does not begin at all. Yet, in a sense, this is also where we must stay throughout our Christian lives. As we have seen, we can never say "goodbye" to the cross, or move on to seemingly more important things.

In chapter 11 we will explore further what it means in practice to keep living under the cross in our fight against sin in our lives. For now, however, we close by noting simply how the cross can help us to be sure of God's love for us.

In our early days as Jesus' followers, we often have many doubts. What if I keep on sinning? Am I really "saved"? Am I part of God's family? Such questions are quite understandable. After all, if sin is as deeply ingrained with us as we learned from Paul's words in Romans above, then it is only to be expected that we should fall again and again into its trap. We are hardly likely to become perfect overnight! Instead, our new life in Jesus helps us to begin to recognize the reality of sin in places we had never seen it before. This can be very discouraging. So we can keep feeling we have failed too badly or have not been committed enough.

God knows all this, but he encourages us to keep coming back to the cross.

- He wants us to realize that Jesus died for all our sin – no sin is so terrible that somehow Jesus did not die for that sin.

- He wants us to see that Jesus loves us totally. Even if we had been the only person in the world, he would still have died for me: he is "the Son of God, who loved me and gave himself for me" (Galatians 2:20).

So we are not to worry whether we are good enough. Instead, we can have a humble assurance, knowing that we now truly belong to God and also that we will go to be with him when we die. He is now fully committed to us, and Jesus "always lives to intercede" for us, because our names are "written" in the "Lamb's book of life" (Hebrews 7:25; Revelation 13:8). Indeed, Jesus the Good Shepherd knows each of his followers by name and has promised that "no one will snatch them out of my hand" (John 10:28).

So, when we continue to sin against God – as we will each day – we must learn to return to the cross. The apostle John recorded Jesus' words, assuring believers that they had truly "crossed over from death to life" and would "not be judged" (John 5:24). Yet John knew we would continue to sin. So he wisely wrote:

> *The blood of Jesus, his Son, purifies us from all sins. If we claim to be without sin, we deceive ourselves and the truth is not in us. If we confess our sins, he is faithful and just and will forgive us our sins.*
>
> 1 John 1:7–9

Every day, we need God's forgiveness. And every day we can receive it through the cross. "The Lord's... compassions never fail. They are new every morning" (Lamentations 3:22–23). So the second building block in the Christian life is to keep coming to the cross of Jesus – to accept his forgiveness and to receive his love.

Building block 2

Accept his forgiveness – Jesus died for you!

3

Welcome His Spirit

---

*I am going to send you
what my Father has promised.*
Luke 24:49

Luke 24 describes one long, memorable day – the first Easter*
Sunday. It was a day full of surprises, from dawn till dusk: visions of
angels, strange encounters on the road, and an in-depth Bible study
with an unrecognized teacher. But before the day was out, Jesus'
followers were in for another surprise. "I am going to send you what
my Father has promised;" Jesus said, "but stay in the city until you
have been clothed with power from on high." Jesus' followers would
be given a special gift – the gift of the Holy Spirit.

After focusing on his death and resurrection, what was the very
next thing Jesus wanted his followers to understand? Answer: the
Holy Spirit. Although the word "Spirit" is not expressly used in Luke
24, this "promised gift" from the Father clearly refers to the Holy
Spirit. We know this because the opening chapters of Luke's second
volume tell us the story of what happened next – when the Holy
Spirit came in power (see Acts 2, printed in full at the start of part
2). Ten days later, Jesus' followers, following his instructions, are
indeed waiting in the city of Jerusalem*. Then suddenly there is a
great noise like "the blowing of a violent wind" and they are all "filled
with the Holy Spirit." The Holy Spirit has come upon them.

We call this event Pentecost*. It marked the launch of Jesus'
church*. It was a clear, unrepeatable sign that Jesus' people from
now on would always be people of the Spirit. We shall be looking at

this event in more detail in part 2, but for now we focus on this earlier promise of Jesus concerning the Holy Spirit in Luke 24. We shall find his words open up for us a surprising new sphere of spiritual reality.

What would we think if someone came up to us in the street and said something like this: "I am going to live inside you!"? We would say they were mad. How can anyone live inside someone else? But Jesus can – and he does! This turns out to be what the promised gift of the Holy Spirit is all about. Jesus lives within each of his followers by means of the Holy Spirit.

So the third building block in following Jesus will be all about welcoming his Holy Spirit within our lives, for the Spirit is the very life of Jesus himself within us. From now on, we are never alone; following Jesus need never be something we do in our own strength. No, we find we have a new engine inside: his powerful Spirit.

Jesus teaches about the coming of the Holy Spirit

What is the basis for this seemingly bizarre idea that Jesus can somehow live within us? Or that the Holy Spirit can be identified in some way with Jesus himself? The answer, once again, is that Jesus himself expressly taught this amazing truth.

A few days earlier, on the night before he died, Jesus had said these puzzling words:

> *Anyone who loves me will obey my teaching. My Father will love them, and we will come to them and make our home with them.*
>
> John 14:23

Back in chapter 1, we saw how the Risen Jesus sees the believer's life as being like a house, and he promises to "come in", when he is asked. Here Jesus is using the same picture and making the same promise: he will come into the home of our lives and he will live within us. In this passage, three new things stand out about Jesus' promise:

- Jesus emphasizes that he will be taking up a fixed residence. He will not be leaving again suddenly, but he will be dwelling (or abiding) with us. We become, as it were, his permanent home!

- God the Father also comes to reside within the believer.
- Jesus makes it clear that this is the work of the Holy Spirit. It will be by means of the Holy Spirit that God and Jesus are able to live within the believer.

Box 3a – Jesus' teaching about the Holy Spirit at the Last Supper

And I will ask the Father, and he will give you another advocate to help you and be with you forever – the Spirit of truth. The world cannot accept him, because it neither sees him nor knows him. But you know him, for he lives with you and will be in you.

I will not leave you as orphans; I will come to you.

The Advocate, the Holy Spirit, whom the Father will send in my name, will teach you all things.

When the Advocate comes... the Spirit of truth who goes out from the Father – he will testify about me.

You are filled with grief because I have said these things. But very truly I tell you, it is for your good that I am going away. Unless I go away, the Advocate will not come to you; but if I go, I will send him to you. When he comes, he will prove the world to be in the wrong about sin and righteousness and judgment.

But when he, the Spirit of truth, comes, he will guide you into all the truth. He will not speak on his own; he will speak only what he hears, and he will tell you what is yet to come. He will glorify me because it is from me that he will receive what he will make known to you.

John 14:16–17, 18, 26; 15:26; 16:6–8, 13–14

From Jesus' other teaching on that night (see Box 3a), we see how he is preparing his followers for his own imminent departure and death. They must not be sad, because he will "come" to them. When we ask how (or in what way) Jesus is coming back, the answer from these verses is clear: by the Holy Spirit. When the Holy Spirit comes to them, this will be Jesus coming back to them.

> When the Holy Spirit comes to them, this will be Jesus coming back to them.

That's why Jesus describes the Holy Spirit as "another advocate". That word "another" literally means "another one of the same kind". Just as Jesus was the great Helper, so the Holy Spirit will be. What Jesus is, the Holy Spirit is. God is not sending someone completely different from Jesus – but another one, just like him!

Jesus also teaches here several other important truths about the Holy Spirit:

- He is able to reveal God's truths to his people.
- He is able to convict people in the "world" of their sin.
- He is to be thought of as a person, not just an impersonal force, because he is "another", like Jesus. Since Jesus was a person, so the Holy Spirit is too.
- Unlike Jesus, however, who was confined to one physical location, the Spirit may dwell in many different people – as many as believe in Jesus – all around the world.
- He is an unseen reality that unbelievers cannot see, know, or understand. This means there is indeed, as the saying goes, "more to life than meets the eye". The physical, visible world is not the sum of all reality. The Spirit is an unseen, but nevertheless real, personal power at work in the world.

The most important point, however, is this: Jesus is able to live within his people by the Holy Spirit. If we are now believers in Jesus, then the Holy Spirit truly lives within us!

The Holy Spirit in the New Testament

In due course, Jesus' followers discovered exactly what he meant. The Holy Spirit came upon them at Pentecost. And then the same things happened for those to whom they preached. These people too discovered this great reality of the Spirit. They had never seen Jesus physically, but they knew him by his Spirit – and his Spirit truly dwelt within them.

Read the book of Acts to see just how the Holy Spirit spread. See what the first Christians were able to accomplish because of Jesus' Spirit within them! Some people have suggested that The Acts of the Apostles (the normal, full title of Luke's second volume) should instead be called "The Acts of Jesus", or "The Acts of the Holy Spirit". For truly, what we are seeing there is the incredible outworking

> The Spirit is an unseen, but nevertheless real, personal power at work in the world.

of Jesus' own life and power through the agency of his Spirit. The Mediterranean world of the first century was hit by a tidal wave of spiritual power and energy, the ripples from which can still be sensed today. And what was the cause of the ripples? Nothing less than the Spirit-empowered life of Jesus, now unleashed on the world through Jesus' Spirit being at work within his followers.

So the New Testament writers often speak about the Holy Spirit (see Box 3b) – and they do so very much from personal experience. This is no merely academic matter, but a profound, life-changing reality, which you too can enjoy. Ask any Christian and they ought to be able to speak about the Holy Spirit at work in their lives.

Box 3b – The apostles' teaching on the Holy Spirit: Three great realities

1. The Holy Spirit is a person

He is not an "it", nor an impersonal force. He is an eternal Person within the Godhead. So the New Testament writers speak of God as "the Father, ... the Son, and... the Holy Spirit" (Matthew 28:19).

2. The Holy Spirit is the power of God

The few Old Testament references to the Spirit use the language of God's "breath" (Hebrew: *ruach*). It is by his "breath" that God speaks his powerful word in creation, and by his Spirit that he inspires the ancient prophets of Israel* (Psalm 33:4–7; 2 Peter 1:21). In the New Testament, Jesus himself is the human being who is "full of the Holy Spirit" (Luke 4:1, 14), and by his Spirit his followers sometimes perform powerful deeds and miracles (Hebrews 2:4; Acts 3:8; 5:9; 13:11; 19:11–12; 28:8). This power of the Holy Spirit is seen, perhaps supremely, in the "miracle" of conversion. Every time someone puts their faith in Christ, this is directly the work of the Holy Spirit, who has been convicting that person, speaking to them and drawing them towards Christ (John 16:8–11; see also 1 Corinthians 12:3). Moreover, the "new birth" that results is also evidence of the Spirit's power (John 3:3–6).

3. The Holy Spirit is the presence of God

God the Father dwells in his majesty and holiness beyond and above our world, yet he is also able to be present within our world by his Spirit. Old Testament believers recognized God's presence in Jerusalem's Temple – it was the "dwelling for his Name". In the New Testament, however, Jesus, as God incarnate*, was God's presence on earth; this means he has replaced the Temple with himself (see Deuteronomy 12:11; Psalm 26:8; John 1:14; 2:19–21). He has also made his church to be a temple, and we ourselves as believers are, as it were, miniature temples (1 Corinthians 3:16; 6:19). This means that God is now present in his world – through living within you and me!

God is offering us this very special gift. To be a Christian is not just about knowing Jesus because of his resurrection, nor just about receiving God's forgiveness through the cross. God has a third great gift for us: we can enjoy God's empowering presence within our lives through the Person of the Holy Spirit.

Common questions

This teaching about the Holy Spirit may leave us, however, with some real questions.

The Spirit within – picture or reality?

Is this talk of the Holy Spirit "living within us" really true? Or is it just a picture? Perhaps it is just a colourful way of speaking? After all, we cannot see the Holy Spirit. So where exactly in our bodies – within our persons – is he supposed to be living?

People in Jesus' day struggled with just this kind of question. We see this in the way a man called Nicodemus responded to some of Jesus' first teaching about the Holy Spirit. Jesus had said to him:

> *The wind blows wherever it pleases. You hear its sound, but you cannot tell where it comes from or where it is going. So it is with everyone born of the Spirit.*
>
> **John 3:8**

Understandably, Nicodemus then replied, "How can this be?" It doesn't seem to make sense! We feel comfortable with what we can see, but we cannot see the Holy Spirit. Nevertheless, just because the Spirit is invisible – like the wind, says Jesus – this does not mean he is not real.

In his subsequent teaching about the Holy Spirit (see Box 3a), Jesus was quite clear that people in the world (that is, people who do not believe in Jesus) will simply never understand the reality of the Holy Spirit: "The world cannot accept him" (John 14:17). Yet their unbelief or cynicism does not deny the Spirit's reality. Jesus went on:

> *"But you know him, for he lives with you and will be in you."*
>
> **John 14:17**

In other words, believers in Jesus will be able to sense his reality.

As to where exactly the Spirit resides within us, perhaps the best way to understand the Bible's teaching is to think of the Spirit dwelling within our "spirits". Paul hints at this when he writes: "though your body is dead because of sin, your spirit is alive because of righteousness" (Romans 8:10, my translation). When we believe in Jesus, it is our spirits within us, which previously were dead, that now come alive – presumably by the operation and presence of God's Spirit within them. We may not see anything, but God is truly present within our spirits. This is not just a picture, however. This is an unseen spiritual reality.

The Spirit's permanence – in every believer?

Is it really true that every believer has the Holy Spirit? Perhaps the Holy Spirit is only for good Christians? Perhaps only for those with special, "miraculous" gifts? Perhaps he comes and goes – sometimes being present within the believer, sometimes not?

Despite what many people say, the New Testament is crystal clear about this. The Spirit dwells within each believer from the moment that person first believes in Jesus – and he never leaves! Yes, we may often grieve him (Ephesians 4:30) and we are encouraged to keep on being "filled with the Spirit" (Ephesians 5:18); yet the Holy Spirit never leaves us. Nor does he wait till we have become mature or seemingly "powerful" Christians. We see this teaching in many places:

> The Holy Spirit dwells within each believer from the moment that person first believes in Jesus – and he never leaves!

- As we have already seen, when people open their lives to him, the Risen Jesus says, "I will come in" and promises to stay or live in them for ever (Revelation 3:20; John 14:16, 23). He remains in us and we become his permanent address. Jesus keeps his promises. These verses do not say, "I will be leaving again very soon afterwards"!

- Paul too teaches very clearly: "If anyone does not have the Spirit of Christ, they do not belong to Christ" (Romans 8:9). By implication, therefore, if we do belong to him, then we do have the Holy Spirit. We cannot be Christ's without his Spirit. So Paul goes on to affirm quite clearly for these believers: "Christ is in you" (8:10).

We are not to doubt that the Holy Spirit is now truly within us. If we have put our trust in Jesus as our Lord and Saviour, if we have asked him to come into our lives, then from that moment the Holy Spirit lives within us. (There is only one episode in the New Testament which suggests that some believers experienced something slightly different, namely, when the Good News first reached the Samaritans*.) We may not always feel this, but it is a fact. And we must begin to build our lives on this amazing spiritual reality: we are God-indwelt people!

We will need to claim this great truth against our own doubting, perhaps when we feel far from God or know we have sinned against him; perhaps too when we see other believers acting in ways that dishonour God, or even hurting us in some way. Whatever we may think, the Spirit is still within them, though he may well be grieving over the situation and their behaviour. The Spirit does not, as it were, come and go, but is rather the Spirit who abides and stays put.

Spiritual "gifts" – all of them for everyone?

There is another situation in which we may need to claim this truth even more. This is when we encounter people who seem "super-spiritual" – those people who imply that we cannot have the Holy Spirit in our lives because we do not do all the "spiritual things" that they do (speaking in tongues*, performing miracles, leading powerful worship, or whatever it may be).

These spiritual things are often referred to as being among the spiritual gifts* and Paul in 1 Corinthians 12–14 encourages us to seek after them: "eagerly desire gifts of the Spirit" (1 Corinthians 14:1). Yet he is also aware that they can cause great arguments and divisions among people. That's why he says the most important spiritual gift is love (1 Corinthians 13:1–13). We are certainly not acting in love if we cause young Christians to doubt the presence of the Holy Spirit in their lives by drawing attention to our own supposedly greater gifting! So Paul teaches here that no believer is without some kind of spiritual gift.

Now to each one the manifestation of the Spirit is given for the common good.

1 Corinthians 12:7

Paul wants us to recognize that it is the Spirit, not we ourselves, who gives these gifts – "he distributes them to each one, just as he determines" (1 Corinthians 12:11). He also stresses that they are always given for "for the common good" (12:7) and that no individual possesses all the gifts. Instead, just as a body has many different parts, so believers have a variety of gifts – with each person's gifts complementing the gifts of others.

So, by all means, ask God for more of the Spirit; yes, seek spiritual gifts. But also be wary of those people who draw attention to their own gifts. Above all, never doubt that the Holy Spirit is already within you. And, if ever we find ourselves asking God for more of the Spirit, let us remember that we are not asking the Spirit, as though he were absent, to come for the first time. No, we are asking the Spirit, who is already present through our faith in Jesus, simply to reveal more of his presence and power in our lives.

Learning from the Spirit

Jesus wants us to follow him by drawing upon the help of his Holy Spirit, who now lives within us. Here, then, are four key points we should remember about the Spirit's purpose as we get used to living under his direction. What does the Holy Spirit want?

1. The Holy Spirit always wants to point us towards Jesus

Jesus said of the Holy Spirit: "He will glorify me" (John 16:14). The Holy Spirit is fixated with the glory of Jesus. And he wants us to appreciate this glory for ourselves. So, if we want to cooperate with the Spirit, this means we will keep our eyes fixed on Jesus and seek to promote his glory and praise. It means letting the Holy Spirit show us more of Jesus.

> The Holy Spirit is fixated with the glory of Jesus.

The Spirit-filled life will always be a Jesus-focused life.

2. The Holy Spirit wants us to enjoy our relationship with God as our Father

Paul writes:

> *Those who are led by the Spirit of God are the children of God... the Spirit you received brought about your adoption to sonship. And by him we cry, "Abba*, Father."*

Romans 8:14–15

Indeed he goes on: "The Spirit himself testifies with our spirit that we are God's children" (Romans 8:16). In Galatians he says the same: "Because you are his sons, God sent the Spirit of his Son into our hearts, the Spirit who calls out, 'Abba, Father.'" (Galatians 4:6). The Spirit wants us to dare to call God our Father.

For some of us, this may be incredibly difficult. We cannot think of God in this intimate way; indeed we often find it hard to believe he is interested in us at all. For some of us, this may be partly because of our relationship with our own, human father. Some of us come from families where our fathers have been removed from us – through their over-busyness or emotional distance, through divorce, or their death; and some, sadly, have had abusive fathers. Few of us know the liberating power of a father's love for us. This is where the Good News kicks in! Each of us who believes in Jesus now has the living God for our true Father.

> The Spirit wants us to dare to call God our Father.

The Holy Spirit wants to help us sense our Father's love for us, to know deep down his unique delight in us as his children. He wants us to hear addressed to us the same words as God once spoke to Jesus: "You are my Son, whom I love; with you I am well pleased" (Mark 1:11). Jesus was God's "Child" in a unique sense, but we too are now truly God's children through being adopted into his family (Romans 8:15, 23; Galatians 4:5). Jesus has given us "the right to become children of God" (John 1:12; see also 20:17). God wants us to run like a little child into his arms, crying out, "Abba, Dad!" Jesus' followers, because of the Spirit, are to walk through each day knowing they are truly children of their heavenly Father, looking up to his face, and drawing into their inmost beings his deep delight.

3. The Holy Spirit wants to help us to pray

Paul continues:

> *The Spirit helps us in our weakness. We do not know what we ought to pray for, but the Spirit himself intercedes for us through wordless groans.*
>
> **Romans 8:26**

None of us, naturally, finds it easy to pray. Now that the Holy Spirit is actually residing within us, he can help us. Focused times of prayer can become opportunities when we let the Spirit within us do the praying. And our whole lives can be lived "in the Spirit" as we "always keep on praying", as the Spirit leads (Ephesians 6:18).

4. The Holy Spirit wants to enable us to live like Jesus

When we first believe in Jesus, we come to him as Saviour, because we recognize God's judgment upon our human sin. We renounce evil and choose now to go God's way. After that, the Christian life is meant to continue in the same vein – an ongoing and continual turning away from sin. How can we do this? We may have good intentions, but we are all so weak!

This is where the Spirit comes to our rescue. For not only can the Spirit reveal to us what Jesus would do, he can also then give us the strength to do it. We will return to this key point in chapter 10, but for now we note that this is perhaps the most important of the Spirit's desires – to help us live as Jesus would want us to. This dependency on God's Spirit will need to become a daily feature of our lives.

> This dependency on God's Spirit will need to become a daily feature of our lives.

Every believer in Jesus has the Spirit of Jesus within them. All of us must learn to love Jesus' Spirit, recognizing his presence with us, and walking each day in his power and strength. The third key building block for growing as a Christian is therefore to welcome God's Spirit daily – for already, through our faith in Jesus, he is living within us.

As we look back over these first three chapters, we can sense what a great foundation we have been given in the Good News:

- In chapter 1 we saw how God is now with us: because of the resurrection, Jesus is alive today and able to meet with us.

- In chapter 2 we saw that God is for us: because of Jesus' cross, we can now be God's friends, forgiven and holy in his sight.

- Now in chapter 3 we see that God is also in us: because the Holy Spirit is given to every believer in Jesus Christ.

God with us, God for us, God in us! Now there's a slogan worth remembering – perhaps reciting to yourself every morning. These great truths are a solid, immoveable foundation on which we can build our Christian lives.

Building block 3
Welcome his spirit – Jesus lives in you!

Feed on His Scriptures

Jesus explained to them what was said in all the
Scriptures concerning himself.
They asked each other, "Were not our hearts burning
within us while he... opened the Scriptures to us?"
Luke 24:27, 32

The Risen Jesus is laying down good foundations for his followers. He teaches about the three great realities at the heart of Christian faith (his resurrection, the cross, and the Spirit), but there is more. On several occasions during that first Easter Day, as recorded in Luke 24, he draws the attention of his followers to the importance of something else: the Holy Scriptures.

The Scriptures (literally, the "writings") were what we now call the "Old Testament". They were ancient texts, received by God's people through the centuries, in which they believed God was truly speaking with his people – written by human beings, but actually inspired by God. On the road to Emmaus, Jesus now goes through "all the Scriptures",

> The Scriptures, expounded by Jesus, bring sheer and utter delight.

explaining how they spoke of his own suffering and glory. Later, back in Jerusalem with his followers, he does the same: as he went through "the Law of Moses, the prophets, and the Psalms", he "opened their minds so they could understand the Scriptures" (Luke 24:44–45). And the result of this extended Bible study, led by the Risen Jesus, is that the disciples find their hearts burning with excitement. The Scriptures, expounded by Jesus, bring sheer and utter delight.

The Risen Jesus is giving us here a vital clue about what it will mean to be his followers once he has departed. Scripture will be central. So the fourth building block in following Jesus is to learn about him through the Scriptures and to give to the Bible the importance which Jesus himself gave to it. Those who love Jesus should love his Scriptures.

Ever since, Jesus' followers have found the Bible to be a source of endless encouragement. Here they have found promises to claim, truths to ponder, examples to heed, and prayers to repeat. Here we find the whole counsel of God, which enlarges our minds; here we find food that sustains our hearts and strengthens our wills. So let us feed on his Scriptures.

A surprising lesson

Jesus wants us to make use of this amazing, God-given resource. Yet his insistence on this here in Luke 24 is all the more remarkable for three slightly different reasons:

1. The Scriptures are important, even though we now have the Risen Jesus

Conceivably, Jesus could have said something like this: "Now I am back from the dead, you have something far more exciting to focus on than an old book!" Yet he says no such thing. The resurrection is indeed life changing, but the Bible is not thereby rendered redundant. If anything, we need it all the more – both to learn how Jesus' coming fits into the Old Testament, but also to help us in our ongoing relationship with this now-Risen Jesus.

Sadly, we can easily go wrong at this point. We come to know Jesus, but sometimes we then think that we have an independent hotline to God which does not need the guidance of the Scriptures. "Who needs the Bible and its difficult words, when you've got direct access to Jesus himself?" The danger, however, is that we then start following an imaginary Jesus, suited to our own likings.

Some people start following a "gentle Jesus, meek and mild", who never speaks out strongly against sin. Others follow a Jesus who (not surprisingly) ends up endorsing all their own prejudices and agendas. Either way, Jesus becomes merely a pale reflection of our own preferences. Instead of following Jesus, it's we who now are taking the lead; we start making Jesus in our image! To avoid all this, what we need is to be following the authentic, awesome Jesus revealed to us in the Bible.

In other words, we need the Scriptures to keep us on the straight and narrow way because the Scriptures alone reliably teach us about Jesus as he really is. Effectively, Jesus is saying something like this: "You need me, but you also need the Scriptures. I am the truth, but they are truth too. Follow me by submitting to them."

> The Scriptures alone reliably teach us about Jesus as he really is.

2. The Scriptures are important, even though we now have the Holy Spirit

This too might come as a surprise. The Risen Jesus has been promising his disciples the gift of his Spirit (as seen in chapter 3); yet he insists this gift does not make the Bible unnecessary. The Risen Jesus knows such thinking may lead us down a false track – not because the Holy Spirit will mislead us, but because we ourselves may misinterpret what the Spirit is saying. Here again, without the guiding control of the Scriptures our sinful hearts may begin to follow our own desires.

So, before returning to his Father, Jesus makes clear that he is leaving not just the gift of his Spirit but also the equally precious gift of the Scriptures. Yes, the one gift might be coming to Jesus' followers in a sudden new way at Pentecost, while the other had taken centuries to produce; even so, both the receiving of God's Spirit and the reading of the written Scriptures are vitally important for God's people. They must not be played off against one another.

Again, the one may bring us an experience of God's love into our hearts, the other a knowledge of God's truth to our minds, but wise followers of Jesus will relish both. In other words, those who truly love God's Spirit will love God's Word, and those who truly love his Word will love his Spirit.

3. The Scriptures are important, precisely because of the example of the Risen Jesus

Note Jesus' own remarkable attitude towards the Bible's truth and authority. Jesus here demonstrates how his whole ministry had been fashioned by the Scriptures. In going to the cross, he had been inspired by prophecies and patterns found in the Bible: the Scriptures had been his own hope and these he had now fulfilled. Jesus was truly a person under the authority of Scripture.

If this was true of the Risen Lord, how much more should it be true of us? What was true for Jesus should now be equally true for Jesus' followers.

In the light of Luke 24, therefore, we are presented by Jesus with some key questions:

- Do we love the Bible? If we value the resurrection, the cross, and the Spirit, do we also value the Scriptures?
- Do we ever elevate our own experience (of Jesus or the Spirit) above the Bible? Or will we always test it against the teaching of Scripture?
- As Jesus' followers, will we follow Jesus' example and submit ourselves to the Bible's authority? Will we seek to believe its truth and obey its commands?

Scripture according to Jesus

In chapter 9 we will focus in more detail on how we can obey the teaching of Scripture, but for now we need to examine our attitude to Scripture itself. What is the Bible? Why should we give it this pivotal importance? Why does it have such authority? Put more technically, what should be our doctrine of Scripture?

As already indicated, a vital clue here will be to observe the attitude of Jesus.

Box 4a – The God who speaks his Word: Old and New Testament references

The psalmists praise God for his revelation

Our God is in heaven;
  he does whatever pleases him.
But their idols are silver and gold,
  made by human hands.
They have mouths, but cannot speak,
  eyes, but cannot see.

                                                                 Psalm 115:3–5

The precepts of the Lord are right,
  giving joy to the heart.
The commands of the Lord are radiant,
  giving light to the eyes...
They are more precious than gold,
  than much pure gold;
they are sweeter than honey,
  than honey from the honeycomb.
By them your servant is warned;
  in keeping them there is great reward.

                                                              Psalm 19:8, 10–11

Your word, Lord, is eternal;
  it stands firm in the heavens...
Oh, how I love your law!
  I meditate on it all day long...
How sweet are your words to my taste,
  sweeter than honey to my mouth!...
Your word is a lamp for my feet,
  a light on my path...
All your words are true;
  all your righteous laws are eternal.

                                              Psalm 119:89, 97, 103, 105, 160

God's word through the prophets

As the heavens are higher than the earth,
  so are my ways higher than your ways
  and my thoughts than your thoughts...
So is my word that goes out from my mouth:
  It will not return to me empty,
but will... achieve the purpose for which I sent it.

Isaiah 55:9, 11

These are the ones I look on with favour:
  those who are humble and contrite in spirit,
and who tremble at my word.

Isaiah 66:2

Is not my word like fire... and like a hammer that breaks a rock in pieces?

Jeremiah 23:29

Peter and Paul's approach to the Old Testament

No prophecy of Scripture came about by the prophet's own interpretation of thing. For prophecy never had its origin in the human will, but prophets, though human, spoke from God as they were carried along by the Holy Spirit.

2 Peter 1:20–21

The Holy Scriptures... are able to make you wise for salvation through faith in Christ Jesus... All Scripture is God-breathed and is useful for teaching, rebuking, correcting and training in righteousness, so that the servant of God may be thoroughly equipped for every good work.

2 Timothy 3:15–17

Approaching the Old Testament

First, we should note how Jesus here is in overall agreement with his fellow Jews on this matter. The people of Israel (as seen in Box 4a) had developed a keen understanding of God's Word. They accepted their responsibility to treasure this divine Word and to preserve what had been given to them. Even though sometimes this Word had revealed their disobedience and judged them, yet strangely they still preserved it – precisely because this was a Word which they had not invented for their own comfort but which they sensed they had received from their holy God through his servants.

Jesus himself clearly agreed with this approach. We never see him denouncing this attitude or trying to distance himself from it in some way. Instead there is every indication that Jesus was a person saturated with Scripture, deeply influenced by its prophecies and prayers, keen to explain and defend its teaching, ready to submit to its rules. This submissive approach to Scripture (already evidenced in Luke 24) is seen elsewhere throughout Jesus' life. Here are some examples from the other three Gospels:

Matthew's Gospel

- Jesus makes clear this fundamental priority within his ministry when facing temptation by the Evil One. Three times, he answers Satan* with these solemn words: "It is written..." (4:4, 5, 10).

- In the Sermon on the Mount he asserts categorically that he has not "come to abolish" the Old Testament laws, but rather to "fulfil them" (5:17).

- Later in Jerusalem he chides some of his critics with these words: "You do not know the Scriptures or the power of God" (Matthew 22:29).

- In keeping with this, Matthew himself points out on numerous occasions how events in Jesus' life took place to fulfil what the Lord had said through the Old Testament prophets (e.g. 1:22–23, 2:15, 17, 23).

Mark's Gospel

- When debating with opponents, Jesus quotes some of God's words through the prophet Isaiah: "They worship me in vain; their teachings are merely human rules." And

then he warns: "You have let go of the commands of God...
Thus you nullify the word of God by your tradition that you
have handed down" (7:7–8, 13).

John's Gospel

- Despite claiming himself to be the embodiment of all truth
  ("I am... the truth", 14:6), Jesus also asserts the truth
  of Scripture: "Scripture cannot be set aside" (10:35). In
  praying to God, he simply says: "Your word is truth" (17:17).

- In making the point that merely studying Scripture may
  be futile (if conducted without faith in him), Jesus boldly
  asserts that Scripture's power lies in its capacity to speak
  truly about him: "These are the very Scriptures that testify
  about me" (5:39).

From such comments, we can deduce this startling paradox: Jesus
was himself both subject to Scripture and simultaneously the
subject matter of Scripture. He both obeyed the Scriptures within
his own life and believed that they spoke about him. That's why
in Luke 24 he showed how his ministry had fitted into Scripture's
teaching and also pointed out in all the Scriptures "what was said...
concerning himself". Put another way, although in some senses
he is the Lord of the Word, he does not cease to be the Servant of
the Word. He does not use his own unique authority to demean the
Scriptures but rather bequeaths on them his own authority.

This cuts out, at a stroke, the very common idea that we
can somehow follow Jesus without also following Scripture,
that we can somehow use our elevation of him as a means
of downplaying Scripture. To love Jesus is to love the Word –
the Word which Jesus himself loved, lived by, and died by; the
Word, which he publicly reaffirmed in his teaching, death, and
resurrection.

No wonder, then, that the New Testament writers follow Jesus
with this high regard for the Hebrew Scriptures (see Box 4a again):
they saw them as coming from God with unique authority, seeing all

Scripture as "inspired" by God (or, more accurately translated, "God-breathed"). Behind the human authors of Scripture, they affirmed, was the work of God the Holy Spirit. If the Bible was a human book, it was also a divine book.

This then explains how the apostles* could slip interchangeably from saying "Scripture says..." to saying "God says..." (Galatians 3:8, 22; Romans 4:3; 9:17; 10:19-21). The two amounted to the same thing: What the Scriptures said, God said. These Scriptures were therefore to be received as the "very words of God" (Romans 3:2).

> What the Scriptures said, God said.

It also explains why one of the apostles' key aims in speaking of Jesus was precisely to show how the story of Jesus was the true fulfilment of this longer biblical story. Thus for them, Jesus' coming did not deny Scripture's truth but only affirmed it all the more. The activity and actions of God, which they had witnessed so powerfully for themselves in Jesus, only confirmed that the same God had truly been active in the past (as revealed in the Scriptures). Indeed, truly, his story (Jesus' life, death, and resurrection) was the climax of all history (God's true story for the world as found in the Bible).

Approaching the New Testament

If this is how Jesus and the apostles viewed the Old Testament, then there is a strong argument that this should also be the way we approach the New Testament – the Scriptures left for us by Jesus and the apostles themselves.

The apostles saw the Jesus-event as the true fulfilment of the Old Testament story; they would quickly have seen their own writings (which alone describe and explain that Jesus-event) as a necessary "sequel" within the Scriptures – a second part in God's unfolding drama. Their writings would soon be seen as being on an equal footing with the Old Testament.

This self-consciousness among the apostles (that they were the conveyors of further Scripture) can be seen in several places. Peter views Paul's letters as "Scripture" (2 Peter 3:16) and Paul claims an authority to speak from God (Romans 1:1; Galatians 1:1). Almost certainly, this came about precisely because they were given this role and function by Jesus himself. Since Jesus knew he would never write anything himself, he instead gave this task to his apostles, sending them out on his behalf to act as his special messengers. Effectively, they were commissioned by him to give a truly authoritative account of his life (as it were, as his authorized biographers). They would also be given Jesus' authority to augment his teaching – that is, to draw out the true implications of his coming for those who would respond to the Good News about him. Believers have always needed to know not only the words of Jesus (what he said) but also the works of Jesus (what his coming achieved).

We see this process, this commissioning of the apostles, both in the way in which Jesus first called them (Mark 3:13–15) and also in the way he describes them as his appointed "witnesses" shortly before his departure or ascension* (Matthew 28:16–20, Luke 24:48; Acts 1:8; 10:42). Jesus' apostles were entrusted by him to speak of him truly and authoritatively – not just in real speech or personal testimony, but also, eventually, in writing.

More than that, Jesus gave them an express promise:

> *I have much more to say to you, more than you can now bear. But when he, the Spirit of truth, comes, **he will guide you into all the truth**. He will not speak on his own; he will speak only what he hears, and he will tell you what is yet to cone.*
>
> ### John 16:12–13 (emphasis mine)

The apostles are promised that the Spirit will guide them to speak Jesus' truth to Jesus' people. Firstly, they will not forget anything of importance spoken by Jesus. Secondly, they will be taught any further things that are necessary – those things (the "much more") that Jesus had not been able to say during his lifetime.

It therefore becomes a promise to us. Yet note carefully that his promise is not that we will be led into new truth *beyond* that given to the apostles (which is not necessary), but rather that what the apostles taught in his name is indeed true and comes authoritatively from Jesus by means of his Spirit. The New Testament is therefore the commissioned deposit of Jesus' truth for his followers. As such, we are to receive it *as from Jesus himself*. It is his word to his people, trustworthy and reliable.

> The New Testament is therefore the commissioned deposit of Jesus' truth for his followers.

Indeed, looking at this from God's point of view, one can sense how this faithful account concerning Jesus was always a necessary part and indeed a vital corollary of him ever sending Jesus in the first place. Why would Jesus have bothered to come – let alone to die – if all the people living in later times would find it virtually impossible to find out what he had done? God's great rescue operation would have been wasted – lost for all time! No, within the purposes of God, it was essential that there be an accurate account of Jesus' work.

That authoritative record, so Christians claim, is the New Testament. This means that, while the Old Testament truly prepares us for his coming before the event (as Jesus teaches in Luke 24), the New Testament truly describes that coming after the event. Thus both Old and New Testaments, when combined together, truly teach us about Jesus.

It is in this sense that we can access Jesus only through the Scriptures. Yes, as already noted, he meets us in his risen power by his Holy Spirit, yet we would not know Jesus at all (or recognize that the person we were meeting truly was Jesus) if it were not for the account of him in the Bible. The Scriptures alone have the authority to tell us who he truly is and what his will is for us. Scripture is God's chosen gateway through which we must go, if we want to be confident that we are reaching the real Jesus.

> Scripture is God's chosen gateway through which we must go, if we want to be confident that we are reaching the real Jesus.

In conclusion, then, a Christian approach to Scripture is ultimately rooted in the character of God himself.

- God the Father is a speaking God: he is well able to speak to us, his creatures, and longs to be in relationship with us – revealing himself to us and also his perfect will for us.

- Jesus, God's Son, submits to Scripture: although he is the Lord of the Word with authority over it, he yet places himself under it, giving us an example to follow.

- The Holy Spirit is the One who inspires: he was able to work in (or, better, "breathe upon") the biblical writers in both Old and New Testaments, leading them into all those truths which God wished for us to know.

A non-believer, who denied these great truths about God, might well see the Bible as no different from any other book. Those who believe in this God, however, have these three good reasons (and more) for seeing it quite differently. If we wish to be Jesus' followers, we should follow his example, giving our allegiance to Scripture for his sake and looking to it as God's revealed Word brought to us by his Spirit.

Living under Scripture

So Jesus' followers should have a humble attitude towards the Bible. As God said to ancient Israel, so Jesus says to us:

> *Man shall not live on bread alone, but on every word that comes from the mouth of God.*
> **Matthew 4:4 (based on Deuteronomy 8:3)**

God's word is to be treasured as our staple diet. Jesus' own teaching gives us some pictures here:

The seed

In his parable of the sower (Mark 4:1–20), Jesus teaches us that we are like fields receiving the "seed" of God's word. He is asking us: what kind of soil are we? As God's word goes out, what response will it receive? Will we let other concerns in our lives "choke" its message like weeds, so that we become unfruitful soil? Or will we receive the "seed" humbly so that it grows well?

The vine

Jesus pictures himself as a vine (John 15:5–8): "I am the vine; you are the branches." Again, he is looking for followers who "bear much fruit" but warns that this only happens when people "remain" in him: if we start living without him, he may need to prune us. The secret of a fruitful life, instead, is this: "remain in me" and let "my words remain in you".

Picking up these images, the apostles write very similar commands: "Get rid of all moral filth and the evil that is so prevalent and humbly accept the word planted in you" (James 1:21). "Let the message of Christ dwell among you" (Paul in Colossians 3:16). We are to live under Scripture and also to have its words living within us and among us.

So, as Jesus' followers, we should commit ourselves to read the Bible (or to listen to it) whenever we can. And we should commit ourselves in advance to believe and obey anything that it clearly teaches:

- Where it contains warnings, we will heed them.
- Where it contains promises, we will claim them.
- When it teaches us spiritual doctrines (even about things we have not seen or yet experienced), we will trust them.
- When it contains clear commands, we will obey them.

This last point is of vital importance. Jesus is not looking for mere biblical knowledge but for biblical obedience, bringing our minds and our wills under the Bible's rule. The Bible is a very earthy book. Although it contains so much food for thought, its purpose is always practical too. It wants us not only to think about the truth, but actually to "live out the truth" (a strange phrase coined in 1 John 1:6):

> Do not merely listen to the word, and so deceive yourselves. Do what it says.
>
> James 1:22

The Bible, however, is a vast book and, even for those who come to it with an obedient attitude, there are numerous difficulties to face. In this task, Jesus is well able, as it were, to take us by the hand and guide us in our understanding. Just as he "opened the minds" of those two disciples on the Emmaus road, "so they could understand the Scriptures" (Luke

> Jesus is well able to lead us into his own truth!

24:45), so he can help us today, if only we will ask for his guidance. Jesus is well able to lead us into his own truth!

As we close this chapter, it may be useful to highlight some vital tips for reading the Bible to ensure we approach the task with the right frame of mind.

1. We may have an open Bible, but that does not mean we fully understand it

In other fields of human learning we do not fully grasp everything straight away. The same is true here, as we begin this unique, spiritual type of learning. So, although Jesus is with us, we will always remain learners (or "disciples") in his school. Indeed, the complexities and profundity within the Bible may sometimes be used by God to keep us humbly dependent on him. Our faith is always (as the medieval Christian Anselm of Canterbury said) a "faith seeking understanding". We are not to get dispirited at this point – and certainly not to take up a posture of arrogance towards the text. Instead we may put our unsolved problems in a pending tray, trusting that, if necessary, God will one day help us understand some of these things better. Let's not abandon our belief in the Bible's trustworthiness, but rather dig into it more deeply.

2. We may have a complete (or "finished") Bible, but that does not mean the Holy Spirit has stopped speaking

Christians believe that, within the Old and New Testaments, God has given all the revelation he intends to impart (this is sometimes referred to as the closed canon* of the Bible). The chief reason why Christians make this assertion (that the Bible is now complete) is that God has given us the fullest possible revelation of himself in Jesus. There is nothing better in the pipeline – no further revelation to be expected. If you like, the complete salvation (offered in Jesus) is matched by a complete revelation (found in Scripture).

Yet sometimes those who give this (proper) emphasis to the final authority of Scripture are misheard as implying that they do not believe in the ongoing work of the Holy Spirit. Did the Spirit somehow stop speaking when the Bible's last page was written? Of course not! The Holy Spirit is eternally active, and without his daily work in our lives we could never begin – let alone continue – the Christian life.

> The complete salvation (offered in Jesus) is matched by a complete revelation (found in Scripture).

Moreover, if we ask God for wisdom, God's Spirit may give to us, as individuals, guidance which is related to our particular situations (about what we should do or say). We see examples of this in the Bible itself (Acts 16:6–10) and Jesus expressly promises the help of the Spirit for those standing on trial for their faith (Mark 13:11). James positively encourages us to ask God for this kind of godly wisdom (James 1:5).

However, any such prompting by the Spirit for the benefit of the individual believer is qualitatively different from his inspiring of the Scriptures, for in Scripture we see what the Spirit intended to give to all believers for all time. It might thus be called "universal revelation" in contrast to merely "particular revelation" (that is, words of guidance or encouragement made to individuals or churches* throughout history). It is the Spirit's voice as found in the Scriptures which is authoritative throughout every generation.

Once this distinction is safeguarded, then we are set free to seek the Spirit's voice for today. We will always do so knowing that any such supposed speaking by the Spirit today must be tested against his normative and authoritative speaking in Scripture. We will thus let other believers evaluate our interpretation of what the Spirit is saying to us (as Paul counsels in 1 Corinthians 14:29; see also 1 John 4:1).

Another way of making a similar point is this: we may have the Holy Spirit, but that does not mean we are free to go beyond the Bible. Jesus' promise that his Spirit would lead his apostles into "all the truth" (John 16:13) is often mistakenly read as a promise that the Spirit will lead Jesus' followers today into some further "truth", even if it goes beyond the Scriptures or even against them. This is

> **The Holy Spirit will never contradict Scripture.**

nonsensical. If the Scriptures truly express – albeit in human words – the very mind and will of the Spirit, then we can never claim the Spirit's support for something that is contrary to Scripture. The Holy Spirit will never contradict himself.

The Holy Spirit thus continues to speak and reveal himself to this day; yet this will never go either beyond or against the plain teaching he has already given in the Scriptures.

Instead, the Spirit's main role is to bring the truths of Scripture ever more powerfully into the experience of each believer. Yes, he continues to guide us "into all the truth," but this is into all the truth of those Scriptures that he has already given. All good Christian theology is therefore effectively an elucidation of what is already in Scripture (replaying the Bible's themes afresh in each generation), rather than somehow being a development away from or beyond Scripture.

This leading into truth by the Spirit is in itself no small miracle. After all, however long we may live, we will always need to make fresh discoveries within Scripture, so there really is no need to go beyond it! The Bible at this point is rather like a long cylinder driven down deep into the earth, which has a finite circumference, but which is endlessly deep (see diagram). Using this analogy, one can sense how the Holy Spirit will not take us outside the circumference of Scripture, but he will take us ever further into its inexhaustible depth.

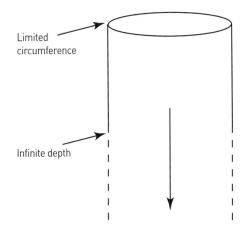

This means that we must resist all our proud attempts to improve upon what we have received. Nor will we give our ultimate allegiance to other possible guides – however helpful they might be. These include our own experience of the Spirit, human reason, or even long-standing Christian tradition. If there are things that God has not revealed to us in the Bible, we should be content and must respect his judgment. Some find an Old Testament verse to be useful here:

> *The secret things belong to the Lord our God, but the things revealed belong to us and to our children forever, that we may follow all the words of this law.*
>
> Deuteronomy 29:29

In other words, trust God for what he has not revealed, and obey him in what he has.

3. We may have the Bible and also the guidance of the Holy Spirit, but that does not mean we no longer need the help of others

Because the Bible is a complex book, we will always need to be learning from others. No single individual will ever grasp it all. In this sense, the Bible belongs to the church*, that is, to all God's people. So we need to learn from those who have studied the Bible faithfully in the past (this is the proper place for valuing and respecting tradition). We also need to submit ourselves to learn from those who teach the Bible in our own day.

Someone might say, "Who needs a human teacher, when we have a divine one – the Holy Spirit?" This attitude is both wrong and dangerous. Yes, as we have seen, the Holy Spirit can indeed speak to us personally through the Bible (see also chapter 8), yet "teachers" are expressly listed as one of Christ's main gifts to the church (Ephesians 4:11), given to us precisely so that we might become mature in our thinking. Therefore, to ignore biblical teachers is not "super-spiritual" but folly. Instead Paul urges: "acknowledge those who... care for you in the Lord and who admonish you"

(1 Thessalonians 5:12). We should gladly place ourselves under the authority of those who teach us the Scriptures; we should value any helpful commentaries on biblical books; and we should submit all our understanding of the Bible to the open scrutiny of others.

Conclusion

Believers in Jesus hang on his every word – given both in the Gospels and through his apostles. We honour the inspired texts of the Old Testament, because Jesus did. And, most importantly, we always study the Scriptures, not for their own sake, but rather to grow in our love for Jesus (John 5:39–40).

Over the years, an organization called The Gideons International has placed over a billion Bibles in hotel rooms and other places. In the introduction to their Bibles, they describe the Bible in the following memorable way:

> *It is supernatural in origin, eternal in duration, divine in authorship, infallible in authority, inexhaustible in meaning, universal in readership, unique in revelation, personal in applications and powerful in effect.*
>
> **The Gideons International**

Let's read the Bible as God's words to us. It is an incredible experience to hear the voice of the living God speaking to us, his people! So, the fourth building block in the Christian life is to ensure we feed ourselves on the Scriptures. They are God's truth, and God's truth brings us his healing and grace, his wisdom and new life.

Building block 4

Feed on his Scriptures – you need God's truth!

Participate in His Meal

*Jesus was recognized by them
when he broke the bread.*
Luke 24:35

For the next lesson in Jesus' "masterclass" on that first Easter Day, we need to use our imaginations a little. Jesus drops a powerful hint, but we may miss it if we are not careful. It all has to do with the precise moment when God allows the Emmaus travellers at last to recognize Jesus. Note how this did not happen as they walked along the road. Instead, it was only when the Risen Jesus "was at the table with them, he took bread, gave thanks, broke it and began to give it to them. Then their eyes were opened and they recognized him, and he disappeared from their sight" (Luke 24:30–31).

Luke then describes their dashing back to Jerusalem to explain to Jesus' other followers "what had happened on the way, and how Jesus was recognized by them," he notes, "when he broke the bread (Luke 24:35). This is the punchline in Luke's story. He wants us to see something significant here, but what is it?

To get Luke's point, we would need to note how Luke speaks elsewhere in his writings about this "breaking of bread" (see below). More importantly, we would need to remember how Jesus himself had already said and done some startling, even shocking, things at certain mealtimes earlier in his ministry (we shall look at the two most important ones in just a moment). There were several previous occasions when he had broken bread with his followers and had hinted that this action of breaking bread would somehow gain a whole new meaning for his followers in the future.

So, even now, when Jesus was recognized in the breaking of bread, his followers would have begun to pick up some of this extra significance. They might sense that, through this moment of revelation, the Risen Jesus was effectively saying to them: "Those special mealtimes I previously shared with you can now continue in a whole new way because I am alive again. Even if you cannot see me, I will be with you, and you will recognize my presence among you. And those puzzling words I said, when breaking bread, will now come into their own – you will now understand what I meant."

So there are hints here in Luke 24 that a fifth building block for those who would be Jesus' followers is to be involved in a special meal of some kind, the meal that would soon be known as the "Lord's Supper". It sounds intriguing! We had better look now in more detail at what exactly Jesus had said at those earlier meals. Two such meals would have stood out in the minds of Jesus' followers – one in Galilee a year or two before, the other in Jerusalem just three days before. We will look first at the second meal – the most recent one.

An earlier meal: The Last Supper

In Luke's Gospel, much of Jesus' teaching takes place in the context of meals, when Jesus is enjoying what some call "table fellowship" with a variety of people (see Luke 7, 11, 14–15). In answering his critics, who noted the unsavoury and "unclean" company he kept at such mealtimes, Jesus speaks about a God who goes out searching for the lost (Luke 15) and tells a parable about a great banquet to which the most unlikely people are welcomed (Luke 14:15–24). Picking up the well-known imagery of his day (which foresaw a great "messianic" banquet to which God would invite all his faithful people in the age to come), Jesus here is hinting that, as Messiah*, he has the authority to host his own banquet and, like a good shepherd, to welcome in those whom he chooses. Indeed, one day, Jesus will host the greatest party of all! The writer of Revelation calls this the "wedding supper of the Lamb" (Revelation 19:5–10). In the meantime, any meal hosted by Jesus will always be a foretaste of that heavenly banquet – open to all who are baptized and have put their faith in him.

These ideas form a powerful background to the meal which Jesus himself hosts once he has arrived in Jerusalem – a messianic banquet indeed, but with some startling differences. Gathered with his small company of followers in a discreet upper room, unnoticed by his enemies, Jesus shares what would be his last supper with his friends. Within a few hours, he would be betrayed to the authorities by one of his followers (Judas Iscariot) and, the next morning, he would be crucified outside the city walls. Not surprisingly, the events of that Thursday evening would be etched on his followers' memories for ever.

It was the season of Passover*. Each year at this time, the nation of Israel* remembered God's great act of rescuing them from Egypt. They longed for God to rescue them again – this time from the Romans. That's why, as we read in Luke 24, Cleopas and his friend are depressed: "we had hoped", they say, that Jesus "was going to redeem Israel" (Luke 24:21). Aware of all this, Jesus now hosted his own Passover meal. Yet, again, this would be a Passover meal with a difference. For, although it would look back to God's past deliverance, Jesus' Passover meal would look forward to a new kind of rescue. And, in the very centre of this whole story, Jesus would place... himself.

> Jesus' Passover meal would look forward to a new kind of rescue.

Within the Passover celebrations, there was always a "breaking of bread" accompanied by a prayer, and also the drinking of some cups of wine, again with prayers and blessings. Suddenly, however, when Jesus gave his followers the bread, he dramatically changed the script. It was a one-liner, not easily forgotten, a sentence that put Jesus and his death right at the centre of human history. He said:

This is my body given for you; do this in remembrance of me.

Luke 22:19

Similarly, when he passed round the wine cup, there were these strange, almost macabre, words:

This cup is the new covenant in my blood, which is poured out for you.

Luke 22:20

Jesus was linking the bread and wine with his own body and blood – and expecting his followers then calmly to eat and drink them!

What could this mean? There are many things in these few short words, but Box 5a highlights some of the more important ones.

Box 5a – The meaning of Jesus' words at the Last Supper

- Jesus was making clear that his death was no accident (see chapter 2). He was talking about it quite openly; he was even planning it. His death, then, would be the result of his own active will (that's why he spoke of giving and pouring out his own body and blood).

- He wanted his followers to remember him in this particular way – not so much for his life and teaching, but rather for his death: "Do this in remembrance of me."

- He wanted to ensure that each of them ate and drank. Jesus' death was something which each person would need to thank him for individually: "Given for you".

- He wanted them to repeat this meal, not just once, but again and again: "Do this" might be better translated as "keep on doing this".

- He was clearly taking up the Passover imagery. Jesus himself would now be the true Passover Lamb (killed in our place, so that God's wrath and judgment could "pass over" us). Jesus would therefore bring to God's people their freedom and rescue – rescue not from Egypt but from slavery to their own sin.

These few words of Jesus were indeed cataclysmic in their effect. Jesus was instituting a dramatic meal that would always remind his followers of his death – the place where Jesus died in our place. As Paul would later affirm, "Christ, our Passover lamb, has been sacrificed" (1 Corinthians 5:7).

This, then, would explain the extra significance we sensed in Luke 24 when (just three days later) the Risen Jesus breaks bread in Emmaus. He is signalling the importance of the meal which he had instituted only a few days earlier; he is also saying that now, because of the resurrection, it will be possible for it to be a meal celebrated with joy and thanks.

Again we need to use our imaginations. If Jesus had remained dead, then perhaps his few followers would have got together occasionally (perhaps for an annual dinner?) in order to have a sad, depressing meal in memory of their dead hero. They would simply be doing what Jesus had commanded, but with heavy hearts and no clear idea as to what it was supposed to achieve.

Yet that is precisely what did not happen! Ever since then, this meal has been celebrated around the world on a remarkably frequent basis. The only possible explanation for this is the resurrection. Only the resurrection could convert this macabre meal into a glorious celebration – of Jesus risen from the dead, of rescue now accomplished, and of sins now forgiven. And the signal that tells us the meal has changed from being something depressing to being a great delight is that moment when Jesus broke bread at Emmaus.

> **Only the resurrection could convert this macabre meal into a glorious celebration.**

The resurrection means we can obey Jesus' command without heavy hearts; remembering Jesus' death was not the end but rather our gateway into new life. Moreover, it also means that we can celebrate this meal in the presence of the Risen Lord himself. For Jesus is alive!

Another earlier meal: The Feeding of the 5,000

The other meal that was so significant in Jesus' ministry took place in Galilee one springtime, a couple of years earlier. Aware of its importance for Jesus' followers, all four Gospel writers record this occasion, when Jesus fed at least 5,000 people from five loaves and two small fish (see, for example, Mark 6:30–44). This miraculous feeding was a clear demonstration of Jesus' spiritual authority and unique power over nature; it also showed his practical compassion for the hungry.

Yet John in his Gospel (6:25–69) records some teaching of Jesus a few days later which gives this miraculous feeding a yet deeper meaning. Jesus begins by chiding his opponents for desiring only physical food; they should be seeking after the "food that endures to eternal life" (verse 27). Then he reveals the startling truth: "I am the bread of life." (John 6:35)

Jesus himself is God's gift of a food that will give eternal life. "Whoever comes to me," he continues, "will never go hungry, and whoever believes in me will never be thirsty." If people wish to have eternal life, being raised to life on the last day (verse 44), then "the work of God is this: to believe in the one he has sent" (verse 29).

Jesus goes further. What does it really mean to "believe in the one he has sent" (that is, in Jesus)? Are people just to believe that he was a great person sent by God? No, Jesus insists, they are to believe in him as the one who came to die, who gave his "flesh" and "blood". So, continuing with the picture of faith as a kind of feeding on him, Jesus says:

I am the living bread that came down from heaven...
This bread is my flesh, which I will give for the life of the
world... Very truly I tell you, unless you eat the flesh of the
Son of Man and drink his blood, you have no life in you.
Whoever eats my flesh and drinks my blood has eternal
life, and I will raise them up at the last day. For my flesh is
real food and my blood is real drink.

John 6:51, 53–55

These words may have made little sense at the time. Indeed, the imagery was so strong and violent that many – even among Jesus' own followers – were appalled (John 6:60). After all, within Old Testament thought, it was wrong to eat any food with blood still in it. Yet here was Jesus seemingly encouraging his hearers to be cannibals!

Jesus, however, is using this graphic language to shock his followers into seeing this important truth: that we cannot be his followers if we do not come to him through his cross. His death for us must be the chief reason for our faith in him. We cannot just applaud him as a great teacher. He insists on being the one who died for us, whose death we need more than we truly know. So he demands that we must feed on him to the extent that we feed on his "flesh" and his "blood".

> We cannot be his followers if we do not come to him through his cross.

Again (as with his words at the Last Supper), the death and resurrection of Jesus would in due course give a new understanding as to what Jesus had meant on this earlier occasion. Moreover, once his followers actually began to do what Jesus commanded – meeting in Jesus' name to break bread and drink wine – these words in John 6 would have been ringing in their ears with a whole new layer of meaning. Jesus' words here would alert them to the fact that they were not just holding a memorial service for their dead hero, nor indeed merely having a meal in the presence of their Risen Master. They were also, in some strange way, being invited to feed on Jesus himself, the very source of their life.

If we apply this to ourselves, then whenever we break bread in Jesus' name, we are to think of ourselves as in some way feeding on Jesus, receiving afresh his powerful life into our lives. The meal is therefore working on two levels. Outwardly, it is an ordinary meal with physical food, which nourishes our bodies. On another (far more important) level, however, it is a spiritual meal with spiritual food, which nourishes our spirits. This is a great mystery – after all, we cannot actually see this spiritual feeding going on – but we should not doubt the power of this spiritual reality. Jesus is inviting us to a meal where he will feed us – with himself!

> Jesus is inviting us to a meal where he will feed us – with himself!

Yet there is a warning. None of this will happen if we are not exercising a real, personal faith in him. John 6 is an extended discourse on the need for faith – it is only "whoever comes to me" who "will never go hungry" (verse 35). There is no automatic magic in the bread and wine themselves. We cannot receive them without faith and expect them, by some mysterious means, automatically to give us eternal life. We can only feed on Jesus by exercising faith in him. If, however, we have put our faith in Jesus, then it is natural that we should want to come and be part of this meal. This is where we can feed on Jesus, and be nourished with the spiritual food that he gives us.

All this explains why, over the years, this meal has come to be called a "sacrament". In Christian thought, a sacrament is a place of divine promise (technically a "means of grace"), where God promises actively to bless his people as they put their faith in him. A sacrament is also an action that has an inner power and spiritual meaning which no one can see: outwardly, we look as though we are eating only bread, but truly and spiritually God is feeding our spirits with Jesus, the Bread of Life. Those who follow Jesus, therefore, will not want to miss out on this sacrament. It is the unique spiritual meal given to us by the Risen Jesus himself.

Key questions about the Lord's Supper

It is for all these reasons that we see the first Christians so frequently breaking bread together. In Acts, we read of the "breaking of bread" (Acts 2:42) and of the believers gathering together in one place "on the first day of the week... to break bread" (20:7). Some of these first meals in Jerusalem may have been ordinary meals. Very soon, however, as the message of Jesus as Lord spread further afield, the pattern developed of celebrating this meal in a special way on a Sunday (the day of his resurrection) – the Lord's Supper on the Lord's day. Ever since, churches have followed this pattern, some having a Sunday Communion* service (or Eucharist*) each week, others at least once a month. Was ever a command so obeyed? For Jesus' meal has been celebrated literally thousands and thousands of times since that first Passover meal in Jerusalem.

Box 5b – A famous description of the Lord's Supper

Was ever another command so obeyed? For century after century, spreading slowly to every continent and country and among every race on earth, this action has been done, in every conceivable human circumstance, for every conceivable human need from infancy and before it to extreme old age and after it, from the pinnacles of earthly greatness to the refuge of fugitives in the caves and dens of the earth.

Gregory Dix, *The Shape of the Liturgy* (1945)

We may still have some important questions here. For example:

- Who can join in this meal? Is it totally open to all?
- And how should we prepare ourselves for it? Are there any things we should avoid or approaches that are unhelpful?

On the first question, the Bible is clear that the meal is intended as a distinctive meal for Jesus' followers. On the one hand, we have seen Jesus' open policy of table fellowship with surprising people (including those termed "sinners" in his day); this clearly demonstrates that his welcome extends to all people, regardless of where they are coming from. On the other hand, we also saw Jesus' insistence in John 6 that faith in him was essential; in his own graphic terminology, there would be no point in people eating the "flesh" of Jesus if they did not have the faith in his death which Jesus was speaking about when he used that very phrase.

In the light of this, the first Christians soon established the simple rule that those attending this meal must first have been baptised. From earliest times, baptism* with water and in the name of the Trinity* has been the sign of entrance into the Christian family (see appendix C). It makes sense to keep this "family meal" within the family. Another way of saying the same thing (since baptism is also seen as a sacrament

> The first Christians soon established the simple rule that those attending this meal must first have been baptised.

given by the Lord to his people) is to observe that only those who have received the sacrament of baptism should go on to receive the sacrament of Communion. This makes eminent sense. (It is worth noting that those churches which practice "infant baptism" normally require people, once they are adults, to go through a further ceremony, known as confirmation*, in which they effectively reconfirm as adults their baptismal vows and express their own faith in Jesus.) Any believer in Jesus, therefore, who has been baptized and has publicly expressed their faith in Jesus, is welcome to start participating in this meal. And, thereafter, they should come to it, on each occasion, with an active and repentant faith in Jesus.

This is also clear from Paul's teaching in 1 Corinthians 10–11, where he emphasizes the importance of people coming to this meal with active faith. Paul's extended teaching here also helps us answer our second question: how should we receive this sacrament? Paul is looking for a repentant spirit and is concerned at what he detects instead in the believers – their arrogance. In fact, the Corinthians were behaving in quite inappropriate ways (for example, some were getting drunk; others were not sharing their food with poorer people). Paul speaks out strongly against this disorder, stressing that we are all equals in Christ and must not put each other to shame (1 Corinthians 11:22).

It is important to note some of his other teaching here:

> *Therefore, my dear friends, flee from idolatry... Is not the cup of thanksgiving for which we give thanks a participation in the blood of Christ? And is not the bread that we break a participation in the body of Christ. Because there is one loaf, we, who are many, are one body, for we all share the one loaf... You cannot drink the cup of the Lord and the cup of demons too; you cannot have a part in both the Lord's table and the table of demons. Are we trying to arouse the Lord's jealousy?*
>
> 1 Corinthians 10:14, 16–17, 21–22

After reminding them of the words Jesus had used at his Last Supper in Jerusalem, Paul then continues:

*For whenever you eat this bread and drink this cup, you
proclaim the Lord's death until he comes.*

*So then, whoever eats the bread or drinks the cup of
the Lord in an unworthy manner will be guilty of sinning
against the body and blood of the Lord. Everyone ought to
examine themselves before they eat of the bread and drink
from the cup. For those who eat and drink without discerning
the body of Christ eat and drink judgment on themselves.*

1 Corinthians 11:26-29

From this, we can draw out the following guidelines for how we
ourselves should receive the Lord's Supper:

1. We should all examine our lives carefully

This is Jesus' meal for sinners who want to be cleansed and forgiven
through his cross. It is not for people who hope they can be forgiven
without turning from their sins, or who do not recognize "the
body of Christ" – Jesus' body broken on the cross for them. Since
Communion services almost always include an act of confession*,
in which we ask God for forgiveness, we should ensure we do this
sincerely. Otherwise, we "eat and drink judgment" on ourselves.

2. We should be aware of the Lord's presence

We do not treat this meal lightly. There is a real "sharing" in the
body and blood of Christ. Even if this is hard to define more exactly,
the Lord Jesus is present by his Holy Spirit and he is opposed to
anything in our lives that stands against him. Though invisible,
Jesus is effectively the true leader or "host" at this meal; we are
meeting, not just in his name, but actually in his presence.

3. We should note that true believers are all part of
Christ's "body"

We are all sharing in the same bread; none of us is more
important than any other – the ground is equal at the foot of

the cross. So we should be united, showing peace, love, and forgiveness to one other. In his teaching, Jesus had emphasized the importance of making peace with our brothers and sisters* before proceeding with our worship of God (Matthew 5:23–24). So we need to take this issue very seriously when we come to this act of worship. Furthermore, Paul teaches here that we are all now members of Christ's spiritual "body" (1 Corinthians 10:17; 12:27). So we need, in this second sense too, to "recognize the Lord's body" as we gather in his name. Each believer is valuable to Christ as a unique member of his body; we should therefore ourselves value each brother or sister "for whom Christ died" (Romans 14:15).

So the fifth building block in following Jesus is to participate in this unique meal, this sacrament of the Lord's Supper. At this point, we can look back and see how, after teaching first about his death and resurrection, the Risen Jesus in Luke 24 was then giving three further gifts to his followers: his Spirit, the Scriptures, and now this sacrament. We are to value each gift in its own way.

Different Christian groups have sometimes emphasized one of these three above the others. This has led over the years to different "streams" appearing in Christ's church (see the epilogue). Partly, this may have come about because these three gifts deliberately touch us at three different points of our human personalities (namely, our spirits, our minds and hearts, and our eyes and bodies). The Risen Jesus, however, clearly wanted us to enjoy each of them to the full, and for every part of our personalities to be touched by his grace.

With regard specifically to the sacrament of the Lord's Supper, this means we should never treat this meal flippantly. Instead, we should see it as an opportunity to meet with the Lord, to enjoy his forgiveness, and to be a visible part of his family. For this is the place where:

- we can come when we are broken and hurting, when we need God's forgiveness or feel unwanted or unworthy;

- we can tell again the great story of Jesus, proclaiming the truths of his resurrection, cross, and Spirit (see chapters 1 to 3);

- we should hear the Bible read and preached (chapter 4); indeed the story of the Scriptures comes alive at the Lord's Supper in a dramatic way, as we find ourselves joining in the action;

- we come together to share in a family meal, meeting with the Risen Jesus and feeding on him in a unique way;

- we are given a foretaste of the great banquet that Jesus is preparing for us in future.

Building block 5

Participate in his meal – this is your spiritual food!

Bear Witness to His Reign

You are witnesses of these things.
Luke 24:48

Jesus' final lesson on that first Easter Sunday was like a "sting in the tail". After unpacking these five aspects of the Good News, he made it plain to his followers that they now had a major task on their hands. The resurrection revealed that Jesus was God's appointed king: it was they who now had to pass on this news to others and do all they could to extend the reach of his kingdom.

Luke helps us to imagine some of the feelings they would have gone through in that upper room (24:41): first, sheer disbelief and incredulity (could this really be Jesus here in their midst?), then joy and excitement (it was true!). But then what? Almost certainly, there came a dawning realization of an awesome, even fearful, responsibility. For if this Good News of the resurrection was not just for them, but was for all people everywhere, then who would be going out into the world with this message? Would it be Jesus himself? No. As if reading their minds, Jesus spells it out plainly: the message about "repentance for the forgiveness of sins will be preached in his name to all nations, beginning at Jerusalem. You are witnesses of these things" (verses 47–48).

Jesus is saying in effect: "This is the message the world has been waiting for, but it's not my job to tell the world – it's yours!" Or, if you like, "My mission has been accomplished. Yours is just beginning!" Indeed, in the parallel account of that first Easter day in the Gospel of John, this is almost exactly what Jesus says: "As the Father has sent me, so I am sending you" (John 20:21).

"Mission" means, literally, being "sent out". So from that moment onwards, Jesus' followers knew he was giving them a new mission in life. The joy of Easter and the task of mission would always go hand in hand. They could not have the one without the other.

> The joy of Easter and the task of mission would always go hand in hand.

This is a startling "reality check". Jesus has performed the unique act of saving the world, but right now, the task of letting the world know about it lies in the hands of a tiny group of men and women in Jerusalem! What if they are not up to it? Jesus has no other plans. His own work is done and he will soon be returning to his Father in heaven – in the event we refer to as his ascension*. The long-term success of his work is invested in those few followers he is leaving behind. What if they fail?

Those men and women in Jerusalem were thus left with a daunting responsibility. For Jesus' sake they had a job to do. But so do we. The message of Jesus' dying love for everyone cannot - must not - stop with us. Jesus is the king, and his kingdom needs to be proclaimed and implemented. If this makes us suddenly feel quite small or afraid, Jesus goes on immediately to talk about the Holy Spirit (Luke 24:49): "I am going to send you what my Father has promised; but stay in the city until you have been clothed with power from on high."

> The message of Jesus' dying love for everyone cannot – must not – stop with us. Jesus is the king, and his kingdom needs to be proclaimed and implemented.

God knows we cannot fulfil this task on our own, so he sends his Holy Spirit. Only the Spirit of Jesus can take this message about Jesus and convert it into a glorious reality – both in our own lives and in the lives of others. As we saw in chapter 3, only Jesus' Spirit can reveal and convey the reality of Jesus' lordship and rule. This means we are not left on our own with this task of mission; instead we have Jesus' outgoing Spirit to lead us, to guide us, and empower us. Yes, the message about "repentance and forgiveness" must be "preached", but the Spirit will do the preaching through us.

So the sixth building block in following Jesus is to get ourselves involved in the mission of King Jesus. It is to let his Spirit guide us outwards – to speak in his name, to show acts of love and compassion which speak deeply of his heart for all, and to do all that we can to bring the world under his just and kindly rule. By our words and actions, we are to bear witness to others that Jesus is the world's true king. Each of us has a part to play in this vital task.

Box 6a – Good news from Jerusalem: "God is king!"

How beautiful on the mountains
*   are the feet of those who bring good news,*
who proclaim peace,
*   who bring good tidings,*
*   who proclaim salvation,*
who say to Zion,
*   "Your God reigns!"*
The Lord will lay bare his holy arm
*   in the sight of all the nations,*
and all the ends of the earth will see
*   the salvation of our God.*
                                                    Isaiah 52:7, 10

After his suffering, he presented himself to them and gave
many convincing proofs that he was alive. He appeared to
them over a period of forty days and spoke about the kingdom
of God... "You will receive power when the Holy Spirit comes
on you; and you will be my witnesses in Jerusalem, and in all
Judea and Samaria, and to the ends of the earth."
                                                    Acts 1:3, 8

In Isaiah 52, the prophet had had a vision of messengers running swiftly away from Jerusalem with good news – the Good News that the God of Israel* was truly king. Now in the short period after his resurrection, as recorded in Acts 1, Jesus teaches the apostles* about how God has become king through him ("he spoke about the kingdom of God") and then sends them out as his messengers and witnesses. Using a different image, they are to be like trumpeters and "heralds" – those who went ahead of ancient armies announcing that a victorious king was approaching. We too are meant to pick up this challenge, going out into the world, giving a clear signal, and proclaiming in word and deed the Good News that there is a new victorious king. Are we ready to run with the message?

God's heart for all people

But is this right? Does God really want us to be proclaiming and building up Jesus' kingdom? A good way to answer our hesitations is to consider the theme of mission in the Bible as a whole. What is on God's heart? We soon discover that God's heart is indeed for all people, and he himself is a "missionary God".

> God's heart is indeed for all people, and he himself is a "missionary God".

We see this in the very first book of the Bible. When human beings turned away from God and fell into sin, God's solution to this universal problem was, strangely, to focus down onto one particular individual, Abram (Genesis 12:1–7). Yet this was not because God was not concerned with the whole world; rather it was his unique strategy to undo the sin that had contaminated it. Thus he gave his chosen servant a new name: he was to be Abraham, which means the "father of many nations" (Genesis 17:5). Through him, God was promising that "all peoples on earth will be blessed" (Genesis 12:3). Right here, back in Genesis, God was showing his concern for all people – ultimately to bring them back to himself.

Thereafter, God chose to focus on the one nation of Israel (Abraham's descendants), for he needed to have one people on earth whom he could teach and who could show forth his distinctive values to the world. Nevertheless, his long-term goal throughout the subsequent centuries of the Old Testament was always to bless the entire world. Israel was to be a people who served God as "priests" (showing forth God's character to the surrounding peoples) and who brought his "light for the Gentiles*"

(Exodus 19:6; Isaiah 49:6). Israel's prophets too, in various ways, clearly predicted a time when non-Jews (the Gentiles) would be brought into God's people – what was sometimes referred to as the ingathering of the nations*. What was not so clear was when God would do this, and how.

The New Testament gives the answer: "when the set time had fully come, God sent his Son" (Galatians 4:4); this was precisely in order that the "blessing given to Abraham might come to the Gentiles" (Galatians 3:14). In other words, Jesus' coming from God into our world was the moment when God's ancient master plan (to bless all people) could at last come into effect. That's why the Risen Jesus says in Luke 24 that the time has come for the Good News to go out to "all nations" (verse 47). He is signalling the long-awaited moment when God's promise to Abraham can at last be fulfilled. We are seeing here God's long-standing (indeed eternal!) agenda of love for his whole world.

> We are seeing here God's long-standing (indeed eternal!) agenda of love for his whole world.

Note too how this message of God's heart for all people will have meant so much to the person who himself wrote down Luke 24. For Luke himself was a Gentile. Almost certainly he had for many years been a God-fearer* – one of those who hovered on the fringes of the synagogue, looking in respectfully but from outside the Jewish race. Then came this brilliant message about Jesus – the Jesus who had died for *all* people. Suddenly Luke knew that he could now become a member of God's people – just as he was! He did not need to undergo circumcision or become a Jew. He simply needed only to have repentant faith in Jesus, Israel's Messiah*.

So in his Gospel, Luke, not unnaturally, is determined to show how Jesus had been truly the Man for Others – the Messiah of Israel who had come to open the kingdom to all. Moreover, Jesus had not been obsessed with his own concerns, but rather had been motivated by love for others. He had mixed with everyone. So Luke portrays him as spending time with both rich and poor, with men and women, with Jews and Gentiles, with notorious sinners and Roman soldiers (see, for example, Luke 7–8). Even when being nailed to the cross in agony, we see Jesus' concern, not for himself, but rather for a thief being crucified alongside him – and even for those who were driving in the nails. "Father, forgive them" (Luke 23:34).

And it was not just Jesus' actions. Luke's selection of the stories Jesus told also reveal Jesus' heart for all people. Think of the story of the "good Samaritan"* (Samaritans were fierce enemies of the Jews: Luke 10:25–37); or the parable of the lost son who was welcomed back by his father (15:11–32); or how Jesus retold the Old Testament story about God healing Naaman, an army commander in charge of Israel's enemies, the Syrians (4:27). All these were deliberately designed by Jesus to shock his hearers into seeing God's concern for all people.

Not everyone liked this message, but Jesus was undeterred and insisted on reaching out to the most unlikely people. When making his final stop before going up to Jerusalem, Jesus went into the house of a hated tax collector, Zacchaeus. When this man repented, Jesus declared, "Today salvation has come to this house." And then he added a vital comment, which for Luke summed up the very heart of Jesus' ministry:

The Son of Man came to seek and to save the lost.

Luke 19:10

For Luke, the Jesus who here welcomed Zacchaeus was the same Risen Jesus who later called his disciples to go out as his witnesses to all nations. Evidently, then, this Jesus has a heart for everyone. His goal is to save people who, without him, are lost.

So, Jesus has a missionary concern, and this truly reflects God's own agenda and passion. God has a deep heart for all people, as seen in two key New Testament verses:

For God so loved the world that he gave his one and only Son, that whoever believes in him shall not perish but have eternal life.

John 3:16

God our Saviour... wants all people to be saved and to come to a knowledge of the truth.

1 Timothy 2:3–4

God wants everyone to know him and to experience his love.

Jesus' mission through his followers

Jesus' mission can only go forward, however, if Jesus' followers themselves take it forward. That's why, earlier in his ministry, Jesus had sent his followers out on what we might call "mission assignments". He needed to train his followers in what it was like to go out in his name. Jesus' words on that occasion reveal how he saw people as being like a harvest in danger of going rotten through never being collected:

The harvest is plentiful, but the workers are few. Ask the Lord of the harvest, therefore, to send out workers into his harvest field. Go! I am sending you out like lambs among wolves.

Luke 10:2–3

Jesus has a strong passion for mission, for bringing people into his inclusive kingdom. And he wants his followers to share this passion too – to play their part in bringing in the harvest.

This is exactly what we see them doing after the resurrection. Luke's second book (The Acts of the Apostles) is all about Jesus' followers going out in his name to all people. They too now have a heart for the lost. They do not stay for long in Jerusalem, but go all around the world. Jesus had repeated his command that they should be his witnesses, testifying that he was the true Messiah of Israel and the ultimate ruler of the world; but now he specified that they would be bearing witness to him "in Jerusalem, and in all Judea and Samaria, and to the ends of the earth" (Acts 1:8). And off they went.

The story told in Acts is an amazing one: truly these were thirty years that turned the world upside down! Yet Acts is written to encourage us to be witnesses too – to pass on the Good News of Jesus to others through our words and through our lives. We see the first Christians:

- speaking about Jesus in Jerusalem, around the Mediterranean, and in Rome, being ready to witness to him before both Jewish and pagan rulers (see Acts 4, 22, 24, 26);
- setting up local communities which cared radically for people in need (2:45; 4:32–37) and sending money to help those caught in a famine (11:28–30);
- talking to complete strangers (8:26–40), accepting invitations into people's homes (10:25–48), and going from house to house with the message that people must repent and have faith in Jesus (20:20–21);
- praying together for boldness (4:23–31) and then sending out some of their number on missionary assignments (13:1–3), who then establish small congregations in remote places and later report back on what has happened (14:23–27);
- proclaiming by whatever means possible that Jesus (not the Roman emperor or anyone else) was the world's true Lord: "These men who have caused trouble all over... saying that there is another king, one called Jesus" (17:6–7).

And this is only what Luke had time to report. There will have been thousands of personal conversations – in homes, in fields, and on the streets – as ordinary believers simply "gossiped the gospel" with their neighbours and friends. There will also have been many acts of kindness as ordinary Christians allowed Jesus' light to shine through them. This is how the church of Jesus grows. This is how the Good News spreads that Jesus is king.

Matthew, in his Gospel, gives us two key statements from Jesus to guide his followers in this task of mission. How do we play a part in God's bringing in his kingdom?

The first statement encourages us that our actions can have a disproportionate and transforming effect on our surrounding culture:

You are the salt of the earth... You are the light of the world. A town built on a hill cannot be hidden... People

do not light a lamp and put it under a bowl... In the same
way let your light shine before others, that they may see
your good deeds and glorify your Father in heaven.
Matthew 5:13–16

Inspired by this vision, Christians through the centuries have got deeply involved in their societies: serving as politicians, encouraging social reform, improving medical conditions, influencing public policy, educating children, campaigning against slavery, and so on. They have caught Jesus' vision of seeking to bring the values of God's kingdom into the here and now – in a way which pleases God and brings praise to his name. If you like, they have prayed, and then tried to implement, the key phrase in the Lord's Prayer: "your will be done on earth as it is in heaven" (Matthew 6:10). Communities and neighbourhoods can be transformed if Jesus' followers commit themselves to such involvement – seeing biblical principles for human society and then working tirelessly to make them a reality. In many contexts, such actions may indeed speak louder than words.

Jesus' second statement, however, balances this, showing us that words too are vitally important – Jesus' followers need to be speaking about him and then teaching people how to walk in his ways.

All authority in heaven and on earth has been given
to me. Therefore go and make disciples of all nations,
baptizing them in the name of the Father and of the
Son and of the Holy Spirit, and teaching them to obey
everything I have commanded you. And surely I am with
you always, to the very end of the age.
Matthew 28:18–20

The resurrection means that Jesus is God's appointed Lord and king over the entire world. People of all nations are to come under his reign and obey his teaching. His followers must themselves obey him, and then they must go out into the world in Jesus' name to help others into this place of obedience. In other words, they must both live in the light and also pass that light onto others – both through what they say and through what they do. And as they do this, they have Jesus' clear promise: "I am with you always."

Hesitating to proclaim Jesus' reign – by word or deed

Some of us may find this exciting. Many of us, however, feel quite weak at this point: "What can I do that would make a difference in society?" Or, "Who am I to speak of Jesus? I wouldn't know what to say!" "And, anyway, I'm not a good advert: I know some non-believers who live a better and more attractive life than I do!"

How *can* we bear witness to Jesus' reign?

Our hesitations are compounded – at least in many Western cultures – by our context. European society, for example, has been enormously influenced by Christian activists in the past, but now so many philanthropic ventures have been taken over by the state (for example, education and healthcare) that the opportunities for Christians to make an appreciable difference can seem harder to find.

Europe's Christian legacy has also had the effect of making many people cynical about matters of faith: religion is branded as responsible for bigotry and violence; people who make truth-claims are dismissed as really just playing power games. Many are also cynical about Jesus; they think they know what Christianity is (and imagine it was long ago discredited), but in fact, they don't. They are often reacting to a distorted stereotype. They think the Christian faith is:

- all about rules – but it's a relationship!
- about losing their freedom – when in fact Jesus offers them true freedom!
- suitable only for a certain kind of person – when in fact it's for everyone!
- a load of myths – when it's rooted in historical truth!
- tied to tradition and the ancient past – when in fact Jesus makes everything new!

Many people also give the appearance of living comfortable lives, seemingly undisturbed about spiritual or personal issues. In fact, of course, many of these same people are miserable and depressed, perhaps outwardly comfortable but inwardly lost – but that's the side of them that we don't see.

Meanwhile, others are indeed going through hard times. In the West they frequently blame God for this, becoming bitter. In the "two-thirds" world, however, where people's suffering is often so much more acute, there is often, paradoxically, a real openness to hearing the Good News. Here too there are barriers: family and tribal commitments, the influence and sometimes hostility of other religious systems, and the time often spent simply fighting for survival.

In these circumstances, all of us are tempted to withdraw. Why try to influence society for good in Christ's name? And why bother to tell others of Jesus? What if they don't think they need forgiveness or greater freedom? What if their suffering is much greater than mine? And (though we don't often admit this) what if this might cause me to suffer for my faith?

We find all kinds of reasons, many of them quite cogent. Despite Jesus' call to be "the light of world", we become brilliant at doing what he told us not to: hiding our light "under a bowl". He called us to be like salt, but too often our salt is left in the saltshaker! Jesus remains the king, nevertheless, and it remains the case that news of his reign needs to be proclaimed in whatever way is possible – challenging unjust authorities, helping those in need, and calling people to come under his rule. We must live out the truth and also speak out the truth. The Good News of Jesus' kingdom is indeed true. People may prefer following lies, but the Good News is God's truth for his world.

> **We must live out the truth and also speak out the truth.**

Moreover, this news about King Jesus also requires us to pass on some important warnings. There is a "broad... road", warned Jesus, which truly leads "to destruction" (Matthew 7:13). God's judgment is a fearful reality which can lead to the "weeping and gnashing of teeth" (Matthew 8:12). Jesus is the king who can dismiss people from his presence and say to them those chilling words: "I never knew you. Away from me, you evildoers!" (Matthew 7:21–23; see also 25:31–46). Paul affirmed that "we must all appear before the judgment seat of Christ" (2 Corinthians 5:10).

So, even if we don't think it is, sin is serious; all rebellion against King Jesus will be treated as such. God has established Jesus as king of the world and eventually "every knee will bow" before him (Philippians 2:10). People may think they are fine, but it isn't necessarily so. Our task, then, is to awaken people to these urgent spiritual realities. We may be unpopular, but truth is true.

Biblical encouragements to witness to Jesus

The rest of this chapter focuses on the issue which, for many of us, is the most difficult: how can we speak about Jesus' reign in a way that is effective and compelling? How do we share the Good News appropriately?

In John's Gospel we are given two good examples which may help us to answer this question.

1. Sharing the Good News is pointing others to Jesus

This is what John the Baptist did (John 1:19–34). First, he was honest about his own limitations: "I am not worthy." Next, he told people to look instead at Jesus: "Look, the Lamb of God, who takes away the sin of the world!" Finally, he added his own personal testimony: "I have seen and I testify that this is God's Chosen One." Here are three simple ingredients: humility of style, a steady focus on Jesus as the unique Saviour, and all backed up by personal endorsement and commitment. Later, John compared himself to the best man at a wedding, whose purpose is not to draw attention to himself but rather to the bridegroom (Jesus):

> *He must become greater; I must become less.*
>
> John 3:30

Our task, then, is not to worry about ourselves (we will be far from perfect), but rather to point people to Jesus and his perfection.

2. Sharing the Good News is bringing people to Jesus

This is what we see in Simon Peter's brother, Andrew. As soon as Andrew heard about Jesus, he at once "found his brother Simon and told him, 'We have found the Messiah'... And he brought him to Jesus" (John 1:41–42). Later, in Jerusalem, we see Andrew doing this again. When some Greek visitors to the city told him they would like to see Jesus, Andrew simply informed Jesus – acting

> Our task is simply to help people get in touch with Jesus.

as the "go-between". Andrew just loved making connections. Like him, our task is simply to help people get in touch with Jesus. We can make the introduction; let Jesus do the rest.

The New Testament gives us some further helpful guidelines:

Be wise in the way you act towards outsiders; make the most of every opportunity. Let your conversation be always full of grace, seasoned with salt, so that you may know how to answer everyone.

Paul's words in Colossians 4:5–6

In your hearts revere Christ as Lord. Always be prepared to give an answer to everyone who asks you to give the reason for the hope that you have. But do this with gentleness and respect, keeping a clear conscience.

Peter's words in 1 Peter 3:15–16

In these commands from Jesus' apostles we learn that we are:

- to be ready at all times – through maintaining an inner reverence for Christ and keeping a clear conscience, living lives that are worthy of him;
- to be full of grace; since God's grace is what we are talking about, we should speak of Jesus with grace, with gentleness and respect;

- to speak of our hope in Jesus – both now and for eternity;
- to be "salty"; that is, we are to be close enough to people to have an effect and also to find creative ways of injecting the light of Jesus into any dark situations we encounter.

In all this, we will need to be prayerful, asking God to guide us to people in whom he is already at work. People cannot come to Jesus, so Jesus teaches, "unless the Father... draws them" (John 6:44); so we will be praying that God's Spirit will be doing his own, unique work of convicting people about Jesus' truth (see John 16:8–11). Also, of course, we will always seek to be sensitive towards people's needs. After all, spreading Good News does not require us to be rude, unkind, or unloving. Ultimately, it's a matter of honestly speaking the truth – the truth about Jesus' reign and the truth that we are his followers. At one level, as someone has helpfully put it, it's all about "one beggar telling another beggar where to find bread".

> It's all about one beggar telling another beggar where to find bread.

Finding the words

What kind of things should we actually say? Are there particular things we can be preparing right now so that we can indeed "make the most of every opportunity?"

At one level, it's important not to be too worried here about developing set formulas or pat answers. Every person and every conversation is unique and we need to respond appropriately. Our goal is simply to live under the rule of Jesus, letting Jesus guide us. We will be trying to discern what Jesus himself might have said or done in this particular situation. After all, Jesus promised his special help and inspiration for those seeking to witness to him, especially in the face of opposition:

> *Do not worry beforehand about what to say. Just say whatever is given you at the time, for it is not you speaking, but the Holy Spirit.*

Mark 13:11

On the other hand, there is no harm in becoming a little clearer in our own minds as to some key things to say. Reading some of the material in appendices A and B might help clarify your own thinking about the faith and how to explain it to another person. Alternatively, you may be able to encourage your friends to read the appendices for themselves – or other books that deal in greater depth with some of their concerns.

Yet we may not have the luxury of so much time. What if someone suddenly asks us about our faith and we realize we only have two minutes left to give a reply?

Here, it's worth getting familiar with a tried and tested summary of the gospel.

The *Why Jesus?* booklets (associated with the *Alpha* course) helpfully summarize the gospel, focusing on what Jesus offers. The materials associated with the *Christianity Explored* course focuses more on the cross and our need for forgiveness.

Two Ways to Live (originating from Australia) develops the theme of this present chapter – that Jesus is king – and challenges people to recognize that they have placed themselves, not Jesus, on the throne of their lives.

There are many others from around the world, adapted for different cultures. Try to find one which fits your culture and which you feel relaxed with. Alternatively, you may find helpful the "gospel presentation" in Box 6b, which presents Jesus' cross as being able to bridge the gap between humans and God.

Whichever presentation you use, it's worth having some Bible verses committed to memory, so that you can speak some of God's words, not merely your own. Remember: Scripture has a unique power.

Another way would be to develop your own summary based on what we covered in chapters 1 to 3. If, as we have seen, the gospel centres upon Jesus (his resurrection, his cross, and his Spirit), then you might want to say something along these lines:

- Through the resurrection, God has established Jesus as king and has revealed that he wants "all people everywhere to repent" and to "come to a knowledge of the truth" (Acts 17:30; 1 Timothy 2:4).

- On his cross Jesus "bore our sins" (1 Peter 2:24) so that, if we repent, God can truly and completely forgive us.

- Eternal life can become ours when we commit ourselves to come under Jesus' rule and to follow him as our Risen Lord. When we do this, he enters into our lives by his Holy Spirit, in keeping with Jesus' promise that God would send us his Spirit – "I will not leave you as orphans; I will come to you" (John 14:18).

Whatever we say, however, the important thing is to be both genuine (speaking what is true to our own experience) and truthful (conveying God's truth from the Bible), always pointing not to ourselves but to Jesus. Remember too the power of personal testimony: people will often be deeply touched and made more open to the Good News if we share honestly with them some of our own experience of God's reality in our lives, and of his faithfulness. Also note that real, lasting change often comes about when people hear the Word of God (in Scripture) as it starts to address them directly.

Box 6b – A gospel presentation: The "bridge" diagram

Diagram 1

GOD   SIN   HUMANKIND

- Many recognize that, if God exists, there is a vast gap (or "chasm") between God and humanity: he is our Creator, we are his "creatures"; he is also "transcendent" – that is, quite distinct from us (Isaiah 40:10–31).

- He is also utterly holy – "your eyes are too pure to look on evil" (Habakkuk 1:13). Human beings, by contrast, are selfish and tainted by moral evil ("there is no one righteous, not even one": Romans 3:10).

- As a result, the Bible teaches that our sinfulness effectively places a barrier between us and God (Isaiah 59:2; see also Genesis 3:23). The gap between us is caused by our sin.

Diagram 2

GOD   Philosophy HUMANKIND
      Religion
      Prayer
      Good Deeds

- Many people, being aware of this distance from God, try to reach out towards him, searching after God – hoping to find him or perhaps to earn his favour.

- Different people may try different tactics. Some will read books on religion or pursue "philosophy" in some way. Others will try to do some of the things Jesus discussed in his Sermon on the Mount (Matthew 5-7), namely being:

  > religiously observant;

  > trying to pray in private;

  > being good and kind to their neighbours.

- Yet there is a basic problem with each of these. However good in themselves, they do not get through to God – because none deal with the fundamental problem of human sin. Put another way, they all fail because (as the diagram makes clear) they all start from humanity's side, not God's; none of them can reach to the other side.

- What is needed, then, is an initiative of God (something which starts from God's side of the diagram) and which deals with the fundamental cause of the gap.

Diagram 3

GOD   HUMANKIND

- This is precisely what the cross is: it is offered by God as his solution to the problem of human sin and wrong-doing. "God presented Christ as a sacrifice of atonement" (Romans 3:25). "Salvation comes from the Lord" (Jonah 2:9), not from ourselves.

- On the cross, God "made him who had no sin to be sin for us, so that in him we might become the righteousness of God" (2 Corinthians 5:21). Jesus effectively (on the diagram) destroys the power of sin by absorbing it onto himself.

- Again, Jesus "suffered once for sins, the righteous for the unrighteous" in order to bring us to God (1 Peter 3:18). Through the cross Jesus is able thereby to remove sin and then bring sinful human beings back across into the presence of God (we can have "access" into God's presence: see Romans 5:2; Ephesians 2:18).

- A bridge has thus been established by Jesus' cross, which can bring us into God's presence and enable us to know him for ourselves.

- The question is: have you walked across that bridge? To do so means simply:

  › acknowledging your need of the bridge (that you are sinful and need God's forgiveness);

  › thanking God for providing that bridge through the cross of Jesus, his Son.

In this way, we play our part in Jesus' great mission, first launched by him in that upper room when he commissioned his followers to go from Jerusalem to "all nations". Some of us may be better talkers and communicators than others. Some may have a particular gift of evangelism in their public speaking or in their friendships. Others, of course, may have a particular calling to spread the kingdom of Jesus through committed social action and practical concern. Each of these is a different gifting which Jesus uses to extend his kingdom. All Jesus' followers are also commissioned with a message which we must be prepared to speak out – if (or indeed when) occasions present themselves.

That's why Peter told Jesus' followers to be "prepared to give an answer to everyone" (1 Peter 3:15). Are we ready? Jesus himself said, "From the one who has been entrusted with much, much more will be asked" (Luke 12:48). If we have been given the great Good News of Jesus, are we going to hoard it to ourselves, becoming like a stagnant pond? Or are we going to give it gladly away, so that others too might be refreshed? In the land of the Bible there are two inland lakes (Lake Galilee and the Dead Sea); the former gives all its water away and so remains fresh; the latter hoards everything it receives and so becomes "dead" and putrid. Which one are we going to be like?

So the sixth and final building block that the Risen Jesus gives to his followers is this: be actively involved in God's mission and bear witness to his reign. Jesus is God's appointed king and we must play our part, by word and deed, in extending his kingdom.

Building block 6

Bear witness to his reign
– others too need to come under his rule.

PART 2

Learning from the Apostles

(Acts 2)

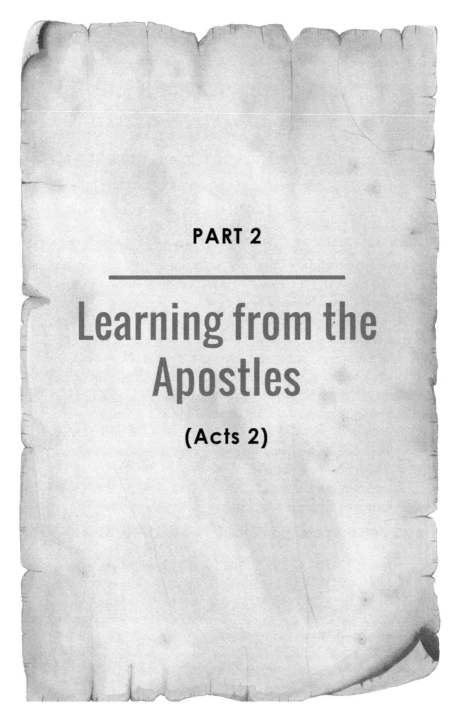

From Luke's Second Book:

The Acts of the Apostles (chapter 2)

The coming of the Holy Spirit (verses 1–8, 11–13)

When the day of Pentecost came, they were all together in one place. Suddenly a sound like the blowing of a violent wind came from heaven and filled the whole house where they were sitting. They saw what seemed to be tongues of fire that separated and came to rest on each of them. All of them were filled with the Holy Spirit and began to speak in other tongues as the Spirit enabled them.

Now there were staying in Jerusalem God-fearing Jews from every nation under heaven. When they heard this sound, a crowd came together in bewilderment, because each one heard their own language being spoken. Utterly amazed, they asked: "Aren't all these who are speaking Galileans? Then how is it that each of us hears them in our native language? ... we hear them declaring the wonders of God in our own tongues!" Amazed and perplexed, they asked one another, "What does this mean?"

Some, however, made fun of them and said, "They have had too much wine."

Peter's message (verses 14–18, 21–28, 31–40)

Then Peter stood up with the Eleven, raised his voice and addressed the crowd: "Fellow Jews and all of you who live in Jerusalem, let me explain this to you; listen carefully to what I say. These people are not drunk, as you suppose. It's only nine in the morning! No, this is what was spoken by the prophet Joel:

'In the last days, God says,
    I will pour out my Spirit on all people.
Your sons and daughters will prophesy,
    your young men will see visions,
    your old men will dream dreams.
Even on my servants, both men and women,
    I will pour out my Spirit in those days,
    and they will prophesy...
And everyone who calls
    on the name of the Lord will be saved.'

"Fellow Israelites, listen to this: Jesus of Nazareth was a man accredited by God to you by miracles, wonders and signs, which God did among you through him, as you yourselves know. This man was handed over to you by God's deliberate plan and foreknowledge; and you, with the help of wicked men, put him to death by nailing him to the cross. But God raised him from the dead, freeing him from the agony of death, because it was impossible for death to keep its hold on him. David said about him:

'I saw the Lord always before me.
    Because he is at my right hand,
    I will not be shaken.
Therefore my heart is glad and my tongue rejoices;
    my body also will rest in hope,
because you will not abandon me to the realm of the dead,
    you will not let your holy one see decay.
You have made known to me the paths of life;
    you will fill me with joy in your presence.' ...

"Seeing what was to come, he spoke of the resurrection of the Messiah, that he was not abandoned to the realm of the dead, nor did his body see decay. God has raised this Jesus to life, and we are all witnesses of it. Exalted to the right hand of God, he has received from the Father the promised

Holy Spirit and has poured out what you now see and hear. For David did not ascend to heaven, and yet he said,

'The Lord said to my Lord:
  "Sit at my right hand
until I make your enemies
  a footstool for your feet.'

"Therefore let all Israel be assured of this: God has made this Jesus, whom you crucified, both Lord and Messiah."

When the people heard this, they were cut to the heart and said to Peter and the other apostles, "Brothers, what shall we do?"

Peter replied, "Repent and be baptized, every one of you, in the name of Jesus Christ for the forgiveness of your sins. And you will receive the gift of the Holy Spirit. The promise is for you and your children and for all who are far off – for all whom the Lord our God will call."

With many other words he warned them; and he pleaded with them, "Save yourselves from this corrupt generation."

Life among the believers (verses 41–47)

Those who accepted his message were baptized, and about three thousand were added to their number that day. They devoted themselves to the apostles' teaching and to fellowship, to the breaking of bread and to prayer. Everyone was filled with awe at the many wonders and signs performed by the apostles. All the believers were together and had everything in common. They sold property and possessions to give to anyone who had need. Every day they continued to meet together in the temple courts. They broke bread in their homes and ate together with glad and sincere hearts, praising God and enjoying the favour of all the people. And the Lord added to their number daily those who were being saved.

Share with Jesus' People

They devoted themselves to... fellowship...
Acts 2:42

In part 1, we saw how Jesus on the first Easter Sunday gave his master plan for his followers. We are to focus on six main things: the resurrection and the cross; the Spirit and the Scriptures; a meal; and our mission in Jesus' name.

Luke now picks up the story to show how his followers responded. Jesus had told them to wait in Jerusalem for something new: the Father's gift of the Spirit. In Acts 2 (see extracts on previous pages) we read the exciting account of what actually happened. Their Easter joy was followed by Pentecost* power.

> **Their Easter joy was followed by Pentecost* power.**

What happened next?

Acts chapter 2 is a great story – a true story of what God did. It was a unique event in the history of the world. Even though we are not to expect the Holy Spirit to do precisely the same for us (touching us with tongues of fire or helping us to speak in foreign languages), we can affirm that this truly happened on that one occasion – especially if we ourselves are those who know the Spirit's presence and power in our own lives. What God was doing here was marking the public launch of Jesus' new people, dramatically vindicating the message of Jesus, and thus confirming his divine intention that we should be people who honour his Son and welcome his Spirit.

God gave to Peter an incredible boldness – the same Peter who, as described in Luke 22, had denied Jesus three times! Peter was thus enabled to launch that witness to King Jesus which Jesus himself had commanded. Here we see happening precisely what Jesus had predicted in Luke 24 (as we saw in chapter 6) – mission in Jesus' name. In one sense, Jesus' mission had been accomplished, but in another sense his mission – that which he can inspire in and through his followers – was only now beginning.

Peter proclaims Jesus as king

Peter's words confirm the pattern of Jesus' teaching which we outlined in part 1 (especially chapters 1 to 3). Note how he focuses on:

- **The new life of Jesus' resurrection.** "God raised him from the dead," Peter says (Acts 2:3). Unlike great King David, "his body [did not] see decay" (verse 31). Death could not hold him in its power. Indeed, he was not only raised from the tomb, but had also now been exalted to the Father's "right hand" – what is now known as his ascension*. God had therefore vindicated him as the anointed king (the Messiah) and the Lord of the world. Peter witnesses to Jesus' unique identity, seen in both his resurrection and ascension.

- **The necessity of Jesus' death.** Even though some of his hearers had been involved with the events leading up to Jesus' crucifixion seven weeks before ("whom you crucified"), Peter does not tactfully omit the cross. Instead he boldly declares that this shameful, unlikely event had been in line with God's plan – his intention to rescue the world. When he then announces God's promise to forgive their sins and to rescue them from the coming punishment, there is an implicit connection to the cross: for the cross was the place where such punishment had been taken by Jesus, precisely to bring about forgiveness of sins (see Luke 24:47; Acts 20:28; and fuller discussion in chapter 2).

- **The new gift of the Holy Spirit.** In the Old Testament, the gift of the Spirit had been limited to certain people, but now this gift was being poured out (by King Jesus!) to all people: to men and women, to young and old, indeed to "all whom the Lord our God will call" (Acts 2:39).

Peter, as instructed by Jesus, is bearing witness to his reign. Note how he simply unpacks the same three great truths that Jesus himself had highlighted in Luke 24 (see chapters 1 to 3). He then backs them up with frequent use of the Scriptures (for example, Joel 2:28–32; Psalm 16:8–11), again as Jesus had strongly encouraged (see chapter 4). The result, perhaps not so surprisingly, is powerful. Peter's hearers, we read, were "cut to the heart". They may have sensed the horror of the cross. They may have been awestruck by the evident power of the Spirit. Or they may have pondered Peter's powerful application of the Scriptures, now fulfilled in the Risen Jesus. In particular, when Peter quoted Psalm 110 ("Sit at my right hand until I make your enemies a footstool for your feet"), they may have sensed the vital importance of not being one of the "enemies" of this King Jesus – who had been so recently exalted by God to his throne in heaven.

Peter gave some straight commands to those who wanted to make a response: "Repent and be baptized, every one of you, in the name of Jesus Christ for the forgiveness of your sins. And you will receive the gift of the Holy Spirit" (verse 38). Here was the punchline, the challenge flowing out from Peter's proclamation of Jesus as king. Many responded on that occasion and many have done so ever since (see chapter 1).

Jesus' followers respond: A vital model for us today

There is more to learn from Acts 2, however. In some important verses (41–47), Luke tells us what these new followers of Jesus did next.

In fact, these few verses will provide the basis for all we are going to be learning together here in part 2, as we learn from the apostles a further six building blocks that are vital for those who want to walk in the ways of Jesus. In other words, by noting how the Holy Spirit guided Jesus' followers, then, we will be guided as to how we should follow him today.

Verse 42 is the key verse:

> *They devoted themselves to the apostles' teaching and to fellowship, to the breaking of bread and to prayer.*
>
> Acts 2:42

Here is a great model for Jesus' followers – a basic blueprint for the church's* life for generations to come:

- apostles' teaching;
- fellowship*;
- breaking of bread;
- prayer.

It is an incredibly well-balanced programme, holding together different strands in the church's life that too easily fly apart: biblical teaching, practical concern for those in need, proper valuing of the Lord's Supper, and commitment to a life of prayer and worship.

The third bullet point is particularly intriguing. For it confirms what we saw (in chapter 5), that Jesus had given his followers this distinctive command to remember his death by "breaking bread" together in his name. Here in Acts, we see them immediately putting this command into practice.

Yet the other three bullet points are fascinating too. From these, we will now in part 2 draw out six further themes that will help us to follow Jesus.

- Here in chapter 7 we will focus on the fellowship (how we should share with our fellow believers).

- In chapter 8 we will focus on prayer (how we should worship God, both individually and corporately).

Then, in the next four chapters, we will look at different aspects of the apostles' teaching.

- Chapter 9 will focus on what the apostles taught us to believe – their doctrines about Jesus and salvation.

- Chapter 10 focuses on what they taught us to do (or the kind of people we are to become) – their teaching about living the Christian life.

- Chapter 11 will focus on the apostles' challenge to resist evil – their lessons about Christian warfare.

- Finally, chapter 12 looks appropriately at what we are to hope for – what the apostles teach us about the future.

Let's look at each in turn to see what it means to truly walk, guided by the apostles' example, in the Jesus Way.

The fellowship of the Holy Spirit: Practical sharing

"Fellowship" is a strange word. What does it mean? We will discover that the very reason it is used so rarely outside Christian circles is precisely because it is trying to describe something unique within Christianity: the unique relationship that exists between believers because they all have something in common – the indwelling presence of Jesus' Spirit.

Peter's message was that those who followed Jesus would surely "receive the gift of the Holy Spirit" (Acts 2:38). This confirms what we said in chapter 3, that every believer has the Holy Spirit dwelling within them. Yet it also explains the great mystery of the church. For the church, unlike any other organization in the world, is made up of people all of whom have the Spirit of their Master living within them! This means that there is automatically a connection between us. When we meet Christians for the first time, we already have something

> The church, unlike any other organisation in the world, is made up of people all of whom have the Spirit of their Master living within them!

in common with them (or perhaps we should say, some*one* in common!). There is a love, a power, and a presence that draws us together: God's Holy Spirit.

This is what those first 3,000 believers discovered when they responded to Peter's preaching. They found that they shared together not just a common faith (in Jesus) but a common life (because of his Spirit within them and between them). The Bible then calls this reality "the fellowship of the Holy Spirit" (2 Corinthians 13:14).

This fellowship is not just a spiritual reality; it should also translate into everyday reality and radical practice. The original Greek word (translated as "fellowship") simply means that which is "common or shared". So fellowship means something like "having or doing things in common" – exactly what we see those first believers putting into practice. Perhaps we will best get the sense of what fellowship means if we use instead the concept of sharing – a concept which sounds much more practical and earthly.

So, after experiencing the Holy Spirit, the first believers immediately "were together and had everything in common" (Acts 2:44). In fact, they decided to go so far as to sell their "property and possessions to give to anyone who had need" (verse 45). This was real, practical sharing. What they now had in Jesus was worth far more than their possessions, so they gladly shared these with other believers who were in real need.

In the same way, our fellowship with other believers should not just be spiritual, but practical. We learn from later in Acts (4:32 – 5:11) that this initial response to the gospel did not require them literally to sell everything – there is not a total ban on possessions or personal wealth. Thus, as the New Testament develops, we see Christians using their money and possessions in different ways to build up their fellow believers (see, for example, 2 Corinthians 8–9). However, there remains here a strong biblical challenge, especially to Christians in the West. In what ways are we sharing our resources with our fellow Christians?

> **In what ways are we sharing our resources with our fellow Christians?**

We also need to hear this challenge whenever we think of the church spreading throughout the world. How are Jesus' followers showing their commitment to one another in practical and financial ways?

So the seventh building block, as we follow Jesus, is to share with Jesus' people. This will mean sharing our care and our lives, showing our love in practical ways, and finding ways of expressing our strong commitment to one another. Every believer has the Holy Spirit dwelling within them. If each of us truly belongs to Jesus, we soon discover that, through him, we now belong to each other!

Jesus' new family: God's commitment to building his people

Some of us, however, may need help becoming convinced that this is part of what it means to be Jesus' followers: "Can I not follow Jesus without having to be so committed to his other followers?" If so, here are two insights from the Bible that can help strengthen our resolve. They come in the form of two questions: how will we respond?

1. Do we consider other believers as members of our new "family"?

Jesus wants us to. On one occasion, when asked a question about his actual human family, Jesus looked around instead at those sitting near him and replied quite forcefully:

> *Who are... my brothers?... Here are my mother and my brothers! Whoever does God's will is my brother and sister and mother.*

Mark 3:33–35

Jesus was establishing a new family – one that was centred on him, and obedient to God.

Family life can be painful for many; this may be because of difficult or broken relationships (sometimes leading to divorce), or because of personal setbacks or tragedy (fuelled in some parts of the world by the AIDS crisis or long-term wars). Even so, most of us recognize the great value of families. It is a horrible thing to be separated from one's family, to lose one's brothers or sisters, or to be orphaned.

Through Jesus, however, each believer has been brought into a new family: the church, the people of God, God's own family. After all, when we are born physically, we are inevitably born into a family (whether we like it or not!). The same is true when we are born spiritually. Jesus taught that believers are "born again" through the work of God's Spirit upon them (John 3:3, 7). One consequence of this new birth is inevitably that we find ourselves in a new family.

> *Those who believed in his name, he gave the right to become children of God.*
>
> John 1:12

This means that we are automatically in a family relationship with everyone else who, through Jesus, is also a child of God.

For most people, this is an exciting part of the Good News. As believers, we find we are no longer on our own. We belong. We have many new brothers and sisters*, and God is our true Father (see chapters 2 and 3). If we have had difficulties in our human families, we now can experience something of what we have missed: the joy of being valued by others, and the delight of being deeply loved by God himself.

For others, however, there is a challenge here. They don't mind following Jesus on their own, but they don't want to share their lives with others. The saying goes, "You can choose your friends but not your family"; what if we find that we don't like those who are in this new family? Can't we opt out?

We cannot have Jesus himself without also having Jesus' people!

No. We cannot have Jesus himself without also having Jesus' people! Jesus is forming a worldwide family, and his followers need to recognize that to belong to Jesus is to belong to his new people.

Moreover, Jesus wants his family to be characterized by love – Jesus' unique kind of love:

A new command I give you: Love one another. As I have loved you, so you must love one another.

John 13:34–35

If so, then we must express this love, even if our fellow believers are people whom we do not naturally like. And we must do so in practical ways. For Jesus' sake, we are called to share with others in Jesus' family. This is something deeper than mere human friendship; this is authentic, family-styled fellowship.

2. Do we realize just how important it is to God himself that he builds a new people?

We are often so individualistic and wrapped up in our own concerns that we forget the big picture: that God is passionately committed to forming a distinct, new people who will reflect his image in the world. We see this divine desire throughout the Bible.

One of the great promises repeated throughout Scripture is when God says:

I will take you as my own people, and I will be your God.

Exodus 6:7

The God of the Bible is a God of relationship. He longs to be in relationship with us; he wants to be our God (see Revelation 21:3). But he doesn't just want to know us as individuals. He also wants to form a people on earth who recognizably belong to him.

That's why, in the Old Testament, there was so much focus on the people of ancient Israel* and also so much teaching on how they should conduct their national life. In those days, these were God's people and they needed to show the world what the living God was like – not least, through the way they cared for each other in their society. God had specially called Israel to be in a covenant* with him – that is, a binding relationship with promises. He wanted this "covenant people" to look different from the other nations. Yet, because of disobedience, things in Israel often went from bad to worse; so the prophets began to predict a time when God would form a remnant of faithful Israelites, who alone would be God's true people (for example, Isaiah 10:22–23).

Then Jesus came. Jesus was himself the perfect, faithful Israelite. In a strange sense, he himself was the "people of God", the true Israel; as the Messiah he embodied in himself the hopes and destiny of the nation. And he began to draw around him a new "remnant". He chose twelve special followers (like the twelve tribes of ancient Israel), telling them that they were now the true "flock" belonging to God (Luke 12:32). He welcomed unlikely people to follow him and shared table fellowship with others. Jesus was recruiting people to his cause. But he was also re-founding the people of God around himself. From now on, God's people would be defined not by their ethnic background, but by faith in him, Jesus the Messiah.

As a result, the New Testament insists that not only Jews, but also Gentiles* must, through Jesus, be allowed into God's people. Jesus had redefined God's people around himself. God's true people, now centred on Jesus, was to be made up of anyone who had faith in him. Jesus was the vine; his followers were the branches (John 15:5). Or, to use some of the apostles' other favourite pictures:

- Jesus is the head; we are all his body (Ephesians 1:23; Colossians 1:19; 1 Corinthians 12:12–27).

- Jesus is the bridegroom; we are his bride (Revelation 21:2; Ephesians 5:25–33).

- Jesus is the chief "cornerstone"; we are the building constructed upon him (Ephesians 2:20; 1 Corinthians 3:11).

- Jesus is the builder; we are his house (Hebrews 3:3–6).

- Jesus is the eldest brother in a family; we are now brothers and sisters in his family (Romans 8:29; Hebrews 2:11–12).

In other words, there is an organic and unbreakable link between Jesus and his new people – as a head to its body, as a vine to its branches, as a brother to his siblings.

This explains why the New Testament writers were so passionate about the "church" – that is, Jesus' new people. They knew that Jesus was passionately committed to his people – indeed organically linked to them! As Paul says:

Christ loved the church and gave himself up for her... for we are members of his body.

Ephesians 5:25, 30

He did this to make her holy... to present her to himself as a radiant church, without stain or wrinkle... No one ever hated their own body, but they feed and care for their body, just as Christ does the church.

Ephesians 5:26–29

Jesus sees the church as his own body, as his bride. He wants her to be beautiful and to reflect his love. He wants those who see the church to see in her something of him – his true grace and love. So, even if we do not always love the church, Jesus clearly does! He loves her, indeed he died for her.

The apostles knew too from the Old Testament that their God was a community-creating God. They saw Jesus' mission as precisely intended to found and form such a

> He wants those who see the church to see in her something of him.

new people for his Father – what we might call "God's new society". On the cross, Paul writes, Jesus "gave himself for us to redeem us from all wickedness and to purify for himself a people that are his very own, eager to do what is good" (Titus 2:14).

All this, then, should dispel any negative views we may have of the church or of being committed to Jesus' people. Once we grasp God's passionate determination to build a people of God, and once we see how Jesus is the organic centre of his church, we should find ourselves with a new resolve to demonstrate our own commitment to Jesus' followers. We should be people who care for each other's needs, do good, and do all we can to build up his church – never tearing it down.

There may still be some occasions when, because of the church's failings, we may feel strongly tempted to join others in saying, "Jesus, yes; church, no!" Yet, if God has called us to himself through Jesus, he is now calling us also to love Jesus' church and to play our part in making it what he wants it to be. The church is, despite its failings, God's new people.

Loving God's people

Acts 2, then, describes several things all at once:

- the launch of the church;

- the establishment of God's new people;

- the founding of Jesus' family;

- the unveiling of his beautiful bride.

The fact that visitors from so many nations heard the Good News in their own tongue is a dramatic signal (given uniquely to mark this one-off event) to demonstrate that this new community will be a truly international one – an inclusive people, crossing boundaries, extending to the world's end, and overturning the mix-up of languages that, in biblical imagery, has cursed the world ever since the tower of Babel (see Genesis 11:1–9).

> They realized that loving Jesus means loving his people.

Acts 2 also shows us our response – that is, what the Holy Spirit wants to bring about in our own lives as a result. Jesus' followers committed themselves to one other in radical ways. They realized how much they had in common because of Jesus and his Spirit, and they then sought to express this fellowship in down-to-earth practice. They realized that loving Jesus means loving his people.

This is not always easy. Indeed the subsequent story in Acts shows some of the difficulties the early Christians had: people backtracked on their commitments or started lying to one other; some began to feel overlooked or neglected by others; differences of strategy emerged; tensions grew between different nationalities and backgrounds (see Acts 5–6; 15). Jesus' followers include many different types of people. Some we will naturally like and understand, others we will not! Also, many are hurting or sick, meaning that the church often feels like a hospital – made up of people who in different ways all need tender, loving care. Yet none of this can negate the vision (displayed before us so clearly in Acts 2) of what God wants to do – and indeed can do – when his Holy Spirit is truly at work among us.

All of this requires us to love. Where can we find sufficient resources for such great love? Not from us, of course, but thankfully from the Holy Spirit.

> *God's love has been poured out into our hearts through the Holy Spirit, who has been given to us.*
>
> **Romans 5:5**

The Holy Spirit, already given to us, now becomes the channel for the outpouring of God's love. This is indeed a gift from God. As Paul explains when talking about the "gifts" of the Holy Spirit, this Christ-like love (known as *agape* love*) is the "greatest" gift that God can place within us (1 Corinthians 13:13). So when he describes this love, we are to read his words – even though they are challenging – as describing that which God's Spirit can produce in us. That is why love is the very first "fruit of the Spirit" mentioned by Paul, when he describes these fruits being produced in the lives of believers (see Galatians 5:22). The same is true as we read some other New Testament passages in which we are commanded to love (see Box 7).

Box 7 – Some New Testament passages on God's call to love and unity

A new command I give you: Love one another. As I have loved you, so you must love one another.

Jesus' words in John 13:34

Love is patient, love is kind. It does not envy, it does not boast, it is not proud. It does not dishonour others, it is not self-seeking, it is not easily angered, it keeps no record of wrongs. Love does not delight in evil but rejoices with the truth. *It always protects, always trusts, always hopes, always perseveres.*

1 Corinthians 13:4–7

Therefore, as God's chosen people, holy and dearly loved, clothe yourselves with compassion, kindness, humility, gentleness and patience. Bear with each other and forgive one another if any of you has a grievance against someone. Forgive as the Lord forgave you. And over all these virtues put on love, which binds them all together in perfect unity.

Colossians 3:12–14

This is how we know what love is: Jesus Christ laid down his life for us. And we ought to lay down our lives for our brothers and sisters. If anyone has material possessions and sees a brother or sister in need but has no pity on them, how can the love of God be in that person? Dear children, let us not love with words or speech but with actions and in truth.

1 John 3:16–18

Whoever does not love does not know God, because God is love... This is love: not that we loved God, but that he loved us and sent his Son as an atoning sacrifice for our sins... No one has ever seen God; but if we love one another, God lives in us and his love is made complete in us... God is love. Whoever lives in love lives in God, and God in them... We love because he first loved.

1 John 4:8, 10, 12, 16, 19

Carry each other's burdens, and in this way you will fulfil the law of Christ.

Galatians 6:2

I in them and you in me – so that they may be brought to complete unity. Then the world will know that you sent me and have loved them even as you have loved me.

Jesus' words in John 17:23

The apostles give these commands, because they know we are disobedient and will not love if not commanded; but they also know that Jesus by his Spirit can supply the resources we need. As Augustine* once said, "Command what you will, O Lord; then give what you command!" With God's help, we can begin to fulfil Jesus' new command to love one other.

Note too how John insists that such loving must be practical – not just in words but also in action. Love actually. The first Christians discovered God had given them a whole new kind of love. If we have recently become a believing Christian, one of the sure signs of this will be the new love which we sense towards other believers. Yet one of the best ways of growing as a Christian is not just to feel this love, but also to put that love into practice! Love, after all, is not to be hoarded to ourselves, but rather to be gladly given away!

So the seventh building block, as we follow Jesus, is all about loving Jesus' followers. We are to share with Jesus' people in practical ways, demonstrating the love of Christ.

Building block 7

Share with Jesus' people – they are now your family!

Worship His Majesty

They devoted themselves to... prayer.
Acts 2:42

The next theme we note from this key verse is that Jesus' followers instinctively began to worship God and to pray. They found that their new commitment to Jesus meant they now had a new relationship, not just with one other (expressed, as we have just seen, in fellowship) but also with God himself. Their lives could not help but be filled with prayer.

Inevitably, their focus was not just horizontal but vertical. Jesus had spoken about the need for us to love our neighbour as ourselves, but he had also made it clear what our first priority was to be: "Love the Lord your God with all your heart" (Mark 12:28–31, based on Deuteronomy 6:4–5 and Leviticus 19:18). Get this relationship right, he was implying, and then your other relationships will fall into place. So what we see in Acts 2 is the Holy Spirit helping those first believers with this vertical dimension: he was helping them to worship.

Even more startling, the Spirit was helping them to worship Jesus. One of the most remarkable things in the early chapters of Acts is how the first believers, despite coming from a Jewish background, found themselves instinctively worshipping Jesus. After all, the very text which Jesus had quoted from Deuteronomy was the same one which underlined Jewish monotheism* – the belief

> The Spirit was helping them worship Jesus.

in only one God: "The Lord our God, the Lord is one... serve him only" (Deuteronomy 6:4, 13). Yet here now were Jewish people worshipping Jesus! This was the clear implication of Peter's words here in Acts 2 which speak of Jesus as the "Lord", exalted to the "right hand of God" (verses 32–36). Such worship would be blasphemous in the eyes of many, but the first believers were led by the Holy Spirit to confess* "Jesus is Lord" and to worship him.

We shall return (in chapter 9) to what this reveals about Jesus' true identity – his somehow being identified with the glorious God who alone is to be worshipped. For now, however, we focus on what this means for Jesus' followers: we are called to a life of worship, and this includes worshipping Jesus himself who shares in God's glory. We are to worship King Jesus in all his royal power; we are to worship his majesty.

Worship, however, does not come easily to us. Jesus' encouragement that we should love God with all our heart implies that, as creatures made by God, we are created to worship him; so our emotions, our thinking, our energies are all designed to work best when they are touched and motivated by love for God. Yet, as sinful people, we so easily worship other people and other things.

Many in the West worship materialism, but Jesus clearly warned what this will do to our hearts:

> *Do not store up for yourselves treasures on earth, where moths and vermin destroy... For where your treasure is, there your heart will be also.*
>
> Matthew 6:19, 21

Other things too can steal our hearts away from God: evil desires, greed, wrong relationships, selfish activities. Indeed, in the Bible, anything which comes between the believer and God is called an "idol" – a false object of our heart's hidden worship. But Jesus is now the one we must worship, and all other idols are to be thrown down in his name. "Dear children," writes the apostle John, "keep yourselves from idols" (1 John 5:21).

So the eighth building block in the Christian life is to ensure that we give time to worship God, keeping Jesus enthroned as the ruler of our lives. When we come to Christ for the first time, this itself is an act of worship – as we "turned to God from idols to serve the living and true God" (1 Thessalonians 1:9). However, this turning to God must then continue on a daily basis, with worship becoming a recognizable hallmark of our lives. Worshipping God is to be a way of life – the very air that we breathe; it is to become part of the very fabric of our personalities. After all, we were created for such worship.

> We were created for worship.

Those first believers spent their time in prayer; indeed they were constantly "praising God" (Acts 2:47). Worship of God flowed over into the whole of their lives, affecting all that they did. As Jesus' followers, our lives are similarly to be characterized by worship.

Worship: The true and living God

This biblical perspective – that worship is about *all* our lives – may come as surprise. Many think that worship is somehow confined to Sundays or whenever we meet together with other Christians (what we do corporately). In fact, it includes what we do *on our own* and indeed what we do with *every part* of our lives.

The word "worship" in English is associated with the word "worthy". Worship, then, is giving God his "worth", acknowledging that, as our Creator, he is worthy of all our praise. Throughout the Bible, there are powerful pictures of God's awesome power and holiness, his majesty and sovereignty. He is portrayed as quite distinct from us his creatures – wholly "other" and transcendent. He is the "God of all grace", the One "from whom all things came and for whom we live" (1 Peter 5:10; 1 Corinthians 8:6). In the Old Testament he is regularly described as "God Almighty", the "Holy One of Israel"* who is "enthroned on the praises of his people" (see, for example, Psalm 22:3; Psalm 91:1; Isaiah 43:3, 14).

In one of the most significant episodes in Scripture, Israel's God is revealed to the prophet Isaiah as "high and exalted", surrounded by angelic beings who endlessly declare his praise:

Holy, holy, holy is the Lord Almighty;

the whole earth is full of his glory.

Isaiah 6:3

Isaiah's response to this vision encapsulates the kind of response which should come from all of us before such a holy God:

"Woe to me!" I cried. "I am ruined! For I am a man of unclean lips."

Isaiah 6:5

It is a graphic picture of what worship should mean before this awesome, awe-inspiring God.

The good news, however, is that this is not the Bible's last word on the subject of worship. Because of God's grace, our worship of him can be transformed from a position of abject abasement to a position of close, even intimate, relationship.

Here, then, are three further points which we must grasp if ever we are to gain a biblical perspective on worship.

1. Worship of the holy God: Present in our midst

Fear the Lord your God, serve him only... Do not follow other gods... for the Lord your God, who is among you, is a jealous God and his anger will burn against you.

Deuteronomy 6:13–15

Here is a classic call within the Old Testament for God's people to worship him; but note the strange idea that this holy God is present among his people. It reveals how God wants to be close to his people, indeed to be at the centre of their life.

Sinful human beings, of course, do not like this. As in the story of Adam and Eve (in Genesis 3), we disobey God's Word, trying to replace the worship of God with ourselves, putting ourselves on the "throne" of our lives. We want ourselves to be "like God" (Genesis 3:5), to usurp his role; we want to place ourselves, not God, at the centre.

Yet God will not let us do this. He will contend with us to regain his rightful place at the centre. This is seen, for example, in the book that follows Genesis in the Bible (Exodus) when, after delivering his people from Egypt and having given them his Ten Commandments, God then gave detailed instructions for the building of a worship space called the tabernacle (Exodus 24–31). Why was this so important? Because God wanted his people to be able to meet with him and to worship him. We might say, God's great acts of redemption and revelation are always designed to foster relationship. The God revealed at Mount Sinai is awesomely holy, but he longs to be worshipped and encountered.

> God's great acts of redemption and revelation are always designed to foster relationship.

Moreover, this tabernacle was to be located at the very centre of Israel's camp. Israel's God wanted to be at the heart of his people's corporate life. This principle is seen again later, when the Temple in Jerusalem is established at the centre of Israel's national life (see, for example, Psalm 48; 122). From this, we learn that the living God wants to be at the very centre of his people, right there in the middle of their community. Thus, although God is all-glorious, he is not a God who is far away. On the contrary, he is the Holy One who yet longs to come awesomely close: God in our midst.

2. Worship of the holy God: Approached through sacrifice

We have confidence to enter the Most Holy Place by the blood of Jesus, by a new and living way opened for us through the curtain... let us draw near to God with a sincere heart and with the full assurance that faith brings.
Hebrews 10:19–22

God's provision of the Temple in Jerusalem also gave his people a place where they could approach him. Despite his holiness and their sin, God established a sacrificial system through which he could forgive them. Relationship was restored through sacrifice. From this, we learn that we cannot just walk into God's presence, but must approach him in the way he himself has determined and with our sins forgiven.

For us, in the light of Jesus' coming and his sacrificial death on the cross (see chapter 2), this now means coming to God only through Jesus' death: "we have been made holy through the sacrifice of the body of Jesus Christ once for all" (Hebrews 10:10). Indeed, because of the cross, we can gain an access into God's holy presence that was only hinted at within the Old Testament period. For when Jesus died, the Temple curtain (which had prevented worshippers from entering the Most Holy Place) was suddenly "torn in two from top to bottom" (Mark 15:38). The final barrier has been broken down. If previously there was effectively a "No Entry" sign, barring the way into God's full presence, then now, through the cross, it says in large letters, "ALL WELCOME!"

New Testament worship is therefore marked by this great theme of our access into God's very presence: "we have confidence to enter the Most Holy Place" (Hebrews 10:19). "Now that we have been put right with God through faith, he has given us access by faith into this experience of God's grace" (Romans 5:1–2, my translation). "For through [Christ] we both have access to the Father by one Spirit" (Ephesians 2:18).

3. Worship of the holy God: By his Spirit

Acts 2 also makes it abundantly clear that true worship can now only be brought about by the agency and presence of the Holy Spirit. Jesus had hinted at this great new reality earlier in his ministry:

> *Yet a time is coming and has now come when the true worshipers will worship the Father in the Spirit and in truth, for they are the kind of worshipers the Father seeks. God is spirit, and his worshipers must worship in the Spirit and in truth.*
>
> John 4:23–24

We are to worship God (as other versions translate this) "in Spirit and in truth". Jesus is teaching that, because of his coming (being himself "the truth"; John 14:6) and the coming of the Spirit, it will now be possible for anyone anywhere to worship God in a way that is acceptable and pleasing. As seen in chapter 3, the Spirit also enables us to call God "Abba*", or "Father" and intercedes for us when "we do not know what we ought to pray" (Romans 8:15, 26). It is the Holy Spirit who makes true worship possible.

Putting all this together, we can sense how God himself has provided the means whereby we can approach him in worship: he longs to come close, but we can only come close to him through Jesus' death and by the Spirit. We also sense the Trinitarian* nature of Christian worship; for this reason, the Greek Orthodox Church defines worship neatly as being "of God the Father, through God the Son, in God the Holy Spirit."

Worship in every aspect of our lives

By means of his Spirit, God is therefore calling people to the worship of Jesus. He wants us to turn from ourselves, abandoning our idols, and to obey him truly. He wants us to be coming into his presence by the cross and (in reverse) to be welcoming his presence among us by his Spirit. God is to be at the centre of our lives.

Once we see this, we realize straightaway that such worship cannot be kept in some small, distinct corner of our lives. No, all our lives are to be given to this worship. If Jesus is not Lord of all, then he is not Lord at all. If becoming Jesus' follower is like opening the front door of our house to him (see chapter 1), we must remember that he must go on to be in charge of the whole house! There are, as it were, no "rooms" (such as our family life or relationships, our hopes or fears) which he may not enter. Consider these words of Paul:

> If Jesus is not Lord of all, then he is not Lord at all.

> *Therefore, I urge you, brothers and sisters, in view of God's mercy, to offer your bodies as a living sacrifice, holy and pleasing to God – this is your true and proper worship.*

Do not conform to the pattern of this world, but be
transformed by the renewing of your mind.

Romans 12:1–2

True worship, we see here, is a response: giving ourselves back to
the God who has shown us his mercy. It is total:
we are to give all of ourselves, including the
physical and practical aspects of our lives (Paul
speaks literally of offering "your bodies"). And

> **Worship covers the whole of life.**

it is continual: we don't just do this in church, but we keep offering
ourselves to God, especially when challenged by temptations and
the standards of this world. Worship covers the whole of life.

These verses also contain a great promise, which moves us
on to see one of the great benefits of such worship. Of course, the
primary reason for worshipping God is simply that our God is worthy
of our worship. Yet God also knows that our worshipping him will
benefit us. True worship, writes Paul, will be the means by which
God can transform us and indeed completely change our minds.
Many people have been damaged in their thinking or wounded in
their spirits, but true worship can lead to healing and to a renewed
mind. How does worship do this?

- It allows God's Spirit within us to be more effective.

- It helps keep Jesus truly at the centre, thus enabling us to
  do what Jesus would do and to think his thoughts.

- It removes our sinful selves from the throne of our lives
  and builds up our resistance towards the Evil One (see
  chapter 11).

- It gives us precious times of knowing how much we are
  loved by God, which then can set us free to be motivated
  not by self but by God's love.

In a word, God wants Christians to be more like Christ; he wants us
to "be conformed to the image of his Son" (Romans 8:29). How does
he do this? By calling us to worship him.

So worship is to be theme of all our lives. That's why Paul can
encourage us to "pray continually" (1 Thessalonians 5:17) – not

because we are reciting prayers all day, but because all our lives are soaked in prayer. All our lives are to be lived in the Lord's presence. He says:

> *And whatever you do, whether in word or deed, do it all in the name of the Lord Jesus, giving thanks to God the Father through him.*
>
> Colossians 3:17

For Paul, the goal is a life of total worship.

Worship on our own: Personal prayer

> *But when you pray, go into your room, close the door and pray to your Father, who is unseen. Then your Father, who sees what is done in secret, will reward you.*
>
> Matthew 6:6

Once we have this vision of all our lives being an act of worship, we can then see the importance of spending some time each day on our own consciously praying to God. For how can we live every moment of our day as worship (when we are also busy with other things), if we never spend some time in worship (when we are not busy with other things)? We are to take into our day the presence of the Lord whom we have already met, and with whom we have been in recent, focused communication.

So Jesus' followers need to find some time each day to talk with him. Many find early mornings are best; others prefer other times of the day, when they know they can be undisturbed and will be fresh enough to focus on God. But, whenever and wherever we pray, we can be sure that such times are very precious in God's sight. He is already there, delighted that we are seeking his face (see Psalm 27:8). We are to give time to this secret, unseen task – something that others will never know much about and for which we will seldom receive human praise. Yet, according to Jesus, this private worship is a vital part of following him; we will be rewarded by God giving us a deeper knowledge of his love and will.

When we talk with God, we can use our own words. Jesus here expressly encourages us not to "keep on babbling like pagans, for they think they will be heard because of their many words" but to pray in a simple and heartfelt way (Matthew 6:7). At the same time, Jesus goes on to give us a model prayer (what is now known as the "Lord's Prayer"), which we would do well to learn, to use frequently, and indeed to develop as the framework for our own further prayers.

Box 8 – Prayer and worship

The Lord's Prayer

Our Father in heaven, hallowed be your name.
Your kingdom come, your will be done,
  on earth as it is in heaven.
Give us this day our daily bread.
And forgive us our sins,
  as we forgive those who sin against us.
Lead us not into temptation,
  but deliver us from evil.
For yours is the kingdom, the power and the glory,
  for ever and ever!
*Amen**

(The modern translation, based on Matthew 6:9–13, which is now used in many churches.)

The PRAY principle – four key ingredients
(both for personal prayer and public worship)

Praise: worship God for who he is and seek to "give thanks in all circumstances" (1 Thessalonians 5:18). See, for example, Psalm 98; 100; 103; 117; 148; 150.

Repent: confess your sins (1 John 1:9) and come to Jesus for forgiveness through his cross. See, for example, Psalm 32; 51; 95.

Ask for others: intercede for other people and difficult situations in which you long for God's kingdom to "come... on earth as it is in heaven" (Matthew 6:10). See, for example, Psalm 20; 107; 121;

see also Paul's prayers in Ephesians 1:15–23; Philippians 1:9–11; Colossians 1:9–14.

... and for Yourself: at the end, ask for yourself for your "daily bread", seek the fruit and gifts of the Spirit in your life, and bring to God any personal concerns of your own. "Cast all your anxiety on him because he cares for you" (1 Peter 5:7). See, for example, Psalm 22; 28; 38; 56; 63.

Paul on prayer

Do not be anxious about anything, but in every situation, by prayer and petition, with thanksgiving, present your requests to God. And the peace of God, which transcends all understanding, will guard your hearts and your minds in Christ Jesus.

Philippians 4:6–7

Note how in the Lord's Prayer Jesus encourages us to begin and end our praying with a focus on God himself – his holiness, his kingdom, and his glory. Note too how we can ask God for things, but these must include forgiveness for sin, and deliverance from evil. Finally, note that we can approach God truly as our Father, but that this is true, not just for us as an individual, but for any who call on God's name through Jesus: he is *"our* Father". This means there is a sense in which we never quite pray this prayer on our own, but are always part of Jesus' wider family.

Jesus has not given us only the Lord's Prayer. There is the whole of the Bible. This too (especially the Psalms, which formed Jesus' own prayer book) can give us words to speak to God when we have no words of our own.

And, of course, the Bible is also the place where we hear God speaking to us. Reading (or even reciting) a few words of Scripture can have a powerful effect, especially when we ask God's Spirit to be our teacher. It's so powerful to sense God speaking to us personally from his word! The Bible is like a letter from a friend, which we should open with enthusiasm. "[He] wakens my ear to listen like one being instructed" (Isaiah 50:4). So, as we open the Scriptures, we will begin to hear God's voice, and this in turn will fuel our prayers.

Some people find the P.R.A.Y. principle (see Box 8) to be a useful structure for their times of personal prayer. Others find keeping a personal journal helps them to look back over previous weeks and to note the answers to their prayers. Some find particular favourite locations are conducive to prayer; others take themselves off on "prayer walks" where they talk with God as they walk. There is no one right way to pray! The important thing is to be both disciplined and reasonably creative, trying out different habits and finding out gradually what works best for you.

Whatever its precise form, then, this personal encounter with the Lord, this private worship of Jesus, is to be the secret powerhouse of our whole lives. For we can hardly be his followers if we never talk to him, tell him we love him, or listen to him for his instructions.

Worship with others: Corporate prayer

Let the message of Christ dwell among your richly as you teach and admonish one another with all wisdom through psalms, hymns, and songs from the Spirit, singing to God with gratitude in your hearts.

Colossians 3:16

Finally, there is that worship which we offer to God when in the company of others – in small groups or in church services. In Acts 2, we see the believers continuing to meet together "every day", "praising God" both in the Temple courts and in their homes (verses 46–47). We can worship God on our own, but "corporate" or communal worship (when Jesus' followers expressly gather in his name) is also vitally important. There are several reasons for this.

First, Scripture tells us that we are not to be "solo" Christians. We are not to "give up meeting together" but rather to "encourage one another" (Hebrews 10:25). Just as burning coals keep warm so long as they stay together, so too we need one another to keep warm in the faith. A piece of coal, even if very hot originally, soon goes cold if left on its own.

More importantly, Jesus gave us this express promise: "For where two or three gather in my name, there am I with them" (Matthew 18:20).

This promise of divine presence ties in with what we learned about the presence of the Holy Spirit (in chapter 3) and about the "fellowship of the Holy Spirit" (2 Corinthians 13:14; see chapter 7). In other words, Jesus by his Spirit is especially present when his followers meet together – this is when this "fellowship of the Holy Spirit" becomes a spiritual reality. We need to meet together so that the Holy Spirit can work between us, and so that Jesus can be seen in the ways we relate to one another. If we do so, then visitors may be able to say (what Paul hoped would be said in Corinth): "God is really among you!" (1 Corinthians 14:25).

So what should Jesus' followers do when they meet together? What are the vital ingredients for an authentic act of corporate Christian worship?

Perhaps the primary thing to be included is the public reading of Scripture and appropriate teaching from the Bible. Thus Paul (in the words from Colossians quoted above) talks about singing and thanksgiving only after he has first mentioned the importance of teaching and instruction. Hence too, in Acts 2, the first thing to which the new believers devote themselves is the "apostles'" teaching (see further in chapters 9 to 12). Christian worship is always a response to God's self-revelation. It is never to be the worship of ourselves or of our own bright ideas, but rather a turning towards God – to what he has said and done. It is always to be a means through which the "word of Christ" may come to dwell in our hearts more powerfully. And for this, we will always need the Bible – together with faithful teaching of the Bible's truths.

> Christian worship is always a response to God's self-revelation.

Once this is firmly in place, however, the P.R.A.Y. principle (see Box 8) may once again be a useful guide. When next in a church service, it might be worth noting if and how these four things are taking place! In addition to the Bible readings and any talk or sermon:

- Are there hymns and prayers which praise God for his words and his deeds? Are there other opportunities too for giving thanks? If it is a Communion* service, there should be a central prayer (the Great Thanksgiving or Eucharist*), in which we thank God for Jesus' death; but on other occasions, someone may share a personal testimony to God's goodness.

- Is there a time for confession*, as together people come humbly before the Lord to repent?

- Are there opportunities to ask God for things, praying both for others and then for yourself? These may occur in more formal and written prayers ("set" prayers*), or perhaps when praying for one another after the service.

There may be other ingredients too. In Colossians, for example, Paul evidently expected a variety of different types of songs (psalms, hymns, sacred songs). Some of these may be more formal, others informal; some may be sung, as it were, to one another to encourage us to praise God, others expressly addressed to God (perhaps speaking in quite intimate and personal ways as we seek to enjoy his presence); some may be drawn from contemporary experience, others more obviously rooted in the Bible. There can be a wide variety here, even before we mention all the variety of accompanying music styles – some of which we may personally love, others of which we may not!

Meanwhile, as we read in 1 Corinthians, Paul clearly expected a wide variety of "spiritual gifts"* to be in evidence. For example:

A message of wisdom... a message of knowledge... faith... gifts of healing... miraculous powers... prophecy... distinguishing between spirits... speaking in different kinds of tongues, and... the interpretation of tongues.

1 Corinthians 12:8–10

Yes, he was concerned about the way these gifts could be abused in ungodly ways, and so spoke about the "greatest gift" – that of love (1 Corinthians 13; see chapter 7). Yet Paul clearly envisaged that Christian worship-gatherings would sometimes include the use of some of these gifts:

> *When you come together, each of you has a hymn, or*
> *a word of instruction, a revelation, a tongue or an*
> *interpretation.*

> 1 Corinthians 14:26

Come to public worship with an attitude of expectancy.

So there may be such signs of God's Holy Spirit at work. This should not surprise us, for the Holy Spirit lives within each believer and wants to help the body of Christ to be a living, dynamic force. Our part may then be simply to come to public worship with an attitude of expectancy and to be ready to share what we think God has been doing in our lives. We are not to be passengers, but must come ready to contribute.

We must also come in a spirit of humility, willing to be taught and led by those in authority, and never in a disruptive spirit:

> *No one should seek their own good, but the good of others....*
> *Everything must be done so that the church may be built*
> *up... For God is not a God of disorder but of peace...*
> *Everything should be done in a fitting and orderly way.*
> 1 Corinthians 10:24; 14:26, 33, 40

As we welcome God's Spirit among us, our goal will always be to do that which is helpful for others and which "builds up" our brothers and sisters in their faith (1 Corinthians 14:17).

The apostles of Jesus want his people to make sure they regularly worship God together. Sometimes we may not feel like it, but that is precisely the point. Worship is not about us and our feelings; it is all about God and his worth. So sometimes worship will indeed be a matter of the will, not just of the heart. Yet, amazingly, so often when we truly give ourselves to worship, our hearts are strangely warmed – we come out feeling quite different. This is a happy by-product of worship, but it is not its primary goal. "Praise the Lord" we are commanded, "and forget not all his benefits" (Psalm 103:2).

So the eighth building block in the Christian life is to give a priority to worshipping the Lord Jesus: we are to worship his majesty. The first believers devoted themselves to prayer, and so should we. Worship is to be our lifeblood. It is what we were made for. And it is what one day, according to Revelation, we will be doing for all eternity:

Day and night they never stop saying:

"Holy, holy, holy
is the Lord God Almighty,
who was, and is, and is to come."

Revelation 4:8

Then I heard every creature in heaven and on earth and under the earth and on the sea, and all that is in them, saying:

"To him who sits on the throne and to the Lamb
be praise and honour and glory and power,
for ever and ever!"

Revelation 5:13

Building block 8

Worship his majesty – it's what you were made for!

9

Follow His Teaching

They devoted themselves...
to the apostles' teaching.
Acts 2:42

We see in Acts 2 that, for the new believers, it was a top priority to discover the "apostles' teaching". They had committed themselves to following Jesus as king but, right now, they only knew a tiny part of his royal truth. We too may have decided to follow Christ – perhaps for a wide variety of different reasons – but there remains so much more to discover about him. So in our final chapters we will unpack more of the apostles' teaching – about who Christ is (Christian belief); about how we should live for him and resist evil (Christian behaviour); and, finally, about what are his future purposes for us (Christian hope).

The example of those first believers is one of humility. They were ready to be taught. In the West today, teachers are often ridiculed and disobeyed – people think they know best and so are difficult to teach. In other cultures, however, teachers are often greatly respected; people value learning and are glad to sit at others' feet, being honest about what they do not know. This humble attitude is the one Jesus is looking for in his followers: "If you love me, keep my commands." (John 14:15)

Those baptized in Jesus' name are "to obey everything [he] commanded" (Matthew 28:20). So those first believers committed themselves in advance to obey anything that the apostles passed on to them from the lips of Jesus. But will we do the same? Will we humbly submit our minds and wills to him – truly sitting at his feet?

Here we hit a strange thing. Luke does not say that those first believers devoted themselves to the teaching of Jesus. No, they devoted themselves to the teaching of the apostles. Partly, this is for the obvious reason that Jesus himself was no longer there in Jerusalem*. Yet it is also Luke's way of making a vitally important point: precisely because Jesus is no longer here, the way we submit to his teaching is to submit ourselves to the teaching of his apostles. We saw in chapter 4 how Jesus commissioned the apostles as his special messengers, authorizing them to teach his truth. So humility before Jesus requires humility before his messengers. For us today (when those messengers have long since died), this means in practice a humility towards that which they have written – that is, the New Testament. We are to be devoted to the apostles' teaching, then, because of our love for Jesus; and this, in turn, will mean that we will love the New Testament (and the Bible as a whole), submitting our minds to its truth and committing ourselves to obeying its commands.

> Because Jesus is no longer here, the way we submit to his teaching is to submit ourselves to the teaching of his apostles.

So the ninth building block as we walk in the Jesus Way is to follow his teaching – not just what Jesus taught during his earthly ministry, but also that which he teaches us through the apostles and the rest of Scripture.

The Creed: A summary of the apostles' teaching

But what exactly did the apostles teach? The New Testament was drawn together over about sixty years (c. AD 30–90) from the works of different authors writing in different contexts and in different styles. It is a colourful book, far from monochrome. This means it is not entirely straightforward to summarize. God has chosen to reveal his will in a document which is far more interesting than, say, a legal code. It is a document brimming with light and life; it is also fundamentally a story, with a fascinating plot line which draws us into its world, and which demands a response.

Yet this living quality of the New Testament must not be taken as meaning that it contains no definite teaching on any subject. No, it gives a coherent answer on all the subjects that God wants us to know about. Ask the New Testament a reasonable question and it will give you an authoritative answer! What it does mean, however, is that, ever since its composition, believers have rightly been trying to summarize the apostles' teaching in brief, systematic ways.

In the early days, these summaries were called "rules of faith", but in due course, they came to be called creeds* (*credo* means "I believe" in Latin). Their intention was never to add to the New Testament but rather to summarize it, expounding its essential inner teaching. They were intended as reliable guides within which to enjoy the New Testament's teaching – effectively warning that those who came up with quite different ideas had misread it.

The same is true today. The Bible is an open book for everyone, but individuals can misinterpret its teaching. The creeds then give us a tried and tested way in which the wider body of Christian believers can hold firmly to the true words of the apostles' teaching (as we are encouraged to do in, for example, 1 Timothy 3:9 or 2 Timothy 1:13). They are safeguards – like fences around playing fields, or like railway lines. Or they are like wise parents, pointing out where true freedom lies: "This truly is what it means – trust us!" In other words, if we are reading the Bible appropriately (with faith in Christ at the centre), then what we will find is the teaching contained in the creeds.

In this chapter, then, we will focus on the text of the so-called Nicene Creed* (see Box 9a). As a creed, its focus is deliberately on what we are to believe (not on Christian practice). Yet it remains a brilliant summary of the apostles' teaching in this particular area, summarized under three main headings.

Box 9a – The Nicene Creed

1. *We believe in one God,*
   the Father, the Almighty,
   maker of heaven and earth,
   of all that is,
   seen and unseen.

2. *We believe in one Lord, Jesus Christ,*
   the only Son of God,
   eternally begotten of the Father,
   God from God, Light from Light,
   true God from true God,
   begotten, not made,
   of one Being with the Father;
   through whom all things were made.
   For us and for our salvation he came down from heaven,
   was incarnate from the Holy Spirit and the Virgin Mary
   and was made man.
   For our sake he was crucified under Pontius Pilate;
   he suffered death and was buried.
   On the third day he rose again
   in accordance with the Scriptures;
   he ascended into heaven
   and is seated at the right hand of the Father.
   He will come again in glory to judge the living and the dead,
   and his kingdom will have no end.

3. *We believe in the Holy Spirit,*
   the Lord, the giver of life,
   who proceeds from the Father and the Son,
   who with the Father and the Son is worshipped and glorified,
   who has spoken through the prophets.
   We believe in one holy catholic and apostolic Church.
   We acknowledge one baptism for the forgiveness of sins.
   We look for the resurrection of the dead,
   and the life of the world to come.
   Amen.*

Believe: In God the Father

The apostles were convinced that they were bringing Good News from the one true God. In their ancient world, where people believed in many "gods", they affirmed that in Jesus Christ we truly see the action of the true and living God. Hence the first section of the Nicene Creed which categorically proclaims Christian monotheism* – that there is only one God.

This God is described as the "maker of heaven and earth, of all that is, seen and unseen". This matches the apostles' teaching that God is our "Creator" (1 Peter 4:19, based on passages such as Genesis 1–2 and Isaiah 40). This is important. It means that we should value God's created world – this planet earth and our environment. It also means that, if God in Jesus is offering us salvation, his purpose will never be somehow to remove us from the created world (as if the created world was bad and inherently evil); no, God plans to bring about a renewed creation (see chapter 12). The God of redemption is also the God of creation, and we should never drive a wedge between the two. God is restoring creation, not abandoning it.

It also means that God is not seeking to destroy that which is human. No, he created us as human beings. Despite what many people think, to become a follower of Jesus never means we become less human. On the contrary, we at last are becoming truly human – as God always intended us to be! We are following Jesus who is the true Human, the most authentic human being that has ever lived (that's why he's described by Paul as the new "Adam" in Romans 5:12–21 and 1 Corinthians 15:45–49).

These were all key points which the early Christians had to defend when faced with some false teachers (known as the Gnostics*) who saw created matter as evil, and who saw salvation as essentially a means of escape from the material world. These Gnostic thinkers often drove another wedge too – this time between the "god" of the Old Testament and the "god" of the New. They caricatured the Old Testament "god" as a lesser god, or a god of evil intent, or a god overly concerned with physical matter.

The apostles would have been horrified at this caricature. The heart of their teaching was that the God seen in Jesus was to be identified 100 per cent with the God known to ancient Israel*. Jesus had brought the Old Testament story to its climax, and Jesus' God was truly "the God of Abraham, the God of Isaac, and the God of Jacob" (see, for example, Matthew 22:32; Acts 3:13). Hence the Creed's use of Old Testament terminology at this point: "One" God (Deuteronomy 6:4); "the Almighty" (Psalm 91:1); "maker of heaven and earth" (Psalm 121:2). Jesus does not introduce us to a new "god" (the Creed is effectively saying), but rather reveals, in a new and powerful way, the God known in the past within Israel.

In fact, this clear identity between the God of Israel and the God of Jesus undergirds everything the apostles teach about God. They deliberately underscore what was revealed in the Old Testament – namely that God is an invisible, eternal, glorious Being, sovereign over his world, utterly faithful in his purposes, holy, righteous, wise, and good. Just as in Old Testament times, so in the New Testament era, God is full of "mercy... and compassion" and "constant love" (for example, 2 Corinthians 1:3, 1 Peter 5:10).

> *I will proclaim my name, the Lord... I will have mercy, and I will have compassion.*
>
> Exodus 33:19

> *The Lord is compassionate and gracious, slow to anger, abounding in love.*
>
> Psalm 103:8

Even so, he is still the one "who judges justly" (1 Peter 2:23). Thus, in both Testaments, God is simultaneously the God of judgment and the God of love. If the New Testament speaks more freely concerning God's love, this is only because God's coming in Jesus has revealed this love so dramatically and in a new, unexpected way. Jesus' coming does not negate God's previous judgment, nor does it deny his previous love.

> In both Testaments, God is simultaneously the God of judgment and the God of love.

What Jesus' coming does introduce – in a way that is not really seen in the Old Testament but is still consistent with it – is the notion of God as Father. This distinctive apostolic teaching is included in the Creed in two senses. First, God is the "Father of our Lord Jesus Christ" (1 Peter 1:3); there is, in the eternal heart of God, a fatherly relationship towards his unique Son. Yet, second, this father's heart now reaches out to include us: as we are adopted by faith into God's family, we too become his sons and daughters, and we can dare to call God "our father" (see chapters 2, 3, and 8). This powerful privilege, brought about through the Good News, is proclaimed at the start of the Creed, because it is the bedrock (and indeed the goal) of the apostles' teaching.

Believe: In God the Son

At the centre of the apostles' teaching was Jesus himself – the fact that this amazing human being was also divine, and that he had entered into the real world of human history for our rescue. This explains why the central, major part of the Creed focuses on the person and work of Jesus – that is, who he truly is and what he truly did.

Concerning the work of Jesus, the Creed is comparatively brief, mentioning his birth, suffering, death, resurrection, and ascension* but with little comment. In its phrases there is clearly a concern to ward off any Gnostic denials about the sombre reality of Jesus' suffering and death: he "was buried" (truly dead, placed in a physical tomb) and this all took place "under Pontius Pilate"* (the Roman governor's name serving to anchor these events in the real, physical world). It also states categorically (though with little explanation) that these events were "for our salvation," "for our sake," and "in accordance with the Scriptures" (for my own explanation, see chapters 1 and 2).

Its greater emphasis, however, is upon the person of Jesus (a topic now known as Christology*) – not least because this was the key point under dispute at the time of the Creed's composition.

The apostles had said many surprising and bold things about Jesus, which the Creed here has to summarize in a few words. While never denying that Jesus was truly human, the apostles had asserted that Jesus must be identified in some way with God himself. They had made this key point in different ways (see Box 9b).

Box 9b – The apostles' teaching on Jesus' identity

- He had been born in a unique way, from a virgin mother, by the power of the Holy Spirit (Matthew 1:20; Luke 1:35).
- He had claimed God's authority to forgive sins and to be the equivalent of a new Temple (Mark 2:5–11; John 2:19–21).
- He "did not sin" (Hebrews 4:15), and so truly and perfectly revealed God's light (John 8:12).
- He had performed numerous "works of power" or "miracles" throughout his ministry (for example, Acts 10:38), and had himself been raised from the dead (see chapter 1).
- He had truly been "sent by God" – but clearly in a way that was different from God's previous "sending" of the prophets (Hebrews 1:1–3; Galatians 4:4; 1 John 4:10).
- He was, in a unique sense, the true Son of God* and shared in God's title as the Lord* (see chapter 1); his status could thus be contrasted with that of mere humans (Galatians 1:1–2).
- He had been exalted to the Father's "right hand" (Acts 2:33; Hebrews 1:3), where he was now "seated on God's throne" and was the rightful object of human worship (Matthew 2:11; 14:33; 28:17; Philippians 3:3; Revelation 5:13; 19:6–10).
- He did things that, according to the Old Testament, belonged to God alone – not least sharing in God's acts of creation and judgment (John 1:3; Colossians 1:16; John 5:27; Philippians 2:11).
- He was an eternal being who, as a king, was establishing an eternal kingdom (Luke 1:32; 1 Corinthians 15:24); so, on occasion, he could appropriately be called "God" (Romans 9:5; John 1:1; 20:28).
- He had been eternally present with God as "the one and only Son" (John 1:14); he was an "exact representation of

[God's] being" (Hebrews 1:3); and was "in very nature God" (Philippians 2:6).

- He then "became flesh" – or (as in many translations) "was incarnate"* (see John 1:1–14). On this last point, the apostles were correcting the false teaching of some Docetic* groups who denied Jesus had truly been human.

The Creed picks up many of these ideas ("Lord", "Son of God", "light", "judge", "kingdom") but gives special emphasis to the aspects of the apostles' teaching mentioned in the last two bullet points – declaring that Jesus was "eternally begotten... not made", and then "was made man." At the time when the Creed was written (and especially in its Greek, not Jewish, context), there was a real need to answer people's questions about Jesus' inherent *being* – who he truly was in his own person. These New Testament verses helpfully answered that question. Other verses had shown how Jesus was effectively functioning as God and sharing in God's actions and activity (still an extraordinary claim, if you stop to think about it, to hear coming from the lips of the apostles who had been born as monotheistic Jews!); but these verses went further and spoke about Jesus' essential *being*. It was not just that he *did* the things of God, but he truly *was* God! Hence the Creed's assertion that Jesus really was "of one substance" (*homo-ousios**) with the Father – a word they coined to express this apostolic teaching that Jesus really did share in God's eternal *being* (or "substance").

So the Creed is teaching precisely what the New Testament also had taught, namely:

- Jesus is unique: truly human but truly divine;

- this God-Man came down from heaven for our salvation... and became a human being;

- he is now seated at the right-hand side of the Father.

This claim for Jesus stands out starkly in our modern world. It's an unpopular truth, making Jesus quite different from other religious leaders and revealing God to be no vague, absent figure but rather someone who has come worryingly close. We might be tempted to think that it would be easier to water down this message. We might think, perhaps – not least when we are accused of arrogance or bigotry – how it would be advantageous to focus on Jesus' brilliant teaching as an authentic human being, while gradually abandoning this bizarre teaching from his apostles about his divinity.

But the Creed puts up a fence here and says, "Don't go there!" It reminds us what Christians down the ages have always believed, as they have (Sunday by Sunday) recited the Creed. And it warns us that any interpretation of the New Testament which overlooks this teaching about Jesus has effectively lost the plot. This is what the apostles taught, and any followers of Jesus today must submit themselves to the apostles' teaching – especially on this vital, central, issue as to who Jesus is! For Jesus does not want us, as his followers, to be concocting our own imaginary ideas about him, but rather to be enjoying the true portrait of him given to us by his special messengers. That way we can truly follow the true Jesus – not our own wishful thinking.

Believe: In God the Holy Spirit – and the Trinity

The Creed's final section begins with a focus on the Holy Spirit. The apostles' full teaching concerning the Holy Spirit was summarized in chapter 3. Here, however, we note that the Creed wants particularly to underline their teaching (seen, for example, in John 14–16) that the Spirit is a divine Person. Thus, although he might be viewed as having a lesser status (he "proceeds from the Father"), the Holy Spirit is yet to be worshipped; indeed he is the effective source of all spiritual life and is to be identified with the Lord.

He has also "spoken through the prophets". This again affirms the eternal nature of the Spirit: he did not come into existence at Pentecost* (as described in Acts 2), but was at work in the Old Testament period, especially in Israel's prophets. It also points us to the truth that God's communication with human beings is always by means of his Spirit (1 Corinthians 2:10–12). Moreover, it underlines that Scripture (both Old and New Testaments) is the place where we find the faithful deposit of the Spirit's communication – God's eternal words for all people, breathed out by the Spirit. For if the Old Testament prophets were truly inspired by the Spirit, how much more is this true of those writing in the days of the new covenant*? As a result, we may fairly conclude: what the Holy Spirit says, God says; and what the Holy Spirit says is now found in Scripture (see chapter 4).

The Creed closes with some brief affirmations about the church* (it is one, holy, catholic*, and apostolic) and about baptism* (for the forgiveness of sins). These affirmations remind us that:

- believers in Jesus must be baptized (see appendix C);

- through this, they are entering into a community, which is to be marked by repentance of sins, by holiness of life, and by faithfulness to the apostles' teaching and mission;

- this community is a worldwide family ("cath-olic" means effectively "all around the world"); believers thus belong to an amazing phenomenon, which is not local but global!

Finally, the Creed closes with an appropriate flourish, looking forward to "the resurrection of the dead, and the life of the world to come" – all revealed to us through the resurrection of Jesus (see chapter 12). Christian belief thus works itself out in action and is a powerful message that affects all our lives: forgiveness from the past, hope for the future, and for the present a life lived in company with all those who have been called to be part of Jesus' new people.

As we look back over the whole Creed, however, what leaps out at us is its threefold structure: it summarizes the apostles' teaching in a threefold form – rooted in the nature of God revealed as Father, Son, and Holy Spirit. This creedal commitment to the Trinity* (God known in three Persons) is often challenged. "Perhaps," it is argued, "this so-called 'trinity' is an unbiblical addition to the Bible, never actually taught in the New Testament!" However, the Creed is accurately reflecting the New Testament, which itself speaks plainly in the direction of the Trinity (see Box 9c).

Box 9c – The apostles' teaching on the Trinity

From Paul

May the grace of the Lord Jesus Christ, and the love of God, and the fellowship of the Holy Spirit be with you all.

2 Corinthians 13:14

There are different kinds of gifts, but the same Spirit distributes them. There are different kinds of service, but the same Lord. There are different kinds of working, but in all of them and in everyone it is the same God at work.

1 Corinthians 12:4–6

God's love has been poured out into our hearts through the Holy Spirit... God demonstrates his own love for us in this: While we were still sinners, Christ died for us... if the Spirit of him who raised Jesus from the dead is loving in you, he who raised Christ from the dead will also give life to your mortal bodies because of his Spirit who lives in you.

Romans 5:5, 8; 8:11 (see also Ephesians 2:18)

From Peter

Praise be to the God and Father of our Lord Jesus Christ... the time and circumstances to which the Spirit of Christ in them was pointing when he predicted the sufferings of the Messiah.

1 Peter 1:3, 11

From John

We live in [God] and he in us: He has given us of his Spirit. And we have seen... that the Father has sent his Son to be the Saviour of the world.

1 John 4:13–14

The verses in Box 9c are worth reading carefully. Although the apostles do not use the actual word "Trinity", it is evident that, at an almost unconscious level, their thoughts about God are taking a threefold form. So, although their experience of God as three Persons

> The apostles would have seen the Trinity as a fundamental truth, underpinning all their teaching.

may have preceded their need to defend this truth (or to describe it with academic formulations), they clearly believed in what we now know as the Trinity. In fact, the apostles would have seen the Trinity as a fundamental truth, underpinning all their teaching. For, if Jesus was not divine, and the Spirit did not truly lead to an encounter with God himself, then their message was not Good News at all.

So Bible-believing Christians are those who know God as Trinity. We remember Jesus' own words when he spoke about the Spirit (see Box 3a) and especially when he said we should baptize people "in the name of the Father and of the Son and of the Holy Spirit" (Matthew 28:19). And we then recognize that the compilers of the Creed were actually being faithful to the apostles' teaching when they too spoke of God in a Trinitarian way. For this is truly who God is!

Conclusion

As Jesus' followers, then, we are to give ourselves to the apostles' teaching. In this chapter, we have seen how the Nicene Creed accurately summarizes some of that teaching, especially what they taught us to believe about God. In the following three chapters, we will unpack some further (perhaps more obviously practical) aspects of the apostles' teaching. For now, however, we close by remembering some words of Jesus that highlight the vital link between his truth and true freedom.

Jesus, who himself is the truth (John 14:16), has ensured that his special messengers, the apostles, also give us truths that are reliable – teaching that comes with Jesus' approval, inspired by the Spirit. He wants us then to give ourselves to this teaching because it ultimately comes from him. Yet this is also because, as he said, "If you hold to my teaching, you are really my disciples. Then you will know the truth, and the truth will set you free" (John 8:31–32). Jesus' truth (and the apostles' teaching about Jesus) is truly liberating. Others may suggest that true freedom comes from doing what we want, but Jesus sees this as a form of slavery: "everyone who sins is a slave to sin" (John 8:34). If we want freedom, it is found instead in serving Jesus and in submitting ourselves to his truth – his service, as they say, is perfect freedom! So...

- Will we, for Jesus' sake, submit ourselves to the apostles' teaching and commit ourselves in advance to believe and obey what they taught?

- Will we pray for those who teach the faith, that they too may be true to this teaching, and ourselves encourage others to follow this teaching?

This is vital. The ninth building block, then, in growing as a follower of Jesus is to ensure we follow his teaching, and so experience the great liberty that it brings.

Building block 9

Follow his teaching – it's the only way to freedom!

Live His Life

Many wonders and signs were performed by the apostles... All the believers... had everything in common... to give to anyone who had need. Every day they continued to meet together... praising God and enjoying the favour of all the people.

Acts 2:43–47

Jesus' first followers, as we have seen from Acts 2, devoted themselves to the apostles' teaching. This would clearly have included instructions, not just about Christian belief, but also about how to live in Jesus' new kingdom and under his rule. What we are seeing in Acts is evidently not just changed minds but radically altered lives. There is a new power, a new purpose, a new praising – altogether a new outpouring of love and life.

We could have guessed as much. In his own life, Jesus had shown a whole new way of being human – living in the power of the Spirit and establishing a pattern for life in God's kingdom. So to be a follower of this Jesus was always going to involve a change of lifestyle – indeed it means having our life turned upside down! And that's what we see in that first community of believers on the day of Pentecost*: the birth of a whole new experiment in risky, Jesus-shaped, living.

> The first Pentecost saw the birth of a whole new experiment in risky, Jesus-shaped, living.

Today, in just the same way, the Risen Jesus wants us to live his way and not ours. It is, after all, the Jesus Way. The opening message of his preaching was: "Repent and believe the good news" (Mark 1:15). Jesus wants people to abandon their own agendas and follow his, to be changed from the inside out, to find both their minds and hearts transformed by his values. So Jesus wants to teach us what to do; as our king, he wants us, his subjects, to obey; as our leader, he wants his followers to... follow. He doesn't just want us to believe the truth, but actually to be and do the truth!

We often squirm at this point. We like to focus on aspects of the Christian faith that suit us well (perhaps God's free forgiveness or his grace) and dismiss its practical challenges. We can even start labelling any who emphasize such obedience as "legalists" or "moralists". Yet Jesus' apostles are quite clear: their frequent teaching about God's grace must never be taken as an excuse to sin or to be careless about our lifestyles; faith in Jesus is vital, but so too is obedience. "The one who loves me," says Jesus, is the one who "has my commands and *keeps* them" (John 14:21).

So the tenth building block in following Jesus is... to follow Jesus! That is, to do what he says, to live our lives as he would live them if he were us – that is, to live his life. In every situation the vital question becomes "WWJD – What Would Jesus Do?" Or, as the apostle John puts it, "Whoever claims to live in him must live as Jesus did" (1 John 2:6). Are we willing to give ourselves to this key aspect of the apostles' teaching?

Walking the talk: Obeying Jesus' commands

In fact, John's words might be even better translated as, "we should walk as he walked". The Bible often uses this picture of "walking" to describe the believer's lifestyle. Clearly, what God wants is walkers, not just talkers. Do we, as they say, "walk the talk"? "Do not merely listen to the word, and so deceive yourselves," writes James, "do what it says" (James 1:22). Or, as Jesus himself had said:

> Not everyone who says to me, "Lord, Lord," will enter the
> kingdom of heaven, but only the one who does the will
> of my Father who is in heaven... Therefore everyone who
> hears these words of mind and puts them into practice

is like a wise man who built his house on the rock... But
everyone who... does not put them into practice is like a
foolish man who built his house on sand.

Matthew 7:21, 24, 26

This severe warning comes at the end of Jesus' Sermon on the
Mount (Matthew 5–7). Box 10a gives us a list of the commands in
that famous sermon together with some recorded by Matthew later
in his Gospel, all of which Jesus expects us to obey.

Box 10a – Challenges for life: A selection of Jesus' teaching from Matthew's Gospel

From the Sermon on the Mount (Matthew 5–7)

*Blessed are the meek... the merciful... the pure in heart... let
your light shine before others, that they may see your good
deeds and glorify your Father in heaven... Anyone who is
angry... will be subject to judgment."*

5:5, 7, 8, 16, 22

*Anyone who looks at a woman lustfully has already
committed adultery with her in his heart... Anyone who
divorces his wife, except for sexual immorality, makes her
the victim of adultery, and anyone who marries a divorced
woman commits adultery... Do not resist an evil person...
Love your enemies and pray for those who persecute you...
Be perfect, therefore, as your heavenly Father is perfect.*

5:28, 32, 39, 44, 48

*Be careful not to practice your righteousness [i.e. giving,
praying, fasting] in front of others to be seen by them... Do
not store up for yourselves treasures on earth... You cannot
serve both God and money.... Do not worry... but seek first his
kingdom and his righteousness.*

6:1, 19, 24, 31, 33

*Do not judge... Do to others what you would have them to do
to you.*

7:1, 12

From later in the Gospel (Matthew 15–28)

For out of the heart come evil thoughts – murder, adultery, sexual immorality, theft, false testimony, slander.

15:19

See that you do not despise one of these little ones... Forgive your brother or sister from your heart.

18:10, 35

For those who exalt themselves will be humbled, and those who humble themselves will be exalted... On the outside you appear to people as righteous but on the inside you are full of hypocrisy and wickedness.

23:12, 28

Whatever you did for one of the least of these brothers and sisters of mine, you did for me.

25:40

Teach them to obey everything I have commanded you.

28:20

Such a list leaves all of us – both then and now – feeling pretty weak (indeed, this may be part of Matthew's point – Jesus' high standards drive us to our knees!). Yet Jesus clearly was insistent. He solemnly told his hearers that their "righteousness" must surpass "that of the Pharisees" (Matthew 5:20). Given that the Pharisees* were the strictest group in Galilee for demanding that people obey the Old Testament Law, it is clear that Jesus is indeed setting the standards extremely high – even impossibly so.

However, in the very heart of Matthew's Gospel, we find another, surprising command which contains a key secret:

Come to me, all you who are weary and burdened, and I will give you rest. Take my yoke upon you and learn from me, for I am gentle and humble in heart, and you will find rest for your souls. For my yoke is easy and my burden is light.

Matthew 11:28–30

Jesus says that, when we believe in him ("come to me") and bring our lives under his control ("take my yoke"), then we will have "rest". How can this be, when his commands seem so heavy?

Living the life: The amazing secret

> We can begin to "live his life" because he himself is "living his life" within us!

The answer, so the apostles affirm, is that he gives us his rest *through placing his own powerful life within us.* Yes, Jesus commands us to live like him – to live our lives as though he were us. Yet we cannot do this in our own strength. That's where the Good News of both the resurrection and the Spirit come to the fore. Jesus is now alive and, by his Spirit, he is able to place his own new life within us. We can begin to "live his life" because he himself is "living his life" within us!

The apostle John is so helpful here. Despite his challenge that believers must walk as Jesus walked (see above), he concludes his letter with exactly this point: "his commands are not burdensome, for everyone born of God overcomes the world" (1 John 5:3–4). Why? Because anyone, who is a child of God, through faith in Jesus (1 John 5:5), now has God's Spirit dwelling in them: "God lives in them and they in God" (1 John 4:15). Believers have a unique resource and power within them: the life of God himself!

> The Christian life is truly meant to be Christ's life – *Christ's life lived in and through us.*

The Christian life is truly meant to be Christ's life – *Christ's life lived in and through us.* We will therefore need Jesus' grace each and every day – not just for our forgiveness but indeed for any living at all! And this remains true, however many years we have been following Jesus. For, as Jesus warned us:

> *If you remain in me and I in you, you will bear much fruit; apart from me you can do nothing.*
>
> John 15:5

That's the key: with Jesus living within us by his Spirit, things become possible that previously were beyond our reach.

What we are seeing in Acts 2 (and indeed throughout the whole book of Acts) is the outworking of Jesus' own life and power – now released in and through his followers. The ancient world was being hit by a surge of divine life, flowing out through "Jesus-indwelt" believers. Not for nothing, then, did we note in chapter 3 that today some people suggest a better name for The Acts of the Apostles is instead The Acts of Jesus. For it is the story of his continued life and power – now seen within his followers.

Let's observe, then, through studying Box 10b, what happens once Jesus' Spirit is "poured out" (Acts 2:17–18), enabling those first believers to begin to live out Jesus' risen life.

Box 10b – Living Jesus' life: Selections from Acts

Previously timid followers become brave and speak out in his name before crowds and interrogators (2:14; 4:8–21, 29–30; 5:21–32; 17:13–21; 18:12–17).

When suffering persecution, they even find a deep joy within them, "because they had been counted worthy of suffering disgrace for the Name" (5:41; note Stephen's example in 6:8 – 7:60); they find themselves in prison but are able to sleep calmly and sing hymns before they are miraculously rescued (12:6–19; 16:23–40).

Sometimes they are given power to heal, performing "wonders and miracles" (3:6–7; 4:30; 13:11; 14:10; 19:11–12; 20:10).

They ensure, as best they can, that "no one in the group is in need,", selling possessions so that money can be redistributed (4:34–35), and then dealing sensibly with the administrative problems that result (6:1–7).

They go and visit those who previously persecuted them, offering to pray for them in Jesus' name (Ananias in 9:10–19).

Jewish believers begin to risk going into Gentile* homes with Jesus' Good News, believing that, through faith in Jesus, Gentiles can truly become ritually clean and join God's new people (Peter in Cornelius' house in 10:1 – 11:18); later the apostles have a special council at which this risky new policy is confirmed and agreed (15:1–22).

They go far from home, way beyond their comfort zone, speaking Jesus' message in remote locations north of the Taurus mountains in what is now modern Turkey (13:13 – 14:28).

Through it all, when the apostles speak of Jesus, their hearers sense the reality of Jesus in their midst and come to faith in him (2:41); instinctively, people recognize that something of Jesus has rubbed off on these "unschooled, ordinary men" – they realize that they are men who have simply "been with Jesus" (4:13). In fact, what people are noticing is not just the influence of a past Jesus but the indwelling power of a present Jesus!

All this (and much else) was the outworking of Jesus' new life – his resurrection power clearly at work within those first believers by his Spirit. In other words, they did not just preach about the resurrection of Jesus, they literally lived it out. As Paul wrote later, excitedly: "That power is the same as the mighty strength he exerted when he raised Christ from the dead" (Ephesians 1:19–20). Jesus' followers are resurrection people – living out the powerful risen life of Jesus.

> They did not just preach about the resurrection of Jesus; they literally lied it out.

Elsewhere in the New Testament, the apostles give us three (slightly overlapping) images which help us picture this powerful reality of Jesus' risen life within us.

A. Raised to life: We have a new status and identity

The apostles teach us that we have truly been raised to life with Christ. The resurrection of Jesus is not a detached, isolated event. Instead, when we believe in Jesus, God includes us in Jesus' resurrection, by raising us from death to life. Consider these verses from Paul's teaching:

We were therefore buried with him through baptism into death in order that, just as Christ was raised from the

*dead through the glory of the Father, we too may live a
new life... In the same way, count yourselves dead to sin
but alive to God in Christ Jesus.*

Romans 6:4, 11

*You were also raised with him through your faith in the
working of God, who raised him from the dead. When you
were dead in your sins... God made you alive with Christ...
Since, then, you have been raised with Christ, set your hearts
on the things above... For you died, and your life is now
hidden with Christ in God... Christ... is your life.*

Colossians 2:12–13; 3:1, 3–4 (see also Ephesians 2:5)

Believers are now truly alive in Christ. Though we were dead because of our sins, now in God's sight we are forgiven and therefore spiritually alive. This is our new status. So if God now sees us as alive, we ought also to see ourselves in this light: "Count yourselves... alive to God in Christ Jesus" (Romans 6:11). This is reality, not pretence. It may not feel like it, but this is a fact. Your "life", as Paul says, actually is Christ! (Colossians 3:4).

This should affect the whole way in which we see our Christian lives. We are Easter people, raised to new life. Grasp this truth about your new God-given identity in Jesus and you will gain a whole new vision of what it means to follow Jesus: for, rather than being a struggle to become something you are not, the Christian life instead becomes a living out of what you already are! Be who you are! Live out your real destiny and be the person God has now made you to be!

To help us in this, Paul encourages us to think of ourselves as "dead to sin" (Romans 6:11): our old sinful natures are "buried" or "crucified with Christ" (Romans 6:4, 6). If you like, our sinful natures have been mortally wounded and need to be treated as the lifeless things they truly are. Meanwhile, the positive side of this is to see our new selves as linked to the Risen Jesus. As Jesus said, our own lives are now organically dependent on his: "Because I live, you also will live" (John 14:19).

> Rather than being a struggle to become something you are not, the Christian life instead becomes a living out of what you already are!

We are alive in him. So our task is to stay connected to Jesus, like branches within a vine (John 15:5–7). Hence some of Paul's other instructions in Colossians: "Just as you received Christ Jesus as Lord, continue to live your lives in him, rooted and built up in him" (Colossians 2:6–7).

The secret of the Christian life is to live in union with the Risen Jesus.

B. New birth: We are new people deep within

The apostles present us with the imagery of new birth. When we believe in Jesus, they teach, it is not just that we are caught up into his risen life; he also places that resurrection-life into us! This is the "other side of the same coin". We are not just given a new status or identity through the resurrection; we are given a new *life* – we are new people! The Risen Jesus comes to dwell within the believer by means of his Holy Spirit (see chapter 3). This means several things:

- Jesus lives within us.

- Our own spirits, which were dead, come alive.

- We gain a new nature (or "person" or "self") deep within.

- We are "born again" (or, better translated, "born from above") with God's new life placed within us. For, as Jesus himself taught, "no one can see the kingdom of God unless they are born again" (John 3:3).

Consider the samples from the apostles' teaching in Box 10c.

Box 10c – New life, new person

In his great mercy he has given us new birth into a living hope through the resurrection of Jesus Christ from the dead... For you have been born again, not of perishable seed, but of imperishable, through the living and enduring word of God.

1 Peter 1:3, 23

> *And if the Spirit of him who raised Jesus from the dead is living in you, he who raised Christ from the dead will also give life to your mortal bodies because of his Spirit who lives in you.*
>
> **Romans 8:11**
>
> *If anyone is in Christ, the new creation has come.*
>
> **2 Corinthians 5:17**
>
> *The glorious riches of God's mystery... is Christ in you.*
>
> **Colossians 1:27**
>
> *I no longer live, but Christ lives in me.*
>
> **Galatians 2:20 (see also Philippians 1:21)**
>
> *Be made new in the attitude of your minds; and... put on the new self, created to be like God in true righteousness and holiness... which is being renewed in knowledge in the image of its Creator.*
>
> **Ephesians 4:23–24 (see also Colossians 3:10)**

New life is always such an amazing thing. Hardly anyone gets bored with the idea of springtime! Few people are not moved by the sight of a newborn baby! Yet this great miracle of new life is precisely what we see taking place in the life of every believer. If we are truly Jesus' followers, then (despite how we may feel) this miracle has occurred within our lives too. In the Old Testament, the prophet Ezekiel, when picturing a valley of dry bones, saw how the bones suddenly put on flesh and became living people at the very moment when God breathed his Spirit upon them (Ezekiel 37:1–14). In a similar way, Jesus' Spirit can now place his life within us. We experience new birth. Although we were dead, we come to life. We are indeed new people!

So following Jesus becomes a matter of learning to live outwards from this new Jesus-shaped person that God is developing deep within us. God has given us new natures and is creating in us a new, authentic human-ness – what Paul calls our "new self" (our new humanity).

God has brought to life within each believer a whole new person, a *new self* which is fashioned "in God's likeness". This is now the real you – your true, God-given, individual personality. Again the message is: be true to your new self; live out who you truly are in Christ.

This means that (despite what many non-Christians think – and indeed Christians too!) the Christian life is not about trying to be good through our own efforts. It's about living out our lives from the good, new nature that God has created in us. God's Word still gives us clear commands about the direction in which we should go, providing, as it were, the railway lines. Yet the new, God-planted life within us also provides us with a powerful engine to travel along the track! There is a clear pattern laid down for the life of Jesus' followers, but there is also, gloriously, a new power.

> God has brought to life within each believer a whole new person, a *new self* which is fashioned "in God's likeness".

So, as new people, our chief aim is simply to let the new life of Jesus within us shine through.

C. Life in the Spirit: We have a new power

The apostles describe this new life as the presence within us of Jesus' Spirit. When asked how exactly the Risen Jesus can live within us, they would answer that it is by means of the Holy Spirit. We saw this in chapter 3, but now we must focus more on how this can be lived out in practice. For the apostles teach us that, if we are to live Jesus' risen life, we must "live... according to the Spirit" (Romans 8:4). This is the normal Christian life – each and every day. But what does this look like?

We saw above how Jesus wanted his life within us to "bear much fruit" (John 15:5). Paul later gives us a list of this fruit, which significantly he calls the "fruit of the Spirit". He focuses on nine key items: "love, joy, peace, forbearance, kindness, goodness, faithfulness, gentleness, and self-control" (Galatians 5:22–23).

This list may seem daunting – after all, these words describe Jesus' character far better than they describe ours! But that's precisely the point: that same Jesus is now living in us by his Spirit and will produce these fruits in our lives – if we let his Spirit do so. So Paul goes on:

Walk by the Spirit... since we live by the Spirit, let us keep in step with the Spirit.

Galatians 5:16, 25

We are to be controlled, led, and directed by the Spirit.

To be sure, the production of this fruit may take time and cannot be rushed. Moreover, because of our continuing sinfulness, we will often hinder the Spirit's work, indeed grieve him and make him "sad" (Ephesians 4:30). Yet, day by day, there is the opportunity to let the Spirit work. This is the way to bear fruit in following Jesus.

This special resource – the gift of Jesus' Spirit within us – should therefore encourage us every time we hear the apostles giving us instructions and commands about how we should live (see Box 10d).

Box 10d – Life in the Spirit: Holiness

But just as he who called you is holy, so be holy in all you do... Rid yourselves of all malice and all deceit, hypocrisy, envy, and slander of every kind.

1 Peter 1:15; 2:1

Clothe yourselves with compassion, kindness, humility, gentleness and patience. Bear with each other and forgive one another... Forgive as the Lord forgave you. And over all these virtues put on love.

Colossians 3:12–14

Whatever is true, whatever is noble, whatever is right, whatever is pure, whatever is lovely, whatever is admirable – if anything is excellent or praiseworthy – think about such things.

Philippians 4:8

Make every effort to live in peace with everyone and to be holy; without holiness no one will see the Lord.

Hebrews 12:14

> *Love must be sincere... be joyful in hope, patient in affliction, faithful in prayer. Share with the Lord's people who are in need. Practice hospitality. Bless those who persecute you...*
> *If it is possible, as far as it depends on you, live at peace with everyone. Do not take revenge, my dear friends... do not be overcome by evil, but overcome evil with good.*
>
> **Romans 12:9, 12–14, 18–19, 21**
>
> For other New Testament passages on Christian lifestyle, see also Ephesians 4:17 – 6:9; 1 Thessalonians 5:12–22; 1 Peter 4; 1 John 3.

These commands reflect the apostles' brilliant vision for Christian living: life lived in the power of the Spirit. Note their concern for personal holiness; note their vision for building Christian communities; note too their wider vision for showing forth God's kingdom in the world. As Paul says elsewhere, "let us do good to all people" (Galatians 6:10).

This last point makes plain that this wider, less self-absorbed focus is all part of following Jesus. As we saw, those first believers in Acts had a vision for bringing not just their own lives as individuals – indeed not just their small congregations – but the whole world under the saving rule of King Jesus. They were, in Jesus' words, to be "the salt of the earth" (Matthew 5:13), being closely stuck into the world with all its disease and sickness, yet always acting as the agents of new life and healing. We are to be the "light of the world" (Matthew 5:14). So the apostles went out "turning the world upside down" (see Acts 17:6) and they want us to do the same – bringing the power of Jesus' life into every situation we meet, transforming it with his light and love.

> Bring the power of Jesus' life into every situation, transforming it with his light and love.

It's a daunting challenge and we need to heed their words, submitting our sinful wills obediently to God's word as spoken through them. That word was inspired by the very Spirit who now lives within us. So the important point is this: God has given us a powerful resource (through his Spirit) that can enable us to live out this spectacular vision for life (given us in his Word). In other words, the Spirit of Jesus given to us is to bring about the lifestyle of Jesus in us – that lifestyle we see displayed before us in the Gospels and passed onto us in the preaching of his apostles. The Spirit indeed is our "advocate" (John 14:16); the Spirit who commands is also the Spirit that enables. We have been given *principles to observe* but also the *power to obey*.

This spiritual reality underlies everything else the New Testament teaches us about how we should now live for God. New Testament commands, if always demanding, are also enticing expressions of what God's new life in us can bring about; they are invitations to

> We have been given *principles to observe* but also the *power to obey.*

walk in his way and in his God-given strength. We are called to live a new lifestyle, but first we are given a new life! In other words, we don't need to "get a life" – we already have it!

As we close this chapter, let's note that this conviction – that to live the Christian life is *to live out the very life of Jesus which he has already given to us* – should cause us to go back and read the Gospels in a whole new way: not just as a story about a unique human being on his way to a unique death, but also as a revelation of how a truly human life is to be lived. If God wants life to be lived the way Jesus lived it (that is, Jesus' way) and if he has also given us the resources to live that life (by placing Jesus' risen life and Spirit within us), then he will be wanting us to look afresh at Jesus' life – to see how we too can now live life "the Jesus way".

This means we will not so quickly excuse our own sinful lifestyles by saying things like: "Jesus was unique and in a category of his own! I do not have the resources to live like that." Or, in a more sophisticated fashion, "The whole point of Jesus' life was so that God could reveal to us, through Jesus' perfection, our sinfulness and inadequacy; he never meant us to try to emulate or imitate it!" Suddenly those fine-sounding excuses have been undermined: we *do* have the resources and God *does* expect us to imitate Jesus!

It also means we will need to move beyond focusing on Jesus' explicit commands about *our* lifestyles (see Box 10a) to look at Jesus' *own* lifestyle in more depth. What were some of the underlying principles which governed his behaviour? Can we detect particular patterns or rhythms which he observed? Did his lifestyle have a distinctive shape? What indeed was his pattern of life (see Box 10e)?

Box 10e – Jesus' pattern of life: Lived in four directions

One helpful way of summarizing the essential pattern of Jesus' life is to notice how it was characterized by four directions:

- **UP:** This upward direction was seen in Jesus' consistent *worship* of God. From the outset, as seen in his temptations, Jesus spoke of the need to "worship the Lord your God, and serve him only" (Matthew 4:10); he was moved to righteous anger when he saw the Temple in Jerusalem being used for lesser purposes than worship (Matthew 21:12–13); he sought always to do what he saw his Father doing and to bring him glory (see, for example, John 5:19; 12:28; 17:1–4).

- **DOWN:** This downward direction was seen in his *self-denial*. Again, from his temptations onwards, Jesus consistently resisted the easier paths of comfort or popular acclaim but resolutely chose the pain-filled way that would lead to the cross (Matthew 4:1–11; 16:21); he did not serve himself but was the servant of others (Mark 10:45).

- **IN:** This inward direction was seen in the way Jesus guarded his inner heart. The Old Testament book of Proverbs had warned: "above all else, guard your heart; for everything you do flows from it" (Proverbs 4:23). In keeping with this Jesus himself spoke, with evident integrity, about how "a good man brings good things out of the good stored in his heart" and warned that, just as bad fruit comes from a bad tree, so evil actions come from an evil heart (Luke 6:43–45). Jesus knew how important it is for us to guard our hearts.

And that's precisely what we see him doing in his own life: when faced with colossal pressures from outside or from other people (the demands of a teaching and healing ministry; dealing with fierce opposition and eventually the plots upon his life), we see Jesus often retreating for prayer and solitude, seeking time with his Father (Mark 1:35; 3:13; 9:2). He ensured, if you like, that there was pure water at the bottom of his inner well (compare John 4:14; 7:37–39).

- **OUT:** This outward direction was seen in his mission and his commitment to others. People could sense his out-going love and compassion as power went out from him to help those in need: as he went through Galilee and the regions beyond with his disciples (Mark 5:30; 7:24–37); as he spoke of God's concern for the poor and the outcast (Luke 4:18; 6:20; 7:22), and demonstrated this by spending time at meals with people such as Zacchaeus (Luke 7:34; 15:2; 19:1–10).

If these four directions made up the inner pattern of Jesus' life – its inner secret – then these should be hallmarks of our lives too. Jesus' lifestyle is to become our lifestyle. If so, we would do well to note these four directions and to become intentional about walking in them each and every day: upwards in worship, downwards in self-denial; inwards in guarding our hearts; outwards in serving others. Up, down, in, out: there is an inner rhythm to the Christian life when lived the Jesus way.

Yet, as we do this, it's important to remember: this is not a matter of our own unaided intentions or resolute determination and effort, but all about God's grace. Through the gift of his Spirit, God has already placed within us the risen life and power of Jesus! So what we are observing in the Gospels, then, is not something remote from us and far-distant, but something that has now, by God's Spirit, been lodged deep within each one of us. The lifestyle lived by Jesus has now, because of God's grace, become *our* lifestyle! Or, better and more simply, THE LIFE HE LIVED IS THE LIFE HE GIVES.

So the tenth building block in following Jesus is to live his life. At first sight, it sounds so daunting. Yet we have learned that the Risen Jesus is living within us by his Spirit and that the life Jesus lived out in the Gospels is the very same life that has now been placed within us – it has the same pattern and the same power. Living Jesus' life, then, turns out to mean letting Jesus live his life through us. It all becomes possible because, in him, we are truly new persons, raised to new life.

The question is: will we let Jesus live his risen life through us?

Building block 10
Live his life – you are a new person!

Resist His Enemy

Peter replied, "Repent and be baptized, every one of you... for the forgiveness of your sins." With many other words he warned them; and he pleaded with them, "Save yourselves from this corrupt generation."
Acts 2:38, 40

Living for Jesus is not all plain sailing. There may be new resources, as we have seen, but there is also some new opposition. Peter names quite clearly the issue of human sins and wickedness. And those first followers of Jesus soon discovered that evil remained a powerful reality – even in the life of a Spirit-empowered community. Hence, for example, Luke's honest account of the way one couple, Ananias and Sapphira, told lies about their finances (Acts 5:1–11). The coming of the Holy Spirit clearly did not bring about a perfect, sinless church – nor has it ever resulted in a single sin-free "saint"!

The apostles' teaching will therefore have included, not just a positive portrait of how Jesus' followers should live, but also a more negative message, warning them about those things they must firmly resist. If they must repent of their sins at the very start of their Christian lives, they must continue to resist sin throughout their lives. After all, Jesus himself had clearly taught that following him would be tough: "Whoever wants to be my disciple must deny themselves and take up their cross daily and follow me" (Luke 9:23). And he was clear that human beings have a battle on their hands in combating the evil in their lives:

> *For it is from within, out of a person's heart, that evil*
> *thoughts come – sexual immorality, theft, murder,*
> *adultery, greed, malice, deceit, lewdness, envy, slander,*
> *arrogance and folly.*
>
> Mark 7:21–22

So being his follower will always mean turning against the tide, going upstream, resisting evil, and sometimes dealing severely with our own desires and agendas. Yes, it is the way of new life and resurrection, but it is also the way of the cross, death, and self-denial.

The eleventh building block in the Christian life, then, is this: to be on our guard against anything that is opposed to Jesus; to resist his "enemy", that is, anything that is inimical (or contrary) to his truth, his light, or his love. This will involve a frank recognition of the reality and power of evil – both in ourselves and in the world.

Jesus' resurrection is a sure pledge from God that he himself is actively involved in the real world, himself bringing good out of evil, and life out of death. Moreover, Jesus' ascension* is a sure sign that God fully vindicated Jesus, completely endorsing all his goodness, and so is totally opposed to all that is evil. Evidently, if we are going to be vindicated by God in any way, then we will need to side firmly and squarely with Jesus. If Jesus is the embodiment of light, we will need to turn our backs on darkness.

Interestingly, this theme is hinted at in Peter's speech on that first day of Pentecost*. Quoting some Old Testament words (which, intriguingly, Jesus had earlier applied to himself: Mark 12:35–37), Peter portrays God the Father as now effectively saying to Jesus: "Sit at my right hand until I make your enemies a footstool for your feet" (Psalm 110:1 in Acts 2:34–35). Evidently, from Jesus' ascension onwards, human history is going to be an extended period in which God brings Jesus' enemies to be under his feet. Paul later develops this idea, applying this same text to Christ's victory over our greatest enemy, namely death itself

> If Jesus is the embodiment of light, we will need to turn our backs on darkness.

(1 Corinthians 15:27). This gives us an indication that the "enemies" in view here are, of course, not so much individual human enemies, but rather humanity's big, long-term enemies: sin, evil, death, and any spiritual forces of darkness.

We also learn from Peter's words that God is opposed to anything which stands in the way of Jesus and his kingdom and is working towards that day when any such opposition to King Jesus is overthrown. God is firmly opposed to sin, wherever it occurs, and is determined to remove its destructive and negative power from his good creation. Will we turn our backs resolutely on these things in our lives? Will we resist evil in all its forms for Jesus' sake?

Recognizing the real enemy

Yet, before we look at these issues, there is first a more important question: is there a danger that we ourselves could ever be classed as God's enemies? There is. Scripture teaches, "All of us also lived among them at one time, gratifying the cravings of our flesh... we were by nature deserving of wrath" (Ephesians 2:3). This means that, until we repent of our own evil and disobedience, we are under God's judgment and in need of being reconciled to him. Yet, through the gospel, God converts his former enemies into his friends:

> *While we were God's enemies, we were reconciled to him through the death of his Son.*
>
> **Romans 5:10**

The cross becomes the place where our own animosity towards God is dissolved and our status as his enemies removed. "God was reconciling the world to himself in Christ, not counting people's sins against them" (2 Corinthians 5:19).

So the Good News, as some of Peter's hearers found out, is that those who respond to Jesus by faith are thereby automatically removed from being counted as God's enemies. If we have come under the rule of King Jesus, then we have been "rescued... from the dominion of darkness and brought... into the kingdom of the Son he loves" (Colossians 1:13).

Great! But now we need to resist that power of darkness. How do we do this? Despite what some extremists might be tempted to think, such resistance will never involve Jesus' followers taking God's law into their own hands and aiming to harm (or even kill) those whom they judge to be God's enemies. Jesus and the apostles show us clearly that such a radical response is entirely inappropriate. His followers should be the last people to be guilty of "hate crimes".

No, in his Sermon on the Mount, Jesus spoke out against murder – indeed even against thoughts of anger (Matthew 5:21–22). Instead, he encouraged his followers to love their enemies and pray for those who persecuted them (Matthew 5:44) – something he acted out himself when being nailed to the cross, saying, "Father, forgive them" (Luke 23:34). Nor do we see the apostles taking up weapons. "On the contrary," writes Paul, "If your enemy is hungry, feed him" (Romans 12:20). Christians should never "take revenge" (Romans 12:19). On the contrary, as Peter says in his letter, we should be following in the steps of Jesus: "When they hurled their insults at him, he did not retaliate; when he suffered, he made no threats. Instead, he entrusted himself to him who judges justly" (1 Peter 2:23). So, clearly, no physical attacks are ever allowed on a Christian's personal enemies. It is far too easy to assume, wrongly, that our enemy is automatically God's enemy. Such thinking is highly dangerous; as James says:

> *Human anger does not produce the righteousness that*
> *God desires.*

James 1:20

So, if this is the case, which "enemy" of Jesus should we be fighting? The chilling response is this: the chief enemy of Jesus is sin, and the chief place where we should be resisting this enemy is not in other people, but in our own lives. Most of the time, we need look no further! After all, Jesus warned us: "Do not judge... Why do you look at the speck of sawdust in your

Jesus' chief enemy is within – within *us*!

brother's eye and pay no attention to the plank in your own eye?" (Matthew 7:1, 3). Or we might say, we must always be first looking in the mirror – not only through the window. Jesus' chief enemy is *within* – within *us*!

In chapter 2 we saw how seriously the Bible speaks of sin. This deadly disease (that makes us choose our own way, worshipping our own selves rather than God) is within us all, and it can only be cured by the cross of Jesus – where the penalty for sin was borne and where evil in all its forms was decisively conquered. Yet now we notice this further solemn reality. Although, as Jesus' followers, we recognize this account of sin (and so should be coming always to Jesus' cross in repentance, asking for his forgiveness), we continue to be deeply sinful. Though forgiven by God, we are not perfect. As Martin Luther (1483–1546) famously observed, we may be declared "righteous" in God's sight (or "put right" with him), yet at the same time we remain sinners: we are "simultaneously forgiven and sinful" (in his Latin phrase: *simul justus ac peccator*).

It is true that a few interpreters have thought some New Testament verses encourage a belief in the possibility of sinless perfection*. Most of us, however, know only too well that we are not perfect! The truth of our ongoing sinfulness is all too obvious to us – sometimes painfully so. Yet, even if obvious, this still remains a serious state of affairs. God does not stop seeing sin as his enemy, just because the person in whom it is present is now a believer. Sin remains evil, a blot on his good creation. The believer needs to fight it, to resist it, and (when necessary) to repent. This is made clear in many baptism* services (see appendix C): new believers not only renounce evil, but are commissioned to be Christ's "faithful soldier and servant" and to "fight valiantly under the banner of Christ against sin, the world, and the devil*." This is a realistic reminder of what it means to be a follower of Jesus – it's a lifelong battle against evil, in all its forms.

> God does not stop seeing sin as his enemy, just because the person in whom it is present is now a believer.

Sin, the world, and the devil

This threefold description of evil will be a useful one as we now look in some more detail at the apostles' teaching on this "enemy" of Jesus – evil in all its forms – that we must resist.

Sin

Until recently there were baptismal services in which those being baptized were asked to renounce "the world, the flesh, and the devil". However, because the word "flesh"* sounds quite strange to our ears, this has now been rendered instead by the word "sin". But what was "flesh" trying to convey? It was included in baptism services because the apostles used this particular term (*sarx* in Greek) to describe what we might now call our sinful "human nature" – that is, our innate human tendency to be self-centred, rather than God-centred. Let's hear Paul's explanation of this key term in Galatians:

> So I say, walk by the Spirit, and you will not gratify the desires of the flesh. For the flesh desires what is contrary to the Spirit, and the Spirit what is contract to the flesh. They are in conflict with each other, so that you are not to do whatever you want... The acts of the flesh are obvious: sexual immorality, impurity and debauchery; idolatry and witchcraft; hatred, discord, jealousy, fits of rage, selfish ambition, dissensions, factions and envy; drunkenness, orgies, and the like. I warn you, as I did before, that those who live like this will not inherit the kingdom of God.
>
> Galatians 5:16–17, 19–21

For Paul, believers are in a battle. Or, you might say, there's a battle going on in them. He speaks of God's Spirit being within us, but so too is our old human nature (our *sarx*) – and these two, says Paul "are in conflict"! We will never get very far in the Christian life if we do not come to terms with this awkward fact. For, although Jesus has indeed placed his new life within us by

> There are two opposing principles at work within us.

his Spirit, this new life will soon be under attack. In the imagery of one of his parables, we may have received the "good seed" into the soil of our lives, but the soil still produces weeds (Mark 4:13–20). We have been given a "new self," a new Christ-like nature (see above, chapter 10), but our old sinful nature is also alive and kicking. In other words, there is a continual tension within each of us between the flesh and the Spirit, and this tension will be with us till the day we die. There are two opposing principles at work within us. We are in for a long-haul fight.

Box 11 – The apostles' teaching about sinful behaviour

Put to death... whatever belongs to your earthly nature: sexual immorality, impurity, lust, evil desires and greed, which is idolatry... You must also rid yourselves of all such things as these: anger, rage, malice, slander, and filthy language from your lips. Do not lie to each other, since you have taken off your old self with its practices and have put on the new self.

Colossians 3:5, 8–10

Among you there must not be even a hint of sexual immorality, or of any kind of impurity, or of greed, because these are improper for God's holy people... No immoral, impure or greedy person has any inheritance in the kingdom of Christ... Do not get drunk on wine, which leads to debauchery. Instead, be filled with the Spirit.

Ephesians 5:3, 5, 18

Rid yourselves of all malice and all deceit, hypocrisy, envy, and slander of every kind... Abstain from sinful desires, which wage war against your soul... Do not live the rest of their earthly lives for evil human desires, but rather for the will of God. For you have spent enough time in the past doing what pagans choose to do – living in debauchery, lust, drunkenness, orgies, carousing and detestable idolatry.

1 Peter 2:1, 11; 4:2–3

Marriage should be honoured by all, and the marriage bed kept pure, for God will judge the adulterer and all the sexually immoral. Keep your lives free from the love of money.

Hebrews 13:4–5

Everyone should be quick to listen... and slow to become angry... Therefore, get rid of all moral filth and the evil that is so prevalent and humbly accept the word planted in you, which can save you.

James 1:19, 21

This conviction about our sinful human natures (the "flesh") and of their continuing power in believers' lives undergirds the apostles' many strong warnings about sin (as seen in Box 11). These are tough words, giving us a flavour of the New Testament's moral challenge. The apostles covered a wide number of areas, while not ignoring the key area of our sexual behaviour – making it quite clear that all sexual intimacy outside heterosexual marriage (what they would have called *porneia*) is contrary to God's will. And they knew they had to be specific about sin, to name particular sins, and to warn Jesus' followers to resist these things. We must heed their challenge.

The world

In biblical thought, however, "sin" does not simply refer to the evil that exists within our own person (the "flesh"). It also describes the whole web of corruption and evil in human society – what the apostle John calls the "world":

> *Do not love the world or anything in the world. If anyone loves the world, love for the Father is not in them. For everything in the world – the lust of the flesh, the lust of the eyes, and the pride of life – comes not from the Father but from the world. The world and its desires pass away, but whoever does the will of God lives forever.*

1 John 2:15–17

John's use of the word "world" helps us realize the scale of the problem. Sin affects everyone, John is saying, and it has led to a whole way of life that is contrary to God's will. The "world" thus becomes, for John, the place that stands opposed to God. Yes, God loves the created world and human life – indeed "for God so loved the world that he gave his one and only Son" (John 3:16) – but in another sense the "world" must be viewed negatively, referring to human beings in their collective hostility towards God. It is the world in this sense that John calls us to renounce – hence his focus on people's desires and pride. Jesus' followers must be driven by a different desire (for God) and must set their hearts and goals in a different place. We are not to "love the world" but "the Father."

Jesus himself had prayed for his followers not to be "of the world" (John 17:14–16). Similarly, Paul describes how believers should conduct their lives:

> *Do not conform to the pattern of this world.*
>
> **Romans 12:2**

It is not too hard to think what the values and standards of the world are: selfish materialism, ambition, envy, strife, sexual license, etc. We are to get wise, acknowledging that this is the way the "world" operates, choosing not to belong to it, and then cutting a different way through life. As James says: "don't you know that friendship with the world means enmity against God?" (James 4:4).

The devil

There is more. We are not just fighting against our own inner desires or the pressure of an unbelieving world. We are also up against a personal force of evil, called in Scripture by different names: the "evil one" (Matthew 6:13), the "accuser" (Revelation 12:10), the "god of this age" (2 Corinthians 4:4), but especially Satan* (meaning the "adversary") and the devil* (the "slanderer").

Jesus' ministry reveals this surprising truth – that the devil is a real spiritual being. Having been himself tested by the devil at the start of his ministry, Jesus later warns Peter that Satan is luring him away from the truth; on another occasion, he celebrates his followers' success in terms of Satan falling "like lightning", and views his own exorcisms as clear signs that Satan is like a "strong man" who is having his house "plundered". Indeed, Satan is being "driven out" by the arrival of Jesus, and Jesus' death is the moment when the "ruler of this world" is roundly defeated (for references see the glossary under "Devil"). Here is Jesus' blunt summary about the one we are dealing with:

> *He was a murderer from the beginning, not holding to the truth, for there is no truth in him. When he lies, he speaks his native language, for he is a liar and the father of lies.*

John 8:44

The apostles teach the same, describing Satan as eternally sinful, a master of disguise, and someone who blinds people to Jesus' truth. They warn us consistently to be on our guard against him (for references, again see the glossary). In one passage, Paul expressly encourages us to see ourselves as soldiers fighting against the "spiritual forces of evil in the heavenly realms" and standing against "the devil's schemes". We are to put on "the full armor of God" – for example, "the belt of truth" and "the shield of faith" (Ephesians 6:10–16). In other words, Jesus' followers are in a spiritual battle. The Evil One stands opposed to Jesus and is therefore our enemy too.

Jesus' followers are in a spiritual battle.

This is not meant to frighten us. Through his cross, Jesus "disarmed the powers" of the devil and dealt him a killer blow (Colossians 2:15); moreover, Jesus promises that no one will be able to "snatch" his followers from his loving care (John 10:28). Even so, we should not minimize Satan's power. Many things in the world can be explained only by reference to the active involvement of the Evil One. We are not therefore to be ignorant of his strategies. These include things such as temptation and deception. And his influence can be seen not just in individual lives but also corporately – in the way that human institutions, societies, and indeed nations so easily veer towards injustice, oppression, and selfishness.

The Evil One especially loves to "accuse" believers, making us feel guilty. If so, we must come back to the cross, and so find again the truth of our being forgiven and accepted by God. In this and other ways, Jesus' followers must recognize the Evil One and be ready to resist him – not in our own strength, but through the powerful blood of Jesus. Put on God's armour and you will be able to stand firm; or, as James succinctly puts it:

Resist the devil, and he will flee from you.

James 4:7

Practical strategies

Sin, then, is a complex reality. When trying to explain the cause of a particular evil, we may need to use a combination of each of these three explanations from the Bible (the flesh, the world, and the devil) – something we see helpfully explored in the letter of James (see James 1:14–15; 3:14–15; 4:4). Understanding this will help us as we seek to resist the enemy of sin in our own lives. Yes, we must always accept responsibility for our own thoughts and actions. Yet becoming aware – both of the pressures coming to us from the world and of the real intervention of the Evil One – can help us see other factors which are genuinely at work. Indeed, sometimes temptation can lose its grip over us the very moment we recognize in it the wily hand of the Evil One; at that point, echoing Jesus' words, we can say with direct confidence, "Get behind me, Satan!" (Mark 8:33).

Here are some further biblical tips for resisting the enemy of sin in our lives and the lure of temptation.

1. Remember you are not alone

Others have faced the same temptation before. Paul writes: "No temptation has overtaken you except what is common to mankind." Yet he then adds a promise: God "will also provide a way out so that you can endure it" (1 Corinthians 10:13). Even more importantly, we are not alone because Jesus himself has faced these temptations:

For we do not have a high priest who is unable to empathize with our weaknesses, but we have one who has been tempted in every way, just as we are – yet he did not sin.

Hebrews 4:15

2. Reckon your old natures as dead in God's sight

Here is a profound spiritual mystery: it never feels true that our old natures are dead, but they are. We saw in chapter 10 how Jesus' followers have been made alive in Christ and given a new nature (or "self"). However, the converse is true too: "our old self was crucified with him"; so we are to "count yourselves dead to sin" (Romans 6:6, 11). This means we should stop paying attention to our sinful nature (even though it continues to operate within us daily). Instead, we are to see it as effectively nailed to the cross: "those who belong to Christ Jesus have crucified the flesh with its passions and desires" (Galatians 5:24). Not for nothing does Jesus command his followers to "take up their cross daily" (Luke 9:23). In this way, we can start operating from our new selves – given us in Christ – and draw strength from our union with Jesus.

3. Feed your mind and imagination on God's truth

Many believers live depressed lives because they believe lies: they imagine, for example, that they are worthless, unable to be forgiven, always on their own, unable to hear God or to speak with him. Instead, we are to feed on the truth of God's Word, replacing such lies with the liberating truths of Scripture. Jesus himself, when tempted, simply responded by standing firmly on biblical truth: "It is written..." (see Matthew 4:4–10). And Paul, in encouraging us to put on God's armour, begins by having us put on "truth" as a belt. Moreover, since much temptation begins in our imaginations, he advises us to replace with more positive thoughts any evil ideas or images that begin to linger there:

Whatever is true, whatever is noble, whatever is
right, whatever is pure, whatever is lovely, whatever is
admirable... think about such things.

Philippians 4:8

"Therefore... fixing our eyes on Jesus" (Hebrews 12:1–2), let us worship him and place him at the centre of our lives. If we do, the grip of sin will lose much of its power.

4. Remove yourself from situations, if necessary

In the Old Testament, there is a memorable example of this, when Joseph flees from the seductive advances of Potiphar's wife (Genesis 39:12). This is not a sign of weakness but a starkly practical decision. Sometimes this decision is made in advance ("I won't go there!"); sometimes it can only be made once we find ourselves in a situation where remaining true to Jesus is going to be difficult ("It's time to leave!"). The New Testament simply uses the plain language of avoidance: "flee from sexual immorality", "flee the evil desires of youth" (1 Corinthians 6:18; 2 Timothy 2:22).

5. Be disciplined with yourself

Our bodies can develop instincts that go in the direction of the "flesh" but, as we give ourselves to delight in God and let the Spirit work his way outwards through our lives, these instincts can be retrained in the direction of Jesus' kingdom. Hence Paul's call to us to "put to death" our sinful actions by the Spirit (Romans 8:13); hence too his own disciplined approach to his own body (1 Corinthians 9:27). Retraining our instincts may require planned effort and the use of such godly disciplines as study, solitude, silence, and worship.

> Retraining our instincts may require planned effort and the use of such godly disciplines as study, solitude, silence, and worship.

And it can be hard. In particular we will need, as we increasingly come to recognize our own unique areas of temptation and weakness, to distinguish between our innate character and temperament (which we cannot change) and the particular sins which such a temperament is prone to fall into. There's nothing wrong, for example, in being someone who has strong emotions; but, if that is our temperament, we will have to be on our guard about falling too easily into anger. In other words, we will need the wisdom to be gentle about the things we cannot change but resolute and firm in rooting out the sins which, however natural they may seem to us, are still contrary to God's perfect law of love.

6. Keep short accounts with God

In any relationship it's good to prevent grievances building up by ensuring that forgiveness is sought as soon as possible. We are to settle disputes "quickly", Jesus warns us (Matthew 5:25). The same is true with God. If we fail to claim his forgiveness each day, we may soon find we have a vague sense of guilt and that God seems strangely far away. It then gets more difficult to come back to him and, once in this position, we are very prone to falling yet further. Here's a downward spiral which (to mix one's metaphors!) it is worth "nipping in the bud".

7. Don't always stay on the back foot

Meanwhile, there will be times when it is appropriate to challenge evils in the wider society in Jesus' name, promoting God's righteousness and the cause of his justice. Jesus proclaimed that God was king and he himself took that challenge to the rulers of his day and to the heart of his own nation. We need to do the same – defending the rights of those unable to defend themselves from predators in the ocean of life, and announcing in practice that evil shall not have the last word in Jesus' world. It is always good to demonstrate that the "powers" at work in the world have met their match in Jesus, and it's good to show people that there is another way of being human – the way of

> It is always good to demonstrate that the "powers" at work in the world have met their match in Jesus.

love. So, even if the focus of this present chapter has necessarily been on our own individual lives, this should not cause us to forget the big concerns of the Bible for righteousness in human society, and for bringing in the values of that alternative kingdom, the kingdom of God. Thus international peace, fair trade, the relief of poverty – these are all on God's heart; and those who name Jesus as king will need to contend for these things in whatever quarter – humbly but courageously. We need to be proactive agents for the kingdom of Jesus. Where there is suffering, bring his compassion; but, where there is evil, confront it.

Conclusion

> *Join with me... like a good soldier of Christ Jesus.*
>
> 2 Timothy 2:3

The apostles saw the Christian life as a kind of warfare; they clearly taught that, if we are going to be Jesus' followers, we will need to be ready to fight in this spiritual battle. So we are going to need to get wise about the real enemy and to learn how to use the weapons we have been given: "The weapons we fight with are not the weapons of the world. On the contrary, they have divine power to demolish strongholds" and they are to be used in order to "take captive every thought to make it obedient to Christ" (2 Corinthians 10:4–5). There's the vision – to see evil made captive to Christ, and thus to see the enemies of Jesus come at last under his feet (Acts 2:35).

So the eleventh building block in the Christian life is to resist his enemy; and we have seen that Jesus' "enemy" is anything that is evil – what the Bible calls "sin" in all its many forms. As a result, we are to fight this wherever we find it – especially in ourselves and in our own old natures, but also in human society.

As individuals, we are to put on God's special armour and resist the Evil One (see Ephesians 6:10–18). Yet we are also to take courage from the fact that, ultimately, the victory is assured. In the imagery of Revelation, Jesus is the conqueror and his people are victorious: the "great accuser" is overthrown, and evil is removed far from God's people (Revelation 21:8; see chapter 12). So, although in this life the battle will never be over (and we ourselves will remain far from perfect), we can take heart: we are on the winning side! "In this world you will have trouble," Jesus said. "But take heart! I have overcome the world" (John 16:33).

We are therefore to press on towards this victory through the power of the cross. For this is where Jesus overcame all our sins and where the "rulers of this age" were defeated (1 Corinthians 2:8; Colossians 2:15). We keep on coming back to the cross – the place where the Christian life begins and the place where it must always continue.

The question is: are we ready to be soldiers of the cross, playing our part in the Lord's true army? Will we renounce all evil, knowing that it is the enemy of Jesus? Human sin is what caused him to die, and the whole purpose of his coming was "to destroy the devil's work" (1 John 3:8). But the cross was also the place where sin – the flesh, the world, the Devil – was publicly humiliated and defeated. So his followers must fight.

Building block 11

Resist his enemy – all evil was defeated on the cross!

12

Trust Him for the Future

---

*God raised him from the dead, freeing him from
the agony of death... David said about him... "You
will not let your holy one see decay... you will fill
me with joy in your presence."*
Acts 2:24–25, 27–28

One of the most striking things about the opening chapters of Acts
is the upsurge of confidence and hope that is suddenly hitting the
world. The apostles and those first believers are marked by a new,
daring approach to life. A few days earlier, they had been full of fear,
meeting in secret (John 20:19); the Emmaus* disciples had been
"downcast" and talking about their dashed hopes (Luke 24:17, 21);
indeed Peter had denied Jesus three times (Luke 22:54–62). But
now, what a contrast! Throughout Acts 2–7 we see first Peter, next
John, and then all the believers, speaking out boldly in Jesus' name,
risking arrest, and being ready to suffer for Jesus' sake. What can
explain this dramatic change – from cowardice into courage, from
despair into hope?

   Answer: the resurrection of Jesus and the gift of his Spirit. These
two great events have convinced them that their God is powerful
and active, and have also given them a glimpse into the future. In
particular, by looking at Jesus' resurrection, they can see how death
has not been able to "keep its hold on him" (Acts 2:24); this surely
means that, for them too as believers, physical death will not be the
final end – there will be resurrection life beyond the grave. Again,
looking at Jesus' resurrection, they also begin to realize that they

have probably not seen the last of Jesus! This eternal person, now seated for a while at God's "right hand," will one day be back. Thus, a few days later, Peter asserts that this Jesus must remain in heaven, but only "until the time comes for God to restore everything" (Acts 3:21). That's their vision: through the resurrection, God has done a bright, new thing, which is a sure sign that, when Jesus returns, he will one day make all things new. It's enough to fill them with undaunted confidence and with an assured hope.

So, as we give ourselves to the apostles' teaching, a key part of this will be to learn from them about what the future holds – now that Jesus has been raised from the dead. How did they see the future unfolding – for Jesus, for believers, indeed for the world? And in our day, when so many find life meaningless, hopeless, and a recipe for despair, what can the apostles teach us that will bring into our lives a sure basis for optimism and hope?

Their writings in the New Testament (as can be seen in Box 12a) turn out to be shot through with great expectations; they pulsate with bright colours and dynamic energy. Someone has estimated that at least one in twenty verses makes some specific reference to this glorious hope. Evidently, the Christian Good News, unlike most news stories, has something very clear to say about the future.

How is this so? Because the future has been anchored in a solid event in past human history: Jesus' resurrection. In the Bible, the word translated "hope" (despite the way this word is sometimes used in English) does not mean some vague, wishful thinking; rather, it is an attitude built on something fixed, concrete, and reliable. If you like, God, through the resurrection, has revealed his future in seed-form – in outline. In the midst of human history, God has done something which speaks loud and clear about the end of human history. We now know the goal that he has for the future, because of what he has revealed of that future in the past.

> The future has been anchored in a solid event in past human history: Jesus' resurrection.

In that sense, we are to go "back to the future"! Or, to use a biblical image, Jesus' resurrection is the "first fruits" of a harvest still to come – a sure sign of what God will do again in the future, both for individuals and for the world. It is, in other words, his "first instalment" – a down payment on what he pledges will be the future of the world.

As believers in Jesus, then, we are to be infused with a strong dose of hope – a sense that the "best is yet to be". Sometimes life is indeed hard: the suffering in our world is great, and the battle against evil long and tiresome. But there is a light at the end of the tunnel! There is solid ground on which we can stand.

So the twelfth and final building block in following Jesus today is to be grounded in hope – to listen carefully to what his apostles teach us about the future and then to trust Jesus for that future. As we now listen to the apostles as they explain and describe this hope, we will note what they say about God's plans for the world and for believers under three headings: renewal for the world, reunion with Jesus, and resurrection for the believer.

Box 12a – The apostles' teaching: Hope for the future

In his great mercy God has given us new birth into a living hope through the resurrection of Jesus Christ from the dead, and into an inheritance that can never perish, spoil or fade... Therefore... set your hope on the grace to be brought to you when Jesus Christ is revealed at his coming.

1 Peter 1:3–4, 13

We know that when Christ appears, we shall be like him.... All who have this hope in him purify themselves, just as he is pure.

1 John 3:2–3

Now faith is confidence in what we hope for.

Hebrews 11:1

If Christ has not been raised, our preaching is useless and so is your faith... Then those... who have fallen asleep in Christ are lost... But Christ has indeed been raised from the dead, the firstfruits of those who have fallen asleep.
What you sow does not come to life unless it dies. When

you sow, you do not plant the body that will be, but just a
seed... So will it be with the resurrection of the dead. The
body... is sown in dishonour, it is raised in glory; it is sown in
weakness, it is raised in power; it is sown a natural body, it is
raised a spiritual body.

For the trumpet will sound, the dead will be raised
imperishable, and we will be changed... Then the saying
that is written will come true: "Death has been swallowed
up in victory."

                    1 Corinthians 15:14, 18, 20, 36–37, 42–44, 52, 54

Then I saw "a new heaven and a new earth," for the first
heaven and the first earth had passed away, and there was
no longer any sea. I saw the Holy City, the new Jerusalem,
coming down out of heaven from God, prepared as a bride
beautifully dressed for her husband. And I heard a loud voice
from the throne saying, "Look! God's dwelling place is now
among the people, and he will dwell with them. They will be
his people, and God himself will be with them and be their
God. He will wipe every tear from their eyes. There will be no
more death' or mourning or crying or pain, for the old order
of things has passed away. He who was seated on the throne
said, "I am making everything new!"

                                        Revelation 21:1–5

For other related passages, see 1 Corinthians 13:13; Ephesians
1:18; 1 Peter 1:3–9; 3:15 and Colossians 1:3–5.

Renewal for the world

This first theme may come as something of a shock. In the light
of what we have just said, it might be imagined that the Christian
message is all about somewhere else – heaven, not earth. But
in fact, the Bible is an earthy book, and biblical hope, in both Old
and New Testaments, is far more down to earth: "The earth is the
Lord's, and everything in it' (Psalm 24:1). So, although evil has
come into the world, there is the strong hope that this world "will

be filled with the knowledge of the Lord as the waters cover the sea" (Isaiah 11:9). Creation has been damaged, but God will bring about a renewed creation. So, as believers, our individual hopes are to be set within this much larger context of God's agenda for the renewal of his world.

We see Paul making exactly this point in Romans 8:

> *I consider that our present sufferings are not worth comparing with the glory that will be revealed in us. For the creation waits in eager expectation for the children of God to be revealed. For the creation was subjected to frustration, not by its own choice, but by the will of the one who subjected it, in hope that the creation itself will be liberated from its bondage to decay and brought into the freedom and glory of the children of God.*
>
> *We know that the whole creation has been groaning as in the pains of childbirth right up to the present time. Not only so, but we ourselves, who have the firstfruits of the Spirit, groan inwardly as we wait eagerly for our adoption to sonship, the redemption of our bodies.*
>
> **Romans 8:18–23**

According to Paul, God is going to share his glory with his own people; believers in Jesus (those who already have the "first fruits" of God's Spirit) will be revealed as his true children. Yet on that day, creation too will be blessed. Creation has experienced a "bondage to decay"; it groans like a woman in childbirth; but these are the labour pains before a new age, a new creation. This is our hope, but this is also creation's "hope". So, whenever we see painful things in our world, such as decay and death, we are yet to have confidence through the resurrection that this is not God's last word on the subject. If human beings will find their ultimate renewal through Jesus and the Spirit, so too will creation itself.

God, then, is moving the old creation through to a glorious new creation. This conviction can help us view many things in a whole new way:

- We can see our physical world not as something to be abused (because it might one day be discarded), but rather as something to be nurtured and cared for (because God is going to redeem it or "set it free").

- We can sense that the whole process of human history is something through which God is mysteriously at work.

- We can see our own individual human lives, not as something to be dismissed (before we get on and do the real thing – in heaven!) but as something valuable in their own right – as the theatre of God's redeeming work.

The basis for this new perspective on human life and the created world is, again, the resurrection of Jesus. It is precisely when we see God not discarding Jesus' corpse but rather transforming it and renewing it as a physical body, that we realize God is not in the business of discarding his broken, bruised world; rather he has the power and purpose to renew it with his healing love. In contrast to many sub-Christian views, which are often dualist*, the resurrection body of Jesus makes abundantly clear that physical matter is not inherently evil; it is only sin and suffering that are evil. One day, this physical world will see these ugly intrusions on God's good creation visibly removed once and for all. The resurrection of Jesus is a sure sign of God's plan to renew the world; it is his pledge to his decaying old creation that he is bringing in his transformed new creation.

> The resurrection of Jesus is a sure sign of God's plan to renew the world; it is his pledge to his decaying old creation that he is bringing in his tranformed new creation.

The New Testament closes with the great picture book of Revelation (see the extract in Box 12a). As the last book in the Bible, it reworks the imagery used in the Bible's very first book (Genesis). Through Jesus, God has taken history from the old first creation (described in Genesis 1–2) to a new, more glorious creation. When read carefully, its final vision of God's future (in Revelation 21) does not speak of our created world being destroyed, but rather of God renewing it – taking the old and making everything new:

He who was seated on the throne said, "I am making
everything new!"

Revelation 21:5

Thus we should understand the "new earth" described here in the sense of a renewed earth. On that day, the world will be truly redeemed and the old creation brought through into a glorious new creation. Note too that the Christian hope is clearly not so much that we go to heaven; rather it is that heaven now comes to us! This is God's "earthy" plan for the renewal of his created world.

Reunion with Jesus

The resurrection also points us forward to an incredible truth about Jesus himself: not just that he is both "Lord and Messiah*" (Acts 2:36), but that he is coming back! From his resurrection, the apostles could deduce that Jesus was an eternal person who would never die again (see chapter 1). Moreover, from his ascension* into heaven, they would learn that he was now living in God's nearer presence. This, then, clearly meant that, somehow or other, there would be an opportunity to meet him again. Although he had departed from them, this was clearly not the end of the story!

This is precisely what the angels told the apostles at the very moment when Jesus ascended back to heaven: "Why do you stand here looking into the sky? This same Jesus, who has been taken from you into heaven, will come back" (Acts 1:11). And this is why, a few days later, Peter is soon saying to the religious leaders in Jerusalem:

God will send... Jesus. Heaven must receive him until the time
comes for God to restore everything.

Acts 3:20–21

In other words, Jesus will return; his followers can look forward to what is known as his "second coming*"; at that time, they will be reunited with him. What a great reunion!

Jesus had hinted at this awesome truth during his ministry. Presumably, however, his words made little sense at the time

– after all, if his followers could not yet understand his death and resurrection, how much less any talk of a return after that! But now, the Spirit would have brought back to their minds key parts of his teaching, for example:

- his parables about a master returning to find his servants not working (for example, Matthew 24–25, Mark 13:34–37, Luke 21:25–38);

- his warnings to be alert for the appearing of "the Son of Man coming in clouds with great power" (Mark 13:26) and not to be "ashamed" of him on that day (Mark 8:38);

- his puzzling words in the upper room: "I will come to you" (John 14:18, 28).

Although these words may well have had other layers of meaning, the conviction grew that they also referred to Jesus' return at the final end of human history – his "second coming".

But when would that be? They simply did not know. For Jesus himself had made it abundantly clear:

> *But about that day or hour no one knows, not even the angels in heaven, nor the Son, but only the Father...*
> *Therefore keep watch because you do not know when the owner of the house will come back.*

Mark 13:32, 35

Although it was sorely tempting to speculate, trying to discern the "signs of the times", the apostles had to encourage Jesus' followers to live in the keen expectation that Jesus' return might occur at any moment and without prior warning – "like a thief in the night" (1 Thessalonians 4:15 – 5:11). At some point, "the Lord Jesus will be revealed from heaven in blazing fire with his powerful angels" (2 Thessalonians 1:7); believers were to "wait for God's Son from heaven" (1 Thessalonians 1:10). And they were not to worry if believers had already died; those believers would "rise first", so that all the faithful, past and present, could enjoy the Lord's presence together (1 Thessalonians 4:16–17). With this hope so strong in their hearts, it is not surprising that the earliest prayer to have survived from New Testament believers (preserved in Aramaic*) is *"Maranatha – Come, Lord!"* (1 Corinthians 16:22).

Even so, the apostles also prepared people for the possibility of a delay:

> *Scoffers will come... They will say, "Where is this 'coming' he promised?"... But... with the Lord a day is like a thousand years, and a thousand years are like a day. The Lord is not slow in keeping his promise, as some understand slowness. Instead he is patient with you, not wanting anyone to perish, but everyone to come to repentance.*
>
> 2 Peter 3:3–4, 8–9

The reason why Jesus has not yet returned, according to Peter here, is that God wants as many people as possible to respond to his Good News. As Jesus had expressly stated, the Good News had first to be "preached to all nations" (Mark 13:10). So, even though people in Peter's day may be finding this future event quite difficult to imagine, they should not mock the whole idea of Jesus' second coming. The Greek word (*parousia**), which is often translated as "second coming" actually means something more like the "personal, royal presence" of a king. Thus, although Peter did not know the precise method or date, he was convinced that, one day, believers would be in the personal, royal presence of God's appointed king, Jesus. We will be brought "before his glorious presence without fault and with great joy" (Jude 24).

> Peter was convinced that, one day, believers would be in the personal, royal presence of God's appointed king, Jesus.

Elsewhere, the apostles use other images to describe that incredible day when believers will meet with Jesus "face to face": we will be "with Christ" (Philippians 1:23) and ourselves "appear before... Christ" (2 Corinthians 5:10). Paul rejoices that, although at present we do not see things clearly, on that day we will see Jesus face to face (1 Corinthians 13:12); and John rejoices that we will all "see him as he is" (1 John 3:2–3). Jesus himself had prayed that his followers might be with him where he is, so that they could see his "glory" (John 17:24). And, on that day, his prayer will be answered. We will see the king!

Resurrection for the believer

Finally (as these last few verses have indicated), the resurrection of Jesus teaches us something very important about ourselves. Our death is not our end. There is life beyond the grave. Into the darkness of the ancient world, with its despair about the possibility of life beyond death, came the light of Jesus' resurrection. Jesus' coming, the apostles teach, now sets "free those who all their lives were held in slavery by their fear of death" (Hebrews 2:15). In Jesus' resurrection:

> *Christ Jesus... has destroyed death and has brought life and immortality to light through the gospel.*
>
> 2 Timothy 1:10

For those who are fearful of death, Jesus' resurrection is indeed Good News. However, for those who think (or even wish) that death is the end, the resurrection is bad news. Thus many people, neither believing in God nor in life after death, act in a way that Paul condemns: "Let us eat and drink," they say, "for tomorrow we die" (1 Corinthians 15:32). It is a sad way to live – exploiting physical pleasures now, minimizing pain, and never finding any true meaning; life is lived under a black cloud and on a road that, so it appears, leads nowhere. Yet, in the light of the resurrection, it is also a foolish and dangerous way to live, because Jesus' resurrection means not only that death is not the end; it also means that we will all meet Jesus after we die.

Box 12b – The apostles' teaching: Judgment after death

People are destined to die once, and after that to face judgment.

Hebrews 9:27

> We must all appear before the judgment seat of Christ.
>
> **2 Corinthians 5:10**
>
> It is a dreadful thing to fall into the hands of the living God.
>
> **Hebrews 10:31**
>
> God has set a day when he will judge the world with justice by the man he has appointed. He has given proof of this to everyone by raising him from the dead.
>
> **Acts 17:31**
>
> For other related passages, see Matthew 7:23; 25:1–46; John 3:18; 5:27–30; Romans 2:9; 3:19.

For believers in Jesus, however, the resurrection is the best news in the world. It is a pledge and foretaste of eternal life (or life in the "age to come": Mark 10:30). Jesus said:

> *I am the resurrection and the life. The one who believes in me will live, even though they die.*
>
> **John 11:25**

He is acknowledging that believers will still die physically, but promising that they will continue to be alive; a few chapters later, he expressly promises that he is going to "prepare a place" for his followers so that they can be with him (John 14:2–3). "And so," writes Paul, "we will be with the Lord forever" (1 Thessalonians 4:17). If we are truly followers of Jesus, this is now our destiny – to be with him for ever!

It's also worth reading Paul's great chapter about the believer's resurrection body (1 Corinthians 15; extracts given in Box 12a). Because of Jesus' physical resurrection from the dead, believers can look forward to a similar resurrection. Our bodies will not be discarded, but we will be given new "spiritual bodies" – real bodies, but animated by God's Spirit and able to live in God's new creation.

> If we are truly followers of Jesus, this is now our destiny – to be with him for ever!

Living in hope

These three strands make up the confident hope of New Testament Christianity. Because of Jesus' resurrection, we know God has a future – not only for Jesus himself, but also for those who believe in him, and indeed for this world. Jesus will be seen again, we will be given new resurrection bodies, and God will bring this all together in an act of new creation.

We are therefore to be people marked by hope. In Box 12a we saw how the lives of the first Christians were marked by this quality – what Peter calls this "living hope", which can never "spoil or fade". So he tells Jesus' followers always to "be prepared... to give the reason for the hope that you have" (1 Peter 3:15). Similarly, John notes how this hope should cause us to live holy lives (1 John 3:3), while Paul elsewhere encourages us not to grieve in the face of death: we are not to "grieve like the rest of mankind, who have no hope" (1 Thessalonians 4:13).

This should encourage us in our following of Jesus. For there is nothing like a strong tonic of biblical hope to keep us following him – motivated for the journey and inspired by its glorious ending. If tempted to give up, we should lift up our eyes and consider again this great hope which God has given us – found only in Jesus. God wants us to live lives marked, not by insecurity and uncertainty, but by confident hope.

> God wants us to live lives marked, not by insecurity and uncertainty, but by confident hope.

Indeed, the Christian life should be seen as a life lived in the interval between two great fixed points – the victory of Jesus in his death and resurrection (in the past), and the ultimate victory of Jesus (in the future) when we too will be raised. So we can live our lives, as it were, like a trapeze artist walking between these two fixed poles – knowing too that underneath us, like a safety net, are the "everlasting arms" of God (Deuteronomy 33:27).

So, although Jesus warned us that we would suffer in this world (John 16:33), he also assured us that he can give us his peace, which he does not give "as the world gives" (John 14:27). Moreover, we will have many life-decisions to make, but we can bring these to Jesus too. For if Jesus can take care of the future of the whole world, he can surely take care of our individual futures. We may not know our own future in any detail, but we do now know him who holds that future in his hand.

The question is: will we trust him as we go into this unknown future? Or will we doubt his power, his love, or his wisdom? Will we pray for his world and work hard for its renewal and for Jesus' kingdom to come – even on days when evil seems rampant? And will we prepare ourselves for his return – even when there seems to be so long a delay?

To follow Jesus is indeed to set out on a journey, which often can be more difficult than we ever at first imagined. Yet the Bible teaches us that Jesus himself has already run this race:

Let us run... the race... fixing our eyes on Jesus, the pioneer and perfecter of faith.

(Hebrews 12:1–2)

In other words, Jesus has blazed a trail ahead of us. And now (as the one who brings our faith to completion), he is standing at the finishing line, beckoning us forwards.

The twelfth building block in the Christian life, then, is to keep our eyes fixed on Jesus and to reach out our hand, placing it in his, for he is our trustworthy companion. We are to trust him for the future, knowing that he has conquered all that is evil and that our future is safe in his hands.

Building block 12

Trust him for the future – his victory is assured!

Epilogue

You will be well aware by now that I want you to follow Jesus. Also that I think the New Testament is not just a brilliant guide, but a vital one, if we are ever going to follow him truly. Jesus *did* give clear guidance to his apostles; and their own guidance, found in the pages of the New Testament, is a reliable guide for us today.

This book has given you a brief introduction to the apostles' writings in the New Testament, but I hope you will now be motivated to discover its treasures for yourself. For the reasons given in the introduction (not least that many people in the world still may not have access to their own copy of the Bible), I have tried to draw out the meaning of the whole New Testament through the lens of just *two* of its 260 chapters (Luke 24 and Acts 2). I hope this has given you a sense of how powerful this small, ancient book is. But now, if you have the opportunity, how about reading more of it for yourself? Why not look up some of the references already mentioned? Or how about sitting down to read one of the Gospels or one of Paul's letters? These will help you so much in your walk with Jesus. *There is nothing like reading the Bible for ourselves.*

Dividing the material into twelve chapters may also have been useful for various reasons – not least because it provides a framework that could easily be committed to memory. Moreover, it is not just that the first six chapters (in part 1) come directly from the teaching of Jesus, and the second six (in part 2) from the teaching and example of the apostles, his first followers. You will find that these two halves match each other in even closer ways (see the diagram).

In other words, we find that in part 2 we have worked through essentially the same six themes, but in the reverse order. For example, in chapter 1 we focused on the resurrection but concentrated on what it means to meet with the Risen Jesus today; in chapter 12 on what the resurrection means instead for the world and for our future. Again, in chapter 2 we focused on the cross as the place where our sins were forgiven; but in chapter 11 on it as the place where evil was conquered, so that we too must now fight sin and evil. And so on. You may find it helpful to go back through the material and note this pattern.

Bear Witness to His Reign	6	RELATING TO OTHERS	7	Share with Jesus' People
Participate in His Meal	5	WORSHIP	8	Worship His Majesty
Feed on His Scriptures	4	SCRIPTURE	9	Follow His Teaching
Welcome His Spirit	3	SPIRIT	10	Live His Life
Receive His Forgiveness	2	CROSS	11	Resist His Enemy
Enjoy Jesus' Resurrection	1	RESURRECTION	12	Trust Him for the Future

Meanwhile, at several points, we noted the way the different chapters balance each other in some intriguing ways. For example, the first three chapters highlight the Trinitarian* truth of "God *with* us, God *for* us, God *in* us." The second three chapters (4 to 6) have a focus *backwards* (to Scripture in studying), *upwards* (to God in worship) and *outwards* (to others in mission).

Then again, chapters 3 to 5 outline consecutively three main emphases that regularly appear in Christian responses to the message of the cross and resurrection of Jesus: there can be those who give special focus to the Spirit, others to the Scriptures, others to the sacrament of the Lord's Supper (often labelled, rightly or wrongly, as the "charismatic," "evangelical," and "liturgical" emphases). Each of these is very important. Yet the fact that all three are followed in this book by the focus on extending Jesus' kingdom (in mission and service to others), helpfully puts these three emphases within a better context. For there is a danger that, on their own, they can be over-emphasized – that somehow they become ends in themselves. When, however, they are placed within the overriding concern of Jesus' mission to the world, they can resume their proper place.

We must remember that the church (that is, the company of all those seeking to be Jesus' followers) is, in the famous words of a former Archbishop of Canterbury (William Temple, 1881–1944) the only "organization in the world that exists for the benefits of its non-members." The Risen Jesus calls us *inwards* to himself and *upwards* to God, but ultimately he also sends us *out* again in his name. So what we have been studying in this book is not only Jesus' recipe for the transformation of your small world, but his recipe for the transformation of the whole world – that is, *his* world.

If studying these pages helps you in your walk with Jesus, I will be glad, but remember too that Jesus himself is always walking outwards to others. The Jesus Way begins with Jesus and ends with Jesus. Yet, along the way, we are to bring others onto the road, and play our part in implementing his kingdom within his world.

We are to follow Jesus – his way!

Appendix A

Jesus of Nazareth: What Makes Him Unique?

Some readers may still be uncertain about whether it is worth setting out on the Jesus Way. Others may want to encourage their friends to follow Jesus but don't know what they can say that might encourage them to take this matter seriously. Whichever group you find yourself in, here are five things about Jesus which, taken all together, mark him out to be quite unique.

1. No one has ever taught as this man

Those who heard him teach could not believe their ears. Unlike their normal religious teachers, Jesus "taught as one who had authority", (Mark 1:22). Where did this wisdom come from?

So, despite his use of simple illustrations, his teaching has proved enduringly profound: one collection of his sayings (the Sermon on the Mount in Matthew 5–7) is probably the most famous sermon of all time. One of his followers, when some in the crowd were finding Jesus' teaching too challenging, explained why he could not give up following Jesus: "You have the words of eternal life" (John 6:68).

Jesus' teaching was stunningly powerful, exact, and liberating – it brought life. "I tell you the truth...." (John 10:1, 7). It was true and authoritative because it stemmed from his direct and personal knowledge of God. Thus, where others spoke *about* God, this man spoke as though *from* God. In other words, Jesus not only knew *what* he was talking about; more importantly, he knew *who* he was talking about.

2. No one has ever lived as this man

Our closest friends know our own weaknesses all too well. Not so with Jesus. Looking back on his life, hisclosest followers concluded that he had "committed no sin", and that in him there had been no "sin" or "darkness" whatsoever (see 1 Peter 2:22; 1 John 1:5; 3:3–6).

Instead he claimed to be the "light of the world" and challenged his accusers directly: "Can any of you prove me guilty of sin?" (John 8:12, 46). There was no answer. For this reason, none of the charges brought against him, when he was later on trial, focused on any of his supposed moral failings, but focused instead on religious and political disagreements.

What people sensed when they were with Jesus was the perfect combination of attributes that in others are often out of balance: authority, power, strength of character, even gutsy determination, but all these shot through with humility, gentleness, compassion, and grace; holiness but transforming love; a "man of suffering, and familiar with pain" but, simultaneously, a man full of life and the deepest joy (see Isaiah 53:3; Luke 10:21).

3. No one has ever died as this man

Other religious leaders associated with worldwide faiths have died in their beds. Not so Jesus.

His was a life marked by suffering: charged with being an illegitimate child, he was frequently misunderstood and often on the move. Eventually, in his mid-thirties, he was betrayed into enemy hands by one of his friends, given a mockery of a trial, and then sentenced to what has been described as the cruelest death imaginable – crucifixion on a Roman cross. After floggings and beatings (which often were quite enough in themselves to bring about a victim's death), he was strung up on a piece of wood outside Jerusalem's* walls, with nails driven through his wrists and legs – left there to suffocate, unable to breathe, and to die some three hours later.

Yes, there were many others in the ancient world (all of them slaves or political rebels) whom the Romans put through this hideous punishment, but none of them actively chose this path for themselves. Jesus did: he went up to Jerusalem, clearly predicting his death, and actively encouraging others too to "take up their cross". And he asked his followers to remember him afterwards by focusing not on his life but on his death – his broken body and shed blood.

So Jesus' death, though excruciating, was chosen and intentional. His purpose, he said, was "to give his life as a ransom for many" (Mark 10:45); his blood was to be shed "for the forgiveness of sins" (Matthew 26:28). There is much more we could say, but clearly this was a death with a difference, involving desperate pain but for some deep purpose (see chapter 2).

4. No one has ever claimed as much as this man

For all his evident humility, Jesus' teaching constantly forced his hearers to ask: who exactly is this teacher? Who does he think he is?

Within their shared Jewish history, Jesus' hearers had great heroes, ancient institutions, and holy writings; but now Jesus claimed to be "greater than Solomon", "greater than the temple", the one in whom their Scriptures (the Old Testament) were coming true "in their own hearing" (see Matthew 12:42; 12:6; Luke 4:21).

Moses, they believed, had brought down God's revealed Law from Mount Sinai, but now Jesus sat on a mountain and said: "You have heard that it was said to the people long ago...". People were longing for God to become king, but now Jesus, in proclaiming the arrival of God's kingdom, made it clear that he was not only the doorkeeper (who decided who would enter the kingdom) but none other than the king himself (see Matthew 5:21–22; Luke 13:27).

Carefully choosing his words, Jesus claimed to be Israel's* anointed king (Messiah*), the exalted figure known as the "Son of Man" who would judge the world, and the "Son" whom the "Father" (God) was fully trusting. Indeed he dared to use God's name ("I AM" – revealed in Exodus 3:14) and apply it in various ways directly to himself (see Matthew 25:31; Mark 8:29–31; Luke 10:22; John 6:37; 8:12, 58).

Hearing such claims, some ever since have thought him mad or bad, but others, sensing his sanity and sincerity, have concluded that he knew exactly who he was, and also that his claims – however unparalleled in human history – are true.

5. No one has ever been worshipped as this man

Set against his Jewish culture (in which people were trained to proclaim regularly that there was only one God who alone was to be worshipped), it is remarkable that Jesus' first followers clearly felt compelled to worship him. This took place both during his lifetime and immediately afterwards – and indeed has continued to the present day.

After one of his miracles, his followers "worshipped him", and later a follower called Thomas, himself prone to doubt and questioning, was moved to call Jesus "My Lord and my God!" Thereafter, his followers in their writings always bracketed Jesus together with God (calling him the "Lord," the "Son of God"*, etc.) and encouraged others to worship and "glorify" him. No other worldwide faith worships its human founder in this blatant way (see Matthew 14:33; John 20:28; Galatians 1:1; Philippians 2:11, etc.).

* * *

These five factors concerning Jesus suggest that he is indeed unique – in a class of his own. They also explain why no one has ever been followed as this man. Throughout history and to this present day, millions of people have been followers of Jesus. To follow Jesus, then, is not to set out on one's own, but rather to do so in the company of countless others.

Appendix B

The Resurrection of Jesus: Can We Be Sure?

The bodily resurrection of Jesus from death stands at the very centre of the Christian faith. So it's worth looking briefly at some of the arguments which point towards this being a real historical event.

Given that we are dealing here with a one-off event which took place nearly 2,000 years ago, we cannot ultimately provide incontrovertible proof – historical events in that sense are not "provable". Yet there have been serious-minded people (including many people initially prone to skepticism) who have come to the conclusion that this is one of the best-attested facts of ancient history. We would do well to follow their reasoning.

What, then, are the arguments used against the truth of the resurrection and how might we answer them?

Contrary to history and science?

Many objections to the resurrection include catchphrases such as these: "Dead men don't rise!" "Miracles don't happen nowadays – and never did!" Indeed, many of the most thoughtful objections to the resurrection have this form, effectively pointing out that the resurrection, if it occurred, would have been a unique event in the world's history. Such a one-off miracle, we are then told, appears to break the rules of both history and science.

However, that does not necessarily mean that it did not happen. For history and science can only observe what happens – they cannot dictate what happens. On the contrary, if the resurrection did occur, then it means we have to rethink what we mean by "science" and "history".

So, if anyone affirms the truth of the resurrection, this does not mean they are giving up on science. Instead, they are being open to the possibility that God can work in his world – both in regular and observable ways, and also occasionally in ways that break the pattern (often called "miracles"). Moreover, what if, in the resurrection, God was doing something that he will be doing again at some point in the future? In that case, the resurrection would not always remain unique. Jesus' resurrection might instead just be a foretaste of what God will do when he raises others at the end of time. At that point, therefore, there would be many "scientific" parallels to this event – it's just that we have not seen them yet!

Again, if anyone affirms the truth of the resurrection, this does not mean they are giving up on history. Instead, they are simply being open to where the evidence has been leading them. Often, historians have to work back from known historical facts to posit an earlier event which alone explains those later consequences. This is what we see with Jesus' resurrection: there are some surprising things that happen subsequently that demand an adequate explanation. And the best explanation – historically – may be the resurrection of Jesus. Only *this* adequately explains *that*.

Box B contains a list of these surprising things which took place after the resurrection and which demand some kind of historical explanation.

Box B – Questions requiring a historian's answer

- What changed Jesus' fearful and frightened followers into brave and courageous witnesses, ready to die for him?

- Why did they start referring to him as "Lord"* and the "Son of God" when as Jews they declared (in the words of Deuteronomy 6:4) that "the Lord our God, the Lord is one"?

- Why did the first Christians change their day of worship from the Jewish Sabbath (on Saturday) to Sunday? And why did they worship God by sharing in a meal that focused in a macabre way on the cruel death of their founder?

- What explains the rapid spread of this Jewish messianic sect across the Greco-Roman world in the first century? And, if the task of the Messiah* was to rid Israel* of its pagan occupiers and to establish a reign of peace, why did the first Christians proclaim Jesus as the Messiah? Apparently Jesus had achieved neither of these things; instead, his death on a Roman cross strongly suggested that he was a failed Messiah. So what caused Christians to make this absurd claim in the face of this evidence to the contrary?

- Why does the New Testament use a word for "resurrection" (anastasis) which means literally "making to stand upright"? This word never referred to some merely "spiritual" event but to the stark event when a dead body was raised in a physical sense. One group within Judaism (the Pharisees*) firmly believed that this would happen to all God's people at the end of time; other Jews doubted this. Meanwhile, those in the pagan world knew for a fact that it did not happen – "dead men don't rise!" Why did the first Christians use this word – a word inviting ridicule and scorn – when it would have been so much easier to speak of some more mystical experience?

- Why does the New Testament make this startling concept of resurrection (both of Jesus and then of believers) so central in its thinking – especially when compared with the Old Testament, which mentions resurrection so rarely?

All of these are intriguing historical facts from the first century which make very little sense if the resurrection did not happen. Some of them may seem rather technical, yet they are important questions for historians nonetheless. Together, they build up a cumulative case which points back to the resurrection of Jesus as a real event that occurred in real history. Each of them is a manifest fact from within ancient history – no one can seriously deny that these things happened. The question is: why? Go through the list and ask yourself whether any one of these would have happened if Jesus was known to be truly dead and buried.

So Jesus' resurrection, though a unique event, cannot be ruled out in advance as somehow non-scientific or non-historical. Instead, it requires careful investigation.

Just a "spiritual" resurrection?

Moving on, other objections to the resurrection begin to focus instead on raising questions about the early Christians' claims. For example, what if Jesus' followers came to believe in his resurrection by mistake? Perhaps they just got in a muddle? Perhaps Jesus' corpse was still there, but they mistakenly went to the wrong tomb? Yet, even if there was some initial confusion after dawn that Sunday morning, the correct tomb was only a few yards away. And, when you look at Box B again, it's reasonably clear that Jesus' followers were basing their actions on something more than just muddled thinking.

At this point, people often suggest that Jesus' followers were only talking of a "spiritual" resurrection, not a brute physical one. If so, Jesus' followers did not make a mistake as such (believing Jesus was physically raised, when in fact he was still in the tomb). Instead, what they did (on this argument) was sincerely to conclude that somehow he was alive again, but only in some kind of spiritual sense.

This novel idea, however, when examined, turns out to be very vague. Jesus' followers are attributed with notions such as these: that "Jesus was too good to die"; or that they could "still sense his influence" upon their lives. These are nice thoughts, but they fail entirely to explain three things:

- why people then started calling Jesus "Messiah" and "Lord" (when, being dead, he clearly was not!);

- why people were willing to die for this still-dead Jesus;

- why people started talking (as Jesus' followers clearly did, immediately) about ana-stasis – a Greek word which (literally) means "up-standing" – thereby indicating that Jesus "stood up" vertically, no longer being a corpse lying horizontally in a grave.

Jesus' followers repeatedly made these outrageous claims, and stuck to them in the face of strong opposition. Why?

We conclude, then, that Jesus' first followers would never have conceded that Jesus' corpse was still lying in the tomb. Nor could they have started out merely with a notion that Jesus was "alive" in some vague spiritual sense, and then only later become convinced that the tomb had been empty. No, as far as they were concerned, the tomb was empty from the outset. All their talk about a resurrection (a physical "raising up" of a body from the dead) would never have even started – never "got off the ground" – if Jesus' corpse was still in the tomb.

Dealing with the empty tomb

The question then becomes: how come the tomb was empty? We need an explanation. And only three options are possible:

A. Jesus had not truly died; so, once he revived, he walked out of the tomb on his own.

B. Jesus' corpse was stolen.

C. Jesus was raised from the dead by an act of God.

Option A is absurd

Roman soldiers would have ensured any crucified criminal was truly dead before allowing his body to be removed. This is precisely why they pierced Jesus' side before bringing him down from the cross (John 19). What flowed out from the spear wound was serum and water – a sure medical indication (not understood at the time) that death had already occurred. Jesus was clearly dead.

Yet, even supposing that he was not quite dead, we may reasonably ask how likely it is that, after all his suffering (and then thirty-six hours left on a cold, damp slab – without any medical attention), Jesus would somehow revive, push away the entrance stone, and convince people that he had conquered death? To believe this almost takes more faith than to believe in the resurrection!

Option B is very unlikely

Who would want to steal the body? The Roman and Jewish authorities both had a keen interest in suppressing any further interest in Jesus. So they would hardly have stolen the body. And, if they had, then surely they would have produced it as soon as anyone started making these strange claims that Jesus had been raised from the dead: "Oh no, he hasn't – here's the corpse!"

But could Jesus' corpse have been stolen, not by his enemies, but by his friends? This was the first explanation given by the guards and it remained a popular theory among Jerusalem's* populace right up until the time of Matthew's Gospel (see Matthew 28:15).

Yet, although it seemed plausible to ancient critics, it remains most unlikely. For Jesus' followers were in no mood for any heroics involving such risky corpse-snatching. Such activity was a criminal offence and would have brought them immediately to the authorities' attention. That was the last thing they wanted. Nine of Jesus' disciples had been so frightened at the time of Jesus' arrest that they had fled out of the city and over the Mount of Olives – fearing they too would be arrested. No, Jesus' followers were depressed and fearful for their lives.

So they were not going to be stealing Jesus' corpse. And, anyway, what was the point? The grave, which a wealthy follower named Joseph of Arimathea had provided for Jesus, was far better than anything his poor friends from Galilee could have mustered up at short notice. What Jesus' body needed was not a relocating but rather a more thorough anointing – precisely what the women planned to accomplish on the Sunday morning.

This all then explains why, when Jesus' friends first heard the news that his body had disappeared, they were so fearful and distraught. This was not good news at all in their eyes – it was a complete disaster! For they would now be accused of stealing it, and that is precisely what they did not want.

So it seems reasonably clear that the disciples did not steal it. Moreover, if they had stolen it, we would then have to believe that they spent the rest of their lives proclaiming a message about Jesus – at great personal risk to themselves – which they knew to be a complete lie. Once again, this is psychologically implausible. And surely, once persecution came their way, one of their number would have snapped under pressure and leaked the truth. But they never did.

Option C

We are left with the answer that Jesus' followers gave from the outset, namely that Jesus had been raised from the dead by God himself. As we've just seen, they themselves could not believe it at first. So they knew full well that it would sound absurd to others, but there was no other explanation. We too need to ask ourselves: is there an alternative explanation which makes any sense?

Jesus was seen again

Finally, we must not forget that Jesus' followers made this claim for one other vitally important reason: because Jesus himself had met them! On that first Easter* Sunday, according to Luke 24, Jesus "appeared to Simon", to the Emmaus* disciples, and also to those gathered in the upper room. Here's how Paul put it, some twenty years later:

> For what I received I passed on to you as of first importance: that Christ died for our sins, according to the Scriptures, that he was buried, that he was raised on the third day according to the Scriptures, and that he appeared to Cephas, and then to the Twelve. After that, he appeared to more than five hundred of the brothers and sisters at the same time, most of whom are still living, although some have fallen asleep. Then he appeared to James, then to all the apostles... Christ has indeed been raised from the dead.
>
> 1 Corinthians 15:3-7, 20

In other words, there are people still living, says Paul, who can vouch for what we are saying. The resurrection is part of the essential message of Christianity ("of first importance"); there is no Good News without it. And its truth is assured by the simple, but amazing, fact that the Risen Jesus was seen on a number of occasions. These were not hallucinations, nor just a delayed reaction within their grief process. No, these were real encounters with Jesus. Initially, writes Luke, Jesus' followers thought that they were seeing a ghost, but then Jesus proceeded to eat some boiled fish before their very eyes! This was their master, Jesus, now back from the dead.

Luke wants any followers of Jesus – then or now – to be convinced about Jesus' resurrection: a real death was followed by an empty tomb, and then by real encounters with the Risen Jesus. This was not something just in the minds of Jesus' followers (perhaps invented to make them feel better). No, it was something that happened in the real life-story of Jesus himself.

And the consequence is: this same Jesus is alive today. As Paul puts it: "Christ was raised from the dead, he cannot die again; death no longer has mastery over him" (Romans 6:9). The resurrection of Jesus thus turns out to be not just a remarkable event within ancient history. Far more than that, it is the event which brings Jesus from the past into the present – able to meet with people today and to transform their lives.

Appendix C

Baptism for Jesus' Followers: Why is it Important?

At the very end of his ministry on earth, Jesus gave his first followers a clear instruction: "Therefore go and make disciples of all nations, baptizing them in the name of the Father and of the Son and of the Holy Spirit, and teaching them to obey everything I have commanded you" (Matthew 28:19 – 20).

Jesus evidently wants his followers to be well taught but also to be baptized. In *The Jesus Way* we have focused on the first of these, aiming to give a clear summary of Jesus' teaching, but we also need to explain here the meaning of "baptism": what is it and why is it important? Why did Jesus want his followers to go through this ritual?

Joining God's people

The word "baptism" comes from the ordinary Greek word for "washing". However, it came to be used in a restricted sense to apply to a washing done for specifically religious reasons. By the time of Jesus, various such baptisms had developed within Jewish practice, one of which was designed for non-Jews who wished now to belong to God's people (the nation of Israel*). So baptism was, first, all about joining God's people.

This was why John the Baptist's call to his fellow Israelites was – that they needed to be baptized – so controversial: he was effectively saying that, despite belonging by birth to God's historic people, they needed now to *rejoin* God's people – to start all over again. It was no good claiming that they had Abraham as their "father"; each person now had to make their own humble entrance into God's new people (see Luke 3).

So the baptism Jesus commands is an outward sign that we belong to his people – it's like a badge of membership. All Jesus' followers have gone through this same rite of initiation. So, when we ourselves are baptized, we join this group of people who have all been through the same experience. Jesus himself was baptized (by John in the River Jordan – see Matthew 3:13–17) and this has been true for all his followers ever since. In the books of Acts, there are numerous episodes in which we see people responding to the message of Jesus and promptly being baptized (see, for example, Acts 2:41; 8:38; 9:18; 10:48). It is the clear signal that individuals have joined Jesus' new people.

Repenting and receiving the Spirit

When joining any new group or society, we have to make certain commitments, or assent to various beliefs. It's no different here. Baptism can never be just an empty formula, in which we go unthinkingly through the motions, but is meant to be an outward sign of our inner choices and commitments. The very first sermon by the apostle* Peter closes with these important words which make this point:

> *Repent and be baptized, every one of you, in the name of Jesus Christ for the forgiveness of your sins. And you will receive the gift of the Holy Spirit. The promise is for you and your children and for all who are far off – for all whom the Lord our God will call.*

Acts 2:38–39

Peter makes it crystal clear that only those who have repented from their sins should consider getting baptized. The key point in following Jesus is recognizing that he is the one who offers us "forgiveness of sins" (see chapter 2). This means we cannot choose to follow him without recognizing Jesus' offer and our need for that forgiveness: in other words, we have to recognize our sinfulness, repent, and seek his forgiveness. Baptism, then, is the public sign of our more private decision – namely that we have repented of our sins and are now turning from all that is evil. We are turning from darkness to the light of Christ.

As we have seen (in chapter 3), those who come to Christ in this way not only receive God's forgiveness but also receive his Holy Spirit. This second great truth is then reflected in Peter's words: those who repent "receive the gift of the Holy Spirit." Baptism then becomes a sign of this too: that we are not just repentant people who have been forgiven, but also empty people who have now been filled. Of course, the very act of baptism cannot actually bring about this spiritual reality, any more than it can bring us automatically the forgiveness of our sins (these invisible realities only come about through exercising repentant faith in Jesus). Yet baptism remains the outward and visible sign of these great realities, which have truly come about in the life of every one of Jesus' followers.

Baptism therefore has within it a pattern of death and resurrection: dying to sin and then coming to a new Spirit-filled life in Christ. That's why Paul in Romans 6 can speak of us being "buried with him" in our baptism and rising to "new life". We can also see how baptism draws together the three great truths we looked at in the first three chapters of *The Jesus Way*: believing in Jesus as the Risen Lord*, repenting from our sins (for which he died on the cross), and receiving his Holy Spirit.

So, if you have taken those three steps but have not yet been baptized, it's important now to go forward to baptism as soon as possible. This will involve talking with a leader in your local church* and then preparing appropriately for this important event in your new Christian life.

A baptism can be a great time of celebration! It's a way of publicly showing our new commitment to Jesus' way and receiving God's assurance that we are now his. And, once we are baptized, we find we are part of God's new people and can then enjoy coming to the family's "meal" (see chapter

5). Throughout the past 2,000 years, the meal of the "Lord's Supper" has always been preserved as a meal designed only for those who have first been baptized. So here's another reason why baptism is important: if we wish to participate in the "breaking of bread" with other believers, we must first be baptized. No baptism, no meal.

Practical details

Sometimes people can be anxious about what precisely their baptism will involve in practice. Of course, this will vary from place to place, as different churches follow different customs. In terms of its essential ingredients, however, a baptism always involves two things:

- **Some water.** Sometimes people go down into some water, totally submerged, and then come up again; sometimes they are just sprinkled with water. Although different churches have adopted different positions on this point, arguably both practices have biblical support (see, for example, Acts 8:38–39 and 1 Peter 1:2). In fact, the standard practice of the early church seems to have been a combination of the two: baptismal candidates would stand in some running water (perhaps up to their knees) but then have this water scooped up and poured over their heads.

- **A prayer in the name of the Trinity*.** Although the New Testament often talks about people being baptized "in the name of Jesus", Jesus' authoritative words in Matthew 28 (quoted at the start of this appendix) have from the earliest centuries been taken as giving the full formula which should be used: we are to be baptized "in the name of the Father and of the Son and of the Holy Spirit."

Finally, there is the complex issue that some people will have been baptized as an infant, when their parents had them "christened". We cannot go into detail here as to why this practice of infant baptism arose so early in the church's life (it had to do with emphasizing how children are indeed to be seen as belonging in God's people). Yet, if this is true for you and you discover you have indeed already been baptized, then the best practice is to ask if you can now publicly *renew* your baptismal vows as a believing adult. This avoids the need for going through a repeat baptism (as if the first one was ineffective), but gives you the opportunity now to publicly declare your faith in Jesus. In this way, your baptism as a child comes, as it were, to fulfilment – as you now express the repentant faith in Jesus that was presumed (and indeed prayed for!) at the start of your life.

Glossary

Abba

This is the word for "father" in Aramaic (Jesus' mother tongue, still spoken in parts of modern Syria). The Gospels (themselves written in Greek) record four or five Aramaic words, but this word, used by Jesus in praying to God (for example, Mark 14:36), was especially treasured by the disciples – not least because it was a colloquial word used between a child and his father (like "my dad"!). Paul then encourages Christians, as God's adopted children, to address God in these intimate terms (Romans 8:15; Galatians 4:6).

Agape love

This is one of four Greek words for "love". As opposed to mere "friendship" or "sexual love", this *agape* love is a selfless, outgoing concern for others. The apostles saw this as having been revealed supremely in Jesus and urged believers to express this love towards each other (see especially Paul's so-called "hymn to love" in 1 Corinthians 13; see also John 13:34; 1 John 4:7–21).

Amen

This is a Hebrew word meaning "truly" or "so be it". It is a way of affirming and giving assent to what has been prayed – meaning "it's true!" or "Yes, Lord!"

Apostle

An "apostle" is, literally, "one who is sent out" (with a mission or task). In biblical thought the "persons sent" (or commissioned as messengers) were to be received by others with the deference due to the "person who sent them". Jesus expected this for his own "apostles" (Matthew 10:40), so we too should receive his apostles' teaching in the same way as we would receive Jesus himself. The evidence is strong that Jesus appointed an inner band of twelve apostles (reflecting the twelve tribes of Israel:

see Matthew 19:28), but that Paul was effectively added to this number after his conversion (see 1 Corinthians 9:1; 15:9). There will therefore be no new "apostles" (in this strict, historical sense) – even though in every generation there will be many "sent out" into the world in Jesus' name to do pioneering work for the kingdom.

Aramaic, *see Abba.*

Ascension of Jesus, the

Jesus' "ascension", when Jesus finally returned to heaven, is the key event described by Luke between our two key chapters (Luke 24 and Acts 2). According to Acts 1:3, for a period of about "forty days" the Risen Jesus had "appeared to his followers in many ways that proved beyond doubt that he was alive," but this came to an end. For there came a day, when Jesus was on the Mount of Olives near Bethany, that "he departed from them" and "a cloud hid him from their sight" (see Luke 24:50–53; Acts 1:9–12). The New Testament sees this "ascension" as the time when Jesus was exalted to the "right hand" of God (Acts 2:33) and given the "name that is greater than any other name" (Philippians 2:9); it was also when, as a sign of his finished work, he "sat down", sharing the very throne of God (see Hebrews 1:3; Ephesians 1:20–23; Revelation 5:13).

Augustine of Hippo (AD 354–430)

Augustine was a pagan philosopher who was converted to Christian faith while reading Paul's letter to the Romans in a garden in Milan in AD 387. His reflective autobiography (the *Confessions*) looks back on all that led up to this dramatic event. He is widely regarded as one of the greatest intellectuals of all time, and is honoured as one of the four great "doctors" (or teachers) of the ancient church. The phrase "faith seeking understanding" is often attributed to him, but is really a paraphrase of his words in his *Sermon* 43.7, 9: "*Crede, ut intelligas*" (Latin for "believe in order that you may understand"). Meanwhile, the quote on page 139 is from *Confessions* 10.29. Another well-known quote from the *Confessions* is the following:

> *You have made us for yourself, O Lord, and our heart is restless until it finds rest in you.*
>
> Confessions 1.1

Baptism, *see fuller discussion in appendix C.*

Brothers and sisters

The Greek word *adelphoi* (meaning "brothers and sisters") is used over 230 times in the New Testament to describe Christian believers – who have now been brought into God's family as equal members.

Canon

This word (derived from the Greek word for a "rule", "measuring-line", or "benchmark") came to be used for the "boundary line" placed around Scripture, defining which books were to be included within the Bible (and thus "canonical") and which books were to be "ruled out". This was a major issue in the second century AD as the early church gathered together the various books of the New Testament and had to evaluate a wide variety of Christian literature, eventually categorizing non-apostolic works as valuable but "non-canonical".

Catholic

This comes from a Greek word which literally means "throughout [or across] the world". From the early second century AD it was used as a key word to describe the amazing phenomenon of the gospel of Jesus spreading across the world and thus creating a "worldwide" or "catholic" church.

Christology

This refers to the "study of Christ's person", and describes all the debates which seek to answer the question, "who is Jesus?" Despite much debate, the New Testament writings show clear evidence of having a very strong or "high" Christology, asserting that Jesus can be identified in some way with God himself – both in what he *does*, but also in who he essentially *is*. This was then well summarized in the Creed (see chapter 9). See also R. J. Bauckham, *God Crucified* (Grand Rapids, MI: Eerdmans, 1998).

Communion

This is one of the four terms commonly used to describe the meal instituted by Jesus at his Last Supper (see chapter 5). It picks up some words of Paul (1 Corinthians 10:16), which speak of our "participating" in the body and blood of Christ (in older English "communion" had this sense of "participating with"). The other three terms are: "Lord's Supper", which points to the truth that this is a meal, like the original Last Supper, which is hosted by Jesus (but now as the Risen Lord); "Eucharist", which comes from the Greek word meaning "thanksgiving"; and "Mass", which comes from the Latin for "dismissal" and echoes the words used at the end of many such Communion services when people are "dismissed" to their homes.

Over the years different theologies have become associated with each term, though the words themselves do not necessarily require those theologies. Each of the first three has clear biblical support, being used in Paul's discussion of this meal in 1 Corinthians 10–11. For evidence of how the first Christians conducted this meal, see Acts 2:42–46; 20:7; 1 Corinthians 11:17–33; 16:2.

Church

This is the English word used to translate the New Testament word *ekklesia*. Literally the word refers to those who have been "called out". It had been used in ancient Greece to describe the democratic civic "assembly", but also in the Greek version of the Old Testament to describe God's "chosen people". The apostles see all believers as thus "called out" or chosen by God through the gospel.

Confess/Confession

This describes when people "confess" their sins to God, repenting of their wrongdoing. It literally means that they "agree" with God and acknowledge that he is right and they are wrong (see, for example, Psalm 51:3–4). As seen in our opening chapters, it is a necessary part in any first response to the message about Jesus (the one who saves from sins), but it should also form a continual part of a Christian's life (see 1 John 1:9). The apostles also encourage us on suitable occasions to "confess our sins to each another" (James 5:16); in some church traditions this has been formalized into making one's "confession" before a "priest", but, though this may be helpful, it is not something which the Bible requires.

Confirmation

This describes a special service or ritual which those churches who practise infant baptism normally encourage their members to pass through before they are allowed to receive the bread and wine at Communion. It is designed to give people an opportunity as adults to confirm the promises made on their behalf at their baptism. It is also intended as a safeguard to ensure that those who come to Communion are truly believers themselves. For those people who wish publicly to confirm their new-found faith in an even more dramatic way, most churches will also offer a special service for the "renewal of baptism vows" (see appendix C).

Covenant

This is a word frequently used in the Bible to describe the binding agreement and committed relationship which God establishes with his people (originally with Abraham and then with the people of Israel). It is well summarized in the divine promise: "I will be their God and they will be my people" (see, for example, Revelation 21:3). The closest parallel in modern life is the "covenant" that binds together a husband and wife. The apostles teach that Jesus has inaugurated a "new covenant" (as prophesied in Jeremiah 31) and that all believers in Jesus are thus members of God's "covenant" people and living in the era of the "new covenant".

Creed

This is a short summary statement, articulating Christian faith (*credo* is Latin for "I believe"). Several such "creeds" were agreed and then recited regularly during the early church period (see chapter 9). Those used most frequently today are the "Apostles' Creed" (a summary of the apostles' teaching dating to the late second century AD) and the so-called "Nicene Creed" (confusingly, composed at Constantinople in AD 381, though based on an earlier version promulgated at the Council of Nicaea in AD 325). The creeds do not have any authority above the Bible, but have an authority within the church – precisely because they have been shown over the centuries to be true to the Bible. Arguably, the creeds focus more on Jesus' person than on his work (for instance, his death on the cross and what that achieved for us), but this is because the debates about Jesus' person and identity were the most hotly disputed ones at that time. It was also because those compiling the creeds recognized that the achievement of the cross would be severely undermined if Jesus could not be identified in some way with God (see, for example, Romans 5:8; and chapter 2).

Devil, the

There are clear hints concerning the devil (also known as "Satan" or the "Evil One") in the Old Testament (see Genesis 3; Job 1); but the full revelation of his identity waits until the coming of Jesus. For references

to Satan in the context of Jesus' ministry, see, for example, Mark 3:22–
27; 8:33; Luke 4:1–13; 10:18; 22:31; 12:31; 14:30. For references in the
apostles' teaching, see, for example, 1 John 3:8; 2 Corinthians 11:14; 4:4;
Ephesians 2:1–3; 1 Thessalonians 3:5; 1 Timothy 4:1–2, and the accounts
of exorcism in Acts 16:16–18; and 19:13–20. Various pictures are used of
the devil: for example, a snake (Genesis 3:1, 14–15; 2 Corinthians 11:3),
a devouring lion (1 Peter 5:8–9) or a great dragon (Revelation 12:9). He
is described as the "father of lies" (John 8:44) and the "accuser of the
brethren" (Revelation 12:10).

Docetism/Docetic

This is the name for an early Christian movement which argued that
Jesus, though truly God, only appeared to be human (from the Greek
word "to seem/appear"). This is denounced by the apostle John who
insists that Jesus truly came "in the flesh" (1 John 4:2; 2 John 7). This
false teaching, of course, could only emerge once people had accepted
the apostles' teaching about Jesus' divinity (as taught by John himself:
see John 1:1–3, 14; 10:30; 20:28); so its existence confirms the high
Christology that was present in the New Testament period.

Dualism, *see* Gnosticism

Easter

This word (derived from Old English) describes the season in the
church's year which focuses on the resurrection of Jesus (celebrated on
Easter Sunday). The Gospel writers clearly teach that Jesus' resurrection
took place on the "first day of the week" (a Sunday after the Jewish
"Sabbath"/Saturday). They are also clear that this was the first Sunday
after the celebration of the Passover (which took place on the night of
the springtime full moon). From ancient times Christians have therefore
celebrated the resurrection on the first Sunday after the Passover
full moon, but the date of this, of course, changes each year. There is
continued debate as to whether the first Easter Sunday was AD 9 April 30
or AD 5 April 33.

Emmaus

This was a village to the north-west of Jerusalem. Four different
locations have been suggested, with perhaps the most likely being the
area of "Motza" (now a suburb of modern Jerusalem): see my book, *In the*

Steps of Jesus (Oxford: Lion Hudson, 2007), pp. 204–205. If so, the total distance covered by the two disciples (going to Emmaus and then back up to Jerusalem) would have been c. 7.5 miles (12 km).

Eucharist, *see* Communion

Fellowship

This is the most common way of translating the New Testament references to *koinonia*. For an explanation of this term see chapter 7.

Flesh

As discussed in chapter 11, the apostle Paul uses the word "flesh" (*sarx* in Greek) in a specialist sense to speak of the sinful principle which is at work in human beings – in contrast to the "spirit" (*pneuma* in Greek). Believers are to "live according to the spirit," not "according to the flesh": see Galatians 5:16–17; Ephesians 4:22–24, Romans 6:1–11 and especially Romans 8:13.

Gentiles

This is the way we translate into English the word used by Israel in the Old Testament for describing "the nations" – those non-Jews outside Israel. Much of the New Testament is devoted to showing that through the gospel the time has now come for "Gentiles" to enter God's people *as* Gentiles (that is, without their first needing to become Jews): see, for example, Galatians 2:15–21; Acts 15:1–36; Romans 11:13–32; Ephesians 2:11–14.

Gnostics/Gnosticism

Gnosticism was a "heresy" (or "false teaching"), which severely tested Jesus' followers in the generations after the New Testament. Its name comes from the Greek word for "knowledge", because Gnostics developed elaborate systems of mystical paths, which those in the know could follow in pursuit of God. Influenced by Greek philosophy, Gnostic thought was strongly dualistic, setting up a strong contrast between created matter (seen as evil) and the spiritual realm; "salvation" or "enlightenment" was then a matter of escaping into that realm. In the second and third centuries AD Gnostic writers produced many rehashed versions of Jesus' teaching which, arguably, contain very little reliable testimony to the authentic, historical Jesus. For hints of Gnosticism's existence already within the New Testament, see, for example, 1 Timothy 6:20 or Colossians 2:8, 16–23.

God-fearer

This was a word coined to describe the many Gentiles who were "fringe" members of the Jewish synagogue – respecting and valuing Jewish ideals but not wishing formally to convert to Judaism (which for the men would have required circumcision). Almost certainly the author of Luke's Gospel had been a God-fearer, and many of the first converts to Christianity may well have been drawn from their number.

Homo-ousios

As noted in chapter 9, this strange Greek word (translated "of one being with") appears in the Nicene Creed. At the time of the creed's composition some were arguing that Jesus was only "like" God (in Greek, *homoios*), not identical with God (in Greek, *homos*). In these circumstances the creed's compilers coined this new non-biblical word in order to safeguard that which was taught within the Bible – even if using different words – namely that Jesus can be identified with God (see John 1:14, 18; Hebrews 1:3; Colossians 1:15, etc.). The incarnation of Jesus, being unique and unprecedented in human history, naturally required Christians to give new meanings to old words and sometimes (as here) to coin entirely new terminology.

Incarnation/incarnate

This word (derived from the Latin for "in the flesh") picks up the teaching of John's Gospel, which speaks of Jesus as the Word of God who "became flesh" (John 1:14). So the "incarnation" is the unique event in which God entered our human world in the person of his Son, Jesus – sometimes referred to as "God incarnate".

Ingathering of the nations

There are numerous texts in the Old Testament which list Israel's hopes for what God would do in the future. One such hope was that the Gentile nations would acknowledge Israel's God and would be "gathered in" – that is, coming up to Jerusalem and joining his people in worship (see, for example, Isaiah 2:1–4; 19:16–25; 60:1–22; Psalm 87).

Israel

According to Genesis 32:28 this was the name given to Jacob after he had "struggled with God". Thereafter it became the theological name given to his descendants ("the people of Israel") to signify that they were indeed the people of God. In later centuries, these descendants were called by other names (for example, the "Judeans" or "Jews"), but the New Testament writers consistently used the term "Israel" as a one-word title to describe God's covenant people in the Old Testament period. Because Jesus was the Messiah of Israel, they affirmed, all those who now believed in Jesus could be seen as incorporated into "Israel", that is, the people of God in the days of the New Testament (or new covenant): see, for example, 1 Peter 2:9–10; Ephesians 2:19–22. In this book "Israel" is therefore used in this strict theological sense, referring to the ancient people of God and is not a reference to the modern political state which has taken the name "Israel". For some further discussion, see chapters 6, 7, and 8.

Jerusalem

This, the central city in Israel's history, was established as the nation's capital by King David, with its Temple being founded by his son, Solomon (c. 970 BC). By the time of Jesus the city was under Roman occupation, but the Temple had been magnificently renovated by King Herod. The city and Temple formed the natural backdrop for the climax of Jesus' ministry as he asserted his claim to be the nation's true prophet, priest, and king. On his arrival, Jesus wept over the city, knowing that the so-called "city of peace" did not know "what would bring peace" (Luke 19:41–44). Seven weeks later, during the annual summer feast of Pentecost, the city was naturally full of Jewish pilgrims who had come up to worship in their mother-city.

Lord

This would become a key title for Jesus in the New Testament, and the earliest Christian creed (see chapter 9) was simply "Jesus is Lord" (Romans 10:9; 1 Corinthians 12:3). Although the word *kurios* could mean simply a "master" or "boss", it had also served to translate the Hebraic references in the Old Testament to "the Lord, the God of Israel". So the apostles, in applying this title to Jesus so frequently, were evidently identifying Jesus in some way with Israel's God.

Messiah

This is a Hebrew term for "the anointed person". In biblical practice Israel's kings were "anointed" with oil during their coronation, so the term refers to a royal figure. In the two centuries before Jesus, Jewish hope for the arrival of this long-awaited royal king had steadily increased; and it was hoped he would liberate Israel from pagan domination. According to the Gospels, Jesus himself made claims (both explicit and implicit) to be the Messiah – but not in all the senses that were expected. After the resurrection the apostles then assert that, despite some of these disturbed expectations, he was indeed the true Messiah. The Greek equivalent for Messiah is Christos; so when the New Testament writers talk of "Jesus Christ" they are effectively referring to "King Jesus".

Monotheism

"Monotheism" means belief in a single "god", as opposed to "polytheism" (belief in many "gods"), "atheism" (belief in no "god") or "pantheism" (belief that everything is "god").

Nicene Creed, *see* Creed

Parousia, *see* Second Coming

Passover

Passover was one of Israel's three main festivals (along with Pentecost and Tabernacles). The festival celebrated how God, when bringing judgment on Egypt, had "passed over" the Israelites' homes, sparing those houses which were marked by the blood of a lamb (as described in Exodus 12:1–36). Thereafter, each year in the springtime Jewish families would come together for a Passover meal. Jesus' Last Supper was essentially a Passover meal, but with some significant differences – there was probably no lamb on the table (pointing to Jesus being the true "lamb") and it may well have been twenty-four hours ahead of the official schedule (since, by that time, Jesus would be dead). Read more in my book, *The Weekend that Changed the World* (London: Marshall Pickering, 1999), pp. 4–5; and N. T. Wright, *Jesus and the Victory of God* (London: SPCK, 1996), p. 555–59).

Pentecost

This was Israel's second major religious festival, coming seven weeks or fifty days after Passover ("Pentecost" comes from the Greek word for "fifty"). It coincided with the barley harvest and was the time when Israel looked back to the giving of the law at Mount Sinai (Exodus 20). Falling in mid-summer, the festival attracted a large number of international pilgrims from around the Mediterranean, and so was a fitting occasion for the dramatic outpouring of the Holy Spirit (described in Acts 2).

Pharisees

These were religious Jews who belonged to one of the four main groups within the Judaism of Jesus' day (the others, according to Josephus, were the Sadducees, Essenes, and Zealots). They were scattered throughout the land and believed God would vindicate Israel only when the "people of the land" began to practise holiness and more fully obey God's commands. They also believed in the bodily resurrection of God's faithful people at the end of the age. The apostle Paul, before his conversion, had been an ardent Pharisee, probably with strong nationalistic tendencies: see Philippians 3:5–6; also Acts 23:6; 26:5; Galatians 1:13–14.

Pontius Pilate

Pontius Pilate was the Roman governor (or "procurator") in charge of the Roman province of Judea from AD 26 to AD 36. Though based most of the time in the provincial capital on the coast (Caesarea Maritima), he was naturally in Jerusalem during Passover – a season often marked by political unrest. Josephus (the Jewish historian writing c. AD 85) indicates that he was particularly brutal and not afraid to provoke local opposition. His name was discovered in a Latin inscription found at Caesarea in 1961.

Samaritans

The Samaritans lived to the north of Jerusalem around the ancient city of Samaria. Their territory had been within the northern kingdom of Israel but its inhabitants had been taken into exile by the Assyrians in 722 BC (the so-called "ten lost tribes of Israel"). Those living there subsequently were viewed by the Jews as racially mixed and impure, and were remembered for their opposition to the rebuilding of the Jerusalem Temple after the exile. Jesus shocked people with his positive attitude to the Samaritans (Luke 10:33; John 4:27).

So when the message about Jesus begins to reach Samaria (as described in Acts 8:4–17), this is a highly significant moment. Almost certainly, then, this is why the new believers in Samaria appear only to receive the Holy Spirit when the leading apostles arrive from Jerusalem – for this was a strategic moment, with the Spirit being received by the Jews' long-standing enemies. For both pastoral and "political" reasons, this significant breakthrough needed to be witnessed and authorized by the apostles. This delay in receiving the Spirit is quite exceptional within the New Testament and so should not be taken as normative for today.

Satan, *see* the devil

Second Coming

The Greek word often translated as "second coming" is *parousia* (literally "presence"). This word often described people being ushered into the presence of royalty. So, when the apostles speak of Jesus' *parousia*, they are focusing not so much on how Jesus will come again, but simply on the sure reality of his "royal presence" at some point in the future (see Matthew 24:3; 1 Corinthians 15:23; 1 Thessalonians 2:19; 3:13; 4:15; 5:23; 2 Thessalonians 2:1, 8–9; James 5:7–8; 1 John 2:28). Quite conceivably Jesus clarified this teaching about his *parousia* in the forty-day period after his resurrection (Acts 1:3): only now he had come back from the dead, could they understand his future coming back from heaven. Thereafter, the apostles speak of this future hope on numerous occasions, warning both against cynicism about its delay or undue speculation as to its imminence (John 21:23; Colossians 3:4; 2 Timothy 4:1, 8; Hebrews 10:25, 37; 1 John 1:3, 2 Peter 3:4–10).

"Set" prayers

These are simply prayers that have been written down already (as opposed to spontaneous or "free" prayer). They should not be dismissed as less "spiritual" than other prayers – indeed many "set" prayers, having been carefully prepared, prevent people from saying the wrong thing or wasting words (which Jesus warned against in Matthew 6:7). What matters in praying is not spontaneity, but sincerity.

Sinless perfection

Some "holiness" movements within the church have suggested that "sinless perfection" is possible in this life (basing their argument on texts such as 1 John 3:6 or Matthew 5:48). However, texts such as Romans 7:23–24 clearly refer to the reality of ongoing sin in believers' lives. The apostles' teaching thus combines a strong vision for holiness with a sober realism.

Son of God

This is one of the key terms used in the New Testament to describe Jesus. In the Old Testament it had been used to refer either to Israel or to its king, but now it comes to describe Jesus' unique relationship with God as Father (see, for example, Matthew 11:27; 16:16; Romans 1:4; John 1:14; see also Christology).

Speaking in tongues, *see* Spiritual gifts

Spiritual gifts

This translates a word used by Paul in 1 Corinthians (12:1), which simply means "spiritual things". However, Paul goes on to speak about the Spirit's giving of *charismata* ("gifts of grace"), so the concept of "spiritual gift" is close to Paul's intention. Paul lists gifts such as "wisdom" and "prophecy"; he also includes "speaking in tongues" (that is, praying with a special language other than your own mother tongue), while urging people to use this (and every) gift with *agape* love. For other (clearly non-exhaustive) lists of such "spiritual gifts", see also Ephesians 4:11; Romans 12:6–8, perhaps also 2 Peter 1:4–7. These lists affirm that both seemingly "supernatural" and "natural" capacities may be given by the Holy Spirit.

Trinity/Trinitarian

This is the doctrine that God has revealed himself in three persons as Father, Son, and Holy Spirit. Although the word "Trinity" is not itself in the New Testament, there are good reasons for arguing that the New Testament writers were instinctively Trinitarian in the way they spoke of God: see more in Box 9c in chapter 9.

All royalties earned from this book
go towards the work of EFAC Global.

The Evangelical Fellowship in the Anglican Communion was founded in 1961 by John Stott. Its role has become even more critical in recent years.

Through national fellowships in the various provinces of the Anglican Communion, EFAC serves to develop biblical literacy and to encourage effective mission. We are *"Bible People, Gospel People, Church People"*. EFAC works to equip Anglican leaders to stand firm in the apostolic faith, to engage thoughtfully with secular trends, and to articulate a persuasive biblical response. Its affiliated group in England is the Church of England Evangelical Council.

EFAC's Theology Resource Network (TRN) draws senior theologians from all continents. As John Stott was always keen to remind EFAC's early members, Christ gave gifts to his church so that they could be shared. Through the TRN's international membership, insights from many contexts are discussed around the table, and then shared more widely through gatherings and in print.

Jesus prayed in Gethsemane for the future church to be unified – "at one" with its apostolic roots (John 17:20–23). EFAC, under the leadership of an International Council and General Secretary, and through its TRN, national fellowships, and small staff team, seeks to further and advance this true unity.

To learn more, visit **efacglobal.com**.

The Jesus WAY
Courses

Ever since Jesus called his first followers, people have been learning Jesus' way of life in small groups. We see in the Gospels how Jesus drew together an "inner circle" of twelve people who then together were committed to learning from him "along the way".

It was a kind of "mobile classroom" – where they could discuss what Jesus' teaching meant and encourage each other to put it into practice. No doubt they had many questions and made many mistakes, but they stuck together. And the result was transformative! Three years later others noticed how these people, despite their lack of education, had obviously "been with Jesus" and were soon "turning the world upside down" (Acts 4:13; 17:6).

What might happen in our own day if we did the same – learning the Jesus Way together in small groups?

That's why I'm excited about these two courses which have been developed to help us all learn the Jesus Way together. We've put together extra course materials (including a Participant's Workbook and some videos) and would love to see many small groups coming together around the world – whether in homes or churches – so that people can learn the Jesus Way together and then live it out in the world.

Together, let's be those who "walk the Way" and "live His life"!

A. LEARNING THE JESUS WAY (based on chapters 1-6)

Week 1	Look at the Risen Jesus: the first Easter (Luke 24)
Week 2	Enjoy Jesus' Resurrection
Week 3	Accept his Forgiveness
Week 4	Welcome his Spirit
	Half-term
Week 5	Feed on his Scriptures
Week 6	Participate in his Meal
Week 7	Bear Witness to his Reign
Week 8	Conclusion: Listen to Jesus

B. LIVING THE JESUS WAY (based on chapters 7-12)

Week 1	Learn from the apostles: Pentecost (Acts 2)
Week 2	Share with Jesus' people
Week 3	Worship his Majesty
Week 4	Follow his teaching
	Half-term
Week 5	Live his Live
Week 6	Resist His Enemy
Week 7	Trust him for the future
Week 8	Conclusion: Live for Jesus

Features of both courses

Venue: They can take place in your own home or in a local church setting (as part of an adult education programme).

Timing: They can be held at any time of year, in either a four-week format or over nine weeks (with a week off for "half-term" in the middle).

Videos: For each course there is a series of short videos, which introduce the topic and show interviews with Christians from around the world describing their experience.

Workbook: There is a Participants' Workbook, with questions and activities for small groups and individuals.

Teaching resources: And – for church leaders – there are also further Teacher's Resources (with lecture outlines and presentation slides).

Getting started

There are two different packages available to help you get started:

- a Home Group Leader's Package (including the Videos and Participants' Workbook)
- a Church Leader's Package (which also includes the Teacher's Resources)

For full details, please go to my website:
drpeterwalker.com/thejesusway

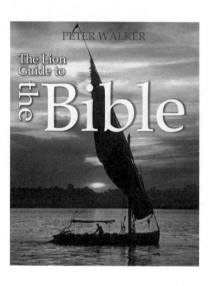

"Dr Walker opens the riches of the Bible
in an accessible and intelligent way."

The Rt Revd George Carey,
former Archbishop of Canterbury

An illuminating tour through the Bible, this handsome hardback is
full of colour illustrations, maps and helpful charts – bringing the
story of God's dealings with his people vividly to life.

Key features include:

- Accessible and engaging text which guides the reader through
  the background of the Bible, and through its 66 books
- Lavish illustrations with over 200 colour photographs, maps,
  timelines and charts
- Over 40 feature boxes providing enhanced material

The Lion Guide to the Bible
ISBN: 978 0 7459 5292 5 (colour hardback, Lion Books)

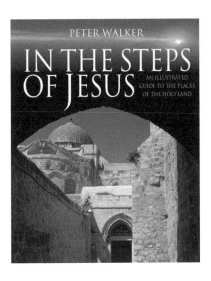

"A fine piece of work... The scholarship informing it is first-class... It's a gem."

The Rt Revd Rowan Williams,
former Archbishop of Canterbury

This book offers readers the opportunity to follow in the steps of Jesus and discover the sites of the Holy Land. Whether you intend to visit the land of the Bible or simply want to learn more about the places were Jesus lived and preached, this book is for you. Designed for the traveller and non-traveller alike, this travel guide...

- follows the chronology of Jesus' life
- covers all the sites Jesus visited in the Gospels
- focuses especially on the Gospel of Luke
- explains historical background, geography and archaeology
- describes and assesses the sites as they are today
- includes photographs, maps, diagrams and timelines

In the Steps of Jesus
ISBN: 978 0 7459 5386 1 (colour paperback, Lion Books)

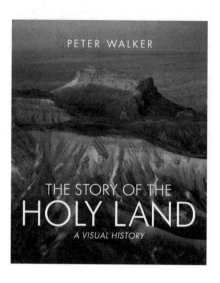

PETER WALKER

THE STORY OF THE
HOLY LAND
A VISUAL HISTORY

"Stunning large-scale photographs, linked and illuminated by an insightful text, encapsulate the 4000-year sweep of the history of the Holy Land in a way that will refresh the expert and instruct the beginner."

**Jerome Murphy-O'Connor,
professor at the École Biblique, Jerusalem, and author of
*The Holy Land: An Oxford Archaeological Guide***

A highly illustrated, visually led guide through the story of the Holy Land, from Bible times to the present day. This book explores the Old Testament and New Testament history of the Holy Land, as well as everything that happened later - the Muslim conquest, the crusades, and the modern rediscovery of biblical sites - unearthing the rich layers of history of this sacred place.

The Story of the Holy Land: a visual history
ISBN: 978 0 7459 8053 9 (colour paperback, Lion Books)